The Price of Money

The Price of Money

A Guide to the Past, Present, and Future of the Natural Rate of Interest

Edited by

Jamie Rush
Tom Orlik
Stephanie Flanders

OXFORD
UNIVERSITY PRESS

OXFORD
UNIVERSITY PRESS

Oxford University Press is a department of the University of Oxford. It furthers the University's objective of excellence in research, scholarship, and education by publishing worldwide. Oxford is a registered trade mark of Oxford University Press in the UK and in certain other countries.

Published in the United States of America by Oxford University Press
198 Madison Avenue, New York, NY 10016, United States of America.

Library of Congress Cataloging-in-Publication Data

Names: Rush, Jamie, author. | Orlik, Tom, author. |
Flanders, Stephanie, author.
Title: The price of money / Jamie Rush, Tom Orlik, Stephanie Flanders.
Description: New York, NY : Oxford University Press, [2025] |
Includes bibliographical references and index.|
Identifiers: LCCN 2025016063 | ISBN 9780197800904 (hardback) |
ISBN 9780197800911 (paperback) | ISBN 9780197800935 (epub) |
ISBN 9780197800942
Subjects: LCSH: Interest rates—United States—History. |
Money—United States—History.
Classification: LCC HB545 .R825 2025 | DDC 332.80973—dc23/eng/20250429
LC record available at https://lccn.loc.gov/2025016063

DOI: 10.1093/9780197800942.001.0001

Paperback printed by Integrated Books International, United States of America

Hardback printed by Bridgeport National Bindery, Inc., United States of America

The manufacturer's authorized representative in the EU for product safety is Oxford University Press España S.A., Parque Empresarial San Fernando de Henares, Avenida de Castilla, 2 – 28830 Madrid (www.oup.es/en).

MIX
Paper
FSC FSC® C183721

Acknowledgments

The natural rate of interest is as elusive as it is important. Tracking it through the theory and the data, and getting the findings down on the page, has been the work of many hands.

First and foremost we'd like to thank all our colleagues at Bloomberg Economics. Many appear as authors of the various chapters of the book. In one way or another, all have contributed along the way.

Also at Bloomberg, we'd like to thank Loly Chan, Kristin Powers, and Randy Shapiro for support getting the project in motion.

Wendy Carlin, Bill Dudley and Stephen King were generous with their time in reviewing plans for the book. Martin Ademmer co-authored the paper on the drivers of the natural rate that underpins a number of chapters. David Wilcox provided valuable feedback. Philip Hubbard shared data that was an important input.

Emily Mackenzie Benitez, Mhairi Bennett, James Cook, Elise Davies, Kayley Gilbert, and Kanimozhi Ramamurthy spotted the potential in the book and shepherded it through the editing and production process.

Last but not least, we'd like to thank our families. So far, their policy of rational inattention to the natural rate has proven to be the correct one.

Contents

List of Figures

List of Tables

List of Contributors

Martin Ademmer is Germany Economist at Bloomberg Economics in Frankfurt, Germany.

Ana Andrade is a European Economist at Bloomberg Economics in London, UK.

Selva Bahar Baziki is Turkey and Sweden Economist at Bloomberg Economics in Ankara, Turkey.

Maeva Cousin is Chief Trade and Climate Economist at Bloomberg Economics in Zurich, Switzerland.

Ziad Daoud is Chief Emerging Markets Economist at Bloomberg Economics in Dubai, United Arab Emirates.

Adriana Dupita is Deputy Chief Emerging Markets Economist at Bloomberg Economics in Sao Paulo, Brazil.

Stephanie Flanders is Head of Economics and Government at Bloomberg LP in London, UK.

Dan Hanson is Chief UK Economist at Bloomberg Economics in London, UK.

Alex Isakov is Russia Economist at Bloomberg Economics in Washington, DC, US.

Eleonora Mavroeidi is a Global Economist at Bloomberg Economics in Paris, France.

Tom Orlik is Chief Economist at Bloomberg Economics in Washington, DC, US.

Stuart Paul is a US Economist at Bloomberg Economics in New York, NY, US.

David Qu is Senior China Economist at Bloomberg Economics in Hong Kong.

Jamie Rush is Director of Global Economics at Bloomberg Economics in London, UK.

Bhargavi Sakthivel is a Global Economist at Bloomberg Economics in Dubai, United Arab Emirates.

Chang Shu is Chief Asia Economist at Bloomberg Economics in Hong Kong.

Jennifer Welch is Chief Geoeconomics Analyst at Bloomberg Economics in Washington, DC, US.

David W. Wilcox is Director of US Economic Research at Bloomberg Economics and Senior Fellow at the Peterson Institute for International Economics, Washington, DC, US.

Eric Zhu is China Economist at Bloomberg Economics in Hong Kong.

1

The Price of Money is Going Up

Jamie Rush, Tom Orlik, and Stephanie Flanders

What's the most important price in the global economy? The price of oil? The price of semiconductors? The price of a Big Mac? More important than any of these is the price of money. For more than three decades it fell. Now it's going up.

Ask most people how the price of money is set, and they'll point to central banks. True, when it comes to direct control of US borrowing costs, it's the high priests of monetary policy at the Federal Reserve (Fed) that are calling the shots. But there's a deeper logic at work. At a fundamental level, the price of money—like the price of anything else—reflects the balance of supply and demand. Higher supply of savings pushes rates down. More investment demand pushes them up.

In economics jargon, the price of money that balances saving and investment while keeping inflation stable has another name—the natural rate of interest, or r^*.

To see why this concept is central to monetary policy, imagine what would happen if the Fed set borrowing costs well below the natural rate. With money too cheap, there would be too much investment, not enough saving, and the economy would overheat—resulting in spiraling inflation. Flipping that around, if the Fed set borrowing costs above the natural rate, there would be too much saving, not enough investment, and the economy would cool—resulting in rising unemployment.

To find out what drove interest rates lower over the final decades of the 20th century and opening years of the 21st, and to forecast where they might be heading, we built a model that captures the major factors driving saving supply and investment demand. Our dataset spans more than a half-century and includes 12 advanced economies that are deeply enmeshed in the global financial system.

Jamie Rush, Tom Orlik, and Stephanie Flanders, *The Price of Money is Going Up*. In: *The Price of Money*.
Edited by: Jamie Rush, Tom Orlik, and Stephanie Flanders, Oxford University Press.
 DOI: 10.1093/9780197800942.003.0001

The model of the natural rate we developed is inspired by the work of Marco Del Negro and his coauthors at the Federal Reserve Bank of New York.[1] The main difference is that our model includes more drivers and allows for spillovers between the 12 economies. We also include more survey data to help sharpen our estimates of how the drivers affect borrowing costs.[2]

It's a radically different approach from the famous Holston-Laubach-Williams model.[3] That model works by taking the temperature of the economy, checking where actual rates are, and triangulating from there to where the neutral rate must be. If the economy is running hot, the neutral rate must be above where actual rates are. If it's running cold, it must be below.

The Holston-Laubach-Williams model is an elegant and intuitive approach to estimating the "where" of the natural rate. What it lacks is much sense of "why." The benefit of our approach is that we can estimate the "where," and rely on the drivers to tell a story about the "why"—explaining the reasons the natural rate has fallen and using forecasts for the drivers to say where it is headed in the future.

Rather than policy rates, we estimate our model on long-term borrowing costs. That's because central banks have increasingly relied on lowering them to support the economy and because the 10-year Treasury bond yield is a crucial benchmark in global markets.

As Figure 1.1 shows, in nominal terms, the natural rate of interest for 10-year US Treasuries fell from about 12% in 1980 to a bit less than 4% in 2015—marking the end of a more than three-decade-long decline and giving way to a brief period of stability. From about 2020, the natural rate began to climb—mainly because governments have piled on debt since the pandemic, raising the supply of safe assets.

A lot of the decline in nominal interest rates since the early 1980s is down to inflation getting squeezed out of the system. Lower long-run inflation expectations have subtracted about 5 ppt from yields over that time period. Stripping inflation out of the picture, we estimate that the real long-term natural rate of interest fell from almost 5% in 1970 to a low below 2% in 2012, before climbing modestly to 2.3% in 2022.

Acknowledging there's substantial risk around the outlook for inflation in the medium term, in what follows, we focus on why the real rate fell and where it might go.

As Figure 1.2 shows, one of the most important reasons for the drop in the natural rate was weaker growth. In the 1960s and 70s, a swelling workforce

[1] Del Negro et al. (2017).
[2] Ademmer and Rush (2024).
[3] Holston, Laubach, and Williams (2017).

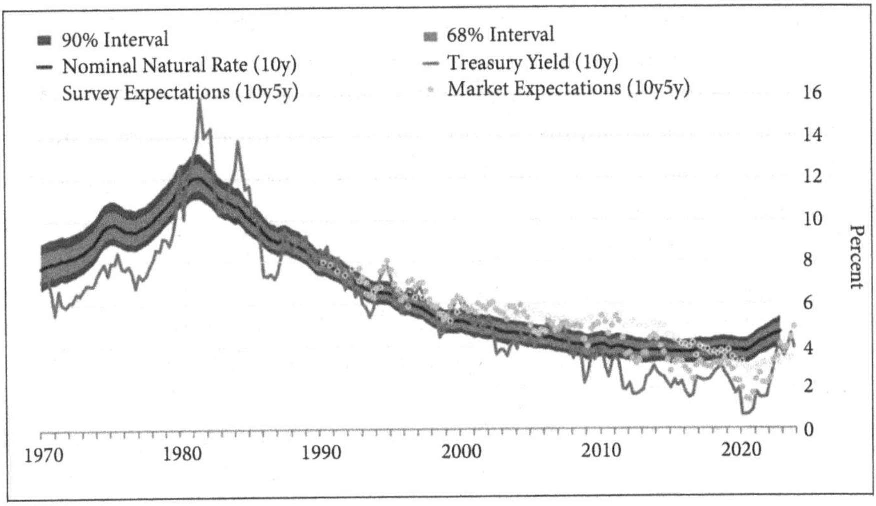

Figure 1.1 The US Natural Rate Has Plunged

Source: Ademmer and Rush (2024), Consensus Economics.

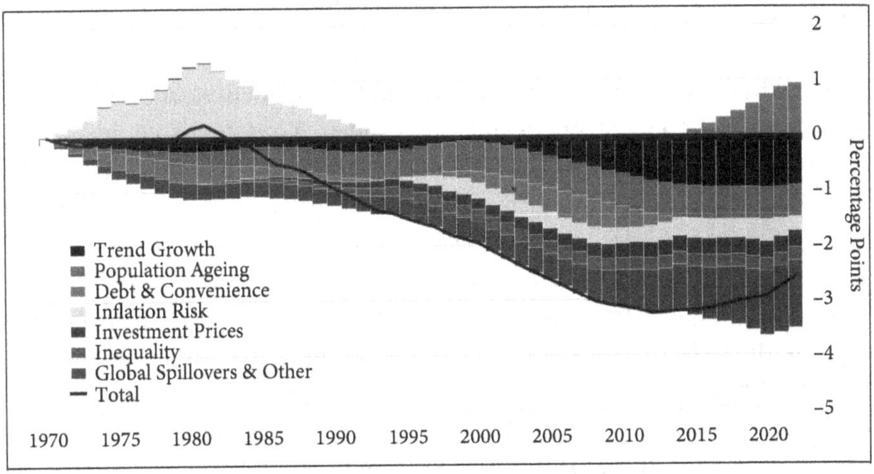

Figure 1.2 Why Money Got Cheap

Source: Ademmer and Rush (2024).

and—in the first part of that period—rapid productivity gains meant average annual growth of gross domestic product (GDP) in the United States was close to 4%. Strong growth created a powerful incentive to invest—lifting the price of money.

By the 2000s, those drivers were running out of steam. In the wake of the Global Financial Crisis (GFC) of 2007–08, average annual GDP growth slumped to around 2%. A more sluggish economy meant the attractiveness of investing for the future was weaker. This dragged the price of money lower.

Shifting demographics contributed in another way. From the 1980s onward, as the baby boom generation started stashing away more funds for retirement, the supply of savings went up, adding more downward pressure on the natural rate.

Other factors also contributed:

- On the saving side of the equation, China's economy was growing fast, running large current account surpluses, and recycling a portion of them into US government bonds.
- In the US, income inequality went up. High earners stashed away a higher share of their income, which further increased the supply of savings.
- On the investment side, computers got cheaper and more powerful, meaning companies didn't have to spend so much upgrading their technology, lowering investment demand and dragging the natural rate lower.

That fall in the price of money had profound consequences for the US economy. Bargain-basement borrowing costs meant households could take on bigger mortgages. In the early 2000s, many bit off more than they could chew. There were lots of reasons behind the subprime mortgage meltdown and GFC. Falling borrowing costs was one of them.

And, as Figure 1.3 shows, cheaper money meant that even as US federal debt almost tripled, from just over 30% of GDP at the turn of the century to more than 90% today, the cost of servicing that debt remained low. That allowed the government to continue spending on education, infrastructure, and the military. For the Federal Reserve, a lower natural rate meant less space to cut rates during recessions, leading to much hand-wringing about the diminished firepower of monetary policy.

All that is changing. Some of the forces that drove the price of money lower are steadying. Others are swinging into reverse. And new vectors are coming into play.

Demographics are shifting. The baby boom generation whose savings helped push borrowing costs down is already exiting the workforce and starting to spend down their retirement funds. Fracturing relations between Washington and Beijing, and a shift in China's exchange rate regime, mean the flow of Chinese savings across the Pacific into US Treasuries has come to an end.

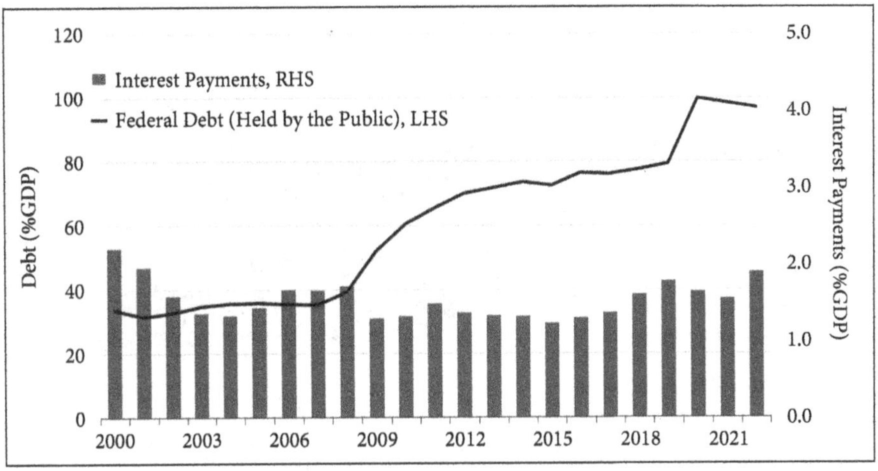

Figure 1.3 Government Got a Free Pass as Rates Dropped
Source: Congressional Budget Office.

US debt leapt as the GFC ripped through the economy, and again as the Covid pandemic struck. Those episodes increased competition for savings, and the Biden administration kept the taps open with the Inflation Reduction Act. Rising debt is already creating upward pressure on long-term borrowing costs.

How high will the natural rate go? Our model shows it already rose from a trough of about 1.7% in the mid-2010s to about 2.3% in 2022. As Figure 1.4 shows, in the years ahead we think it will climb further—hitting a peak of 2.8% in the 2030s. In nominal terms, that means 10-year Treasury yields could settle somewhere between 4.5% and 5%.

And the risks are skewed toward even higher borrowing costs:

- Fractious geopolitics—with Russia's invasion of Ukraine a visceral example—add pressure for more defense spending, making fiscal discipline harder to achieve.
- Flight from a weaponized dollar – following moves to freeze Russia's FX reserves in response to the invasion - reduces demand for US assets.
- The fight against climate change will require massive investment. BloombergNEF estimates getting to a zero-emission economy will cost more than $30 trillion, equal to about 30% of world GDP.[4]
- Leaps forward in artificial intelligence and other technologies might yet boost productivity, resulting in faster trend growth.

[4] BloombergNEF (2022).

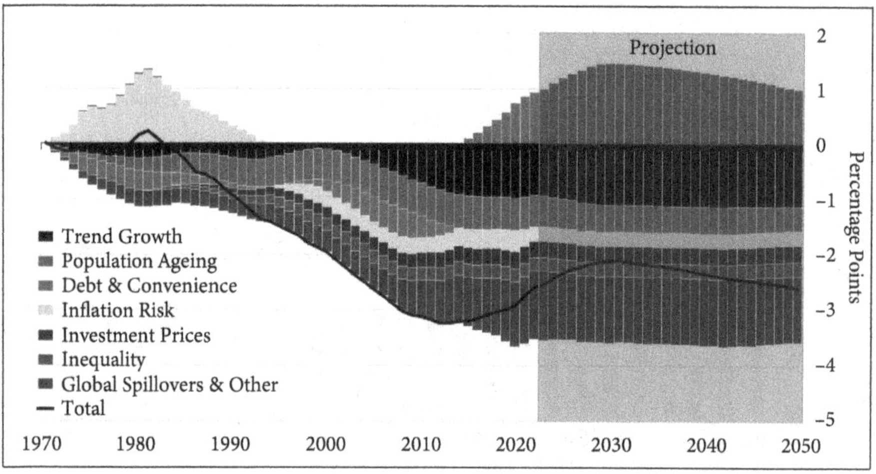

Figure 1.4 Forecasting the Natural Rate
Source: Ademmer and Rush (2024), Bloomberg Economics.

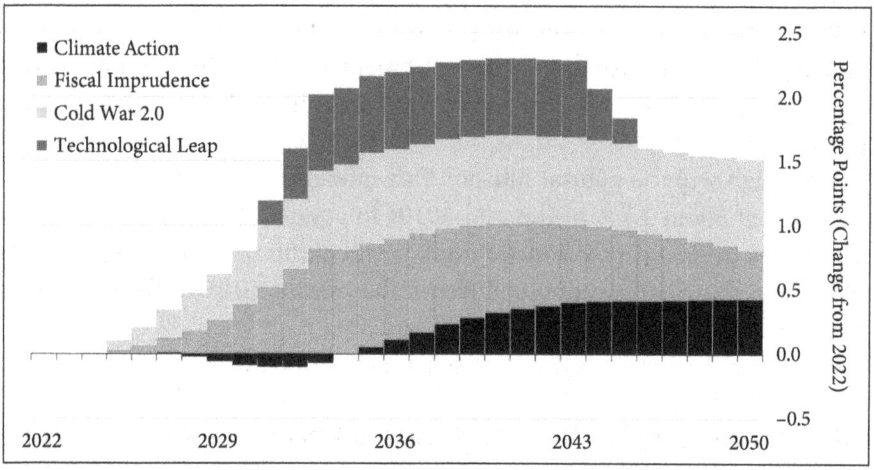

Figure 1.5 Risks Skewed to the Upside
Source: Bloomberg Economics.

High government borrowing, more spending on defense and fighting climate change, and faster growth creating more demand for capital would decrease saving and increase investment, driving the natural rate higher. As Figure 1.5 shows, it's plausible to imagine some combination of these impacts pushing the real natural rate of interest north of 4%, translating to a nominal 10-year bond yield in excess of 6%.

Even in our baseline projection, the shift from a falling to a rising natural rate will have profound consequences for the US economy and financial system.

Some are already evident.

One of the mysteries of the post-pandemic US economy is why 525 basis points (bps) of Fed rate hikes took such a long time to bring inflation back to the 2% target. A higher natural rate is likely part of the answer. Fed hikes lifted the 10-year Treasury rate to around 4.5%. That's more or less in line with our estimate of the natural rate, suggesting that policy wasn't as restrictive as it appeared.

Others will take time to materialize.

Since the early 1980s, house prices in the United States have roared higher, with the decline in interest rates a major contributing factor. With borrowing costs now set to edge higher, that process may come to an end. There's a similar story in equity markets. Since the early 1980s, the S&P 500 has surged upward, powered in part by lower rates. With borrowing costs on the rise, that impetus for ever-increasing equity valuations will be taken away.

Perhaps the biggest loser, though, will be the US Treasury. Even if debt rose no further, higher borrowing costs are set to add 2% of GDP to debt interest payments annually by 2030. If that had been the case in 2022, the year Russia invaded Ukraine, the Treasury would have paid out an extra $550 billion to bondholders—equivalent to two-thirds of the defense budget.

Of course, higher rates create winners as well as losers. Savers with their money in bank accounts and those piling into bonds will get a better rate of return. And a higher natural rate would also mean that when recessions hit, there'll be a little more room in the yield curve for the Fed to squeeze borrowing costs and stimulate growth, restoring some of monetary policy's lost firepower.

After years of falling rates, though, the US—and the world—needs to brace for a reversal. For everyone, from homeowners to 401(k) equity investors to the US Treasury, it's going to be a wrenching transition.

Bibliography

Ademmer, M., and Rush, J. (2024). "Drivers of the Natural Long-Term Rate of Interest (and Why the Economy Hasn't Tanked)." *Oxford Open Economics*, 3, odae012. https://doi.org/10.1093/ooec/odae012

BloombergNEF. (2022). "New Energy Outlook 2022." Bloomberg. https://about.bnef.com/new-energy-outlook-series/

Del Negro, M., Giannone, D., Giannoni, M. P., and Tambalotti, A. (2017). "Safety, Liquidity, and the Natural Rate of Interest." *Brookings Papers on Economic Activity*, 2017(1): 235–316.

Holston, K., Laubach, T., and Williams, J. C. (2017). "Measuring the Natural Rate of Interest: International Trends and Determinants." *Journal of International Economics*, 108: S59–S75.

2

From Wicksell to Bernanke

A Brief History of the Natural Rate of Interest

Jamie Rush and Tom Orlik

The natural rate of interest – the real cost of borrowing that keeps the economy on trend and inflation stable – "might have risen." So said Federal Reserve Bank of Minneapolis President Neel Kashkari, speaking in early 2024. John Williams, his counterpart at the Federal Reserve Bank of New York, and something of an expert on the subject, disagreed, making the case that it "still seemed quite low."

Who was right? For the Federal Reserve (Fed), the US economy, and the world's financial markets, the answer to that question mattered a lot. If it was Kashkari, then even 5.5%—the elevated policy rate reached as the Fed attempted to tame post-pandemic inflation—might not be restrictive enough. Rate cuts were still a long way away. If it was Williams, rates were already plenty high, and cuts could be coming soon.

As it happened, a jump in unemployment over the summer, and a drop in inflation back toward the Fed's 2% target, suggested that Williams was closer to the mark. The Fed kicked off its normalization of policy with a bumper 50-bps rate cut in September 2024. Weeks later, though, sturdy labor market data and robust inflation prints revived talk that policy wasn't as restrictive as it appeared.

The broader point is that the natural rate had shifted from academic obscurity to policy prominence.

From the Fed board to other central banks around the world to the trading rooms of Wall Street investment banks, it had become central to the understanding of monetary policy. Kashkari and Williams disagreed about the level of the natural rate. On its importance, they found themselves in wild agreement.

The journey of the natural rate from academic idea to market driver was long and winding. Along the way, it would pick up inputs from a blaspheming

Jamie Rush and Tom Orlik, *From Wicksell to Bernanke*. In: *The Price of Money*. Edited by: Jamie Rush, Tom Orlik, and Stephanie Flanders, Oxford University Press. © Oxford University Press (2025).
DOI: 10.1093/9780197800942.003.0002

Swedish mathematician, a giant of economic theory who missed the warning signs of the Great Depression, a member of a secret club of Cambridge "apostles," a Hungarian-American polymath, and John Williams himself.

The story starts in Uppsala, a small city near the capital of Sweden.[1] It was there, in 1898, that Knut Wicksell was the first to articulate that "there is a certain rate of interest on loans which is neutral in respect to commodity prices, and tends neither to raise nor to lower them."[2] The idea—which strikes now with the force of common sense—was at the time so revolutionary as to be hard to understand.

Wicksell, Fisher, and Ramsey: The Early Thinkers

In the late-Victorian era, a revolution was underway in economic thought. At the heart of it: recognition that decisions are made at the margin—businesses think about the cost and benefit of building an extra factory, households about the cost and benefit of saving an extra dollar of their income.

Economists already believed that interest rates were linked to growth and that the cost of borrowing should reflect the balance of saving and investment. But thinking was muddled. The idea that too much money chasing too few goods was inflationary had been in circulation since the 16th century. The theory was again expounded in the 19th century and formalized in the 20th, but there was no clear role for interest rates in driving the process.[3]

It fell to a controversial Swedish academic to propel the theory forward. Wicksell was a feminist, puritan, egalitarian, who even blasphemed his way into jail for a short spell. It's easy to understand why his views got a mixed reception. Nonetheless, the unorthodox thinker and PhD mathematician became a respected academic, credited with helping bring analytical rigor to economics.

In his early research, Wicksell furthered understanding of marginal productivity, setting out how inputs to production, like labor and capital, ought to be compensated.[4] In an insight that still holds today, he argued the return on capital—otherwise known as the interest rate—ought to be linked to the marginal product of capital—or how much extra output you get for a little bit of extra investment. Since the marginal product of capital partly reflects

[1] As Obstfeld (2023) points out, Henry Thornton, a British parliamentarian, set out similar views. Still, in our opinion, Wicksell was the first to do so in a way consistent with our modern understanding of the concept.
[2] Wicksell (1898).
[3] See Ricardo (1809) and Fisher (1911).
[4] See a reprint of the earlier work, Wicksell (1954).

technological progress, that also implies a relationship between interest rates and growth.

Wicksell also advanced understanding of the relationship between interest rates and inflation. In his seminal contribution, *Interest and Prices*, published in 1898, he argued that interest rates running below the natural rate create extra demand for loans. After all, if you can borrow cheaply and get a higher return by investing the proceeds, there's money to be made.

The extra demand for loans, Wicksell thought, would be met by banks, adding to the money supply. With more money circulating, but an economy operating with the same supply constraints, the result would be rising prices. His theories caught the attention of the government in his native Sweden, prompting what may have been the first modern experiment with price targeting by a central bank.

Wicksell introduced the concept of the natural rate, set out a link between productivity and real interest rates, and moved forward the understanding of interest rates and prices—no small contribution. Still missing from the framework: an understanding of households' decision-making about how much to spend and how much to save.[5]

The next leap forward came from the American economist Irving Fisher. Fisher was a giant of 20th century economics. In an unfortunate demonstration that no one gets everything right, he's best remembered for an ill-judged claim—nine days before the start of the 1929 Wall Street crash—that stocks had reached a "permanently higher plateau."

Like Wicksell, Fisher believed there was a rate of interest consistent with equilibrium between saving and investment—the key intuition underpinning thinking about the natural rate. And he supported Sweden's price-level targeting policy in the 1930s. But he clashed with Wicksell on what deviations of interest rates from the natural rate meant for prices.

Wicksell believed that any undershoot of interest rates relative to the natural rate would raise prices, partly because of the expansion in the money supply that follows when banks meet the demand for low-cost loans - which raises spending in the economy relative to supply.

Fisher was a firm believer in the quantity theory of money, which says that the price of goods and services will increase in proportion to the supply of money. There was, in his view, no mechanism for interest rates to affect money supply—and so no way for them to move prices. Most economists today side with Wicksell's view over Fisher's.

[5] In later lectures after the publication on interest and prices, Wicksell recognized the importance of saving and investment, referring to a "normal rate of interest" which reflects these influences.

Fisher made other contributions to economic thought that, to this day, underpin our understanding of consumer behavior and have important implications for the natural rate. His great insight, set out in his 1930 book, *The Theory of Interest*, was that the interest rate represents the price of consuming goods now relative to consuming them later on.

He showed that households will optimize their spending depending on how willing and able they are to shift their spending between time periods—which he described as the opportunity to invest income (to save) and how much they prefer to consume something now rather than later—which he referred to as the impatience to spend.

For the natural rate, that was an important development. It suggests the rate is determined not only by the marginal product of capital, as Wicksell supposed, but also by consumer saving preferences. If consumers decide to save more, the supply of savings goes up, and the natural rate falls. If they decide to save less, that dynamic swings into reverse.

Fisher's insight opens up possibilities for all sorts of other factors to play a role in determining borrowing costs. Moving from the decision of an individual about whether to save, to the level of an economy as a whole, factors from income inequality to population ageing, to China's management of its exchange rate all impact the natural rate. Anything that affects world saving has this effect.

Fisher made another contribution, demonstrating that what matters for spending decisions is not the nominal but the real rate of interest—the nominal rate adjusted for inflation. Since high real interest rates during the Great Depression sent the US economy into a deflationary spiral, this is one theory that pretty much all economists now agree with. It underpins models of the economy used by central banks around the world.

Thanks to Wicksell and Fisher, then, economists had a grasp of the key relationships that determine the natural rate of interest and the mechanism by which deviations from it affect inflation. Wicksell had demonstrated that the return on capital should be related to the marginal product of capital and that interest rates below the natural rate could spur bank lending, credit creation and inflation. Fisher's insight solidified understanding of how households' saving choices in aggregate impact borrowing costs.

There was, though, no coherent model that brought Wicksell and Fisher's insights together. That task fell to a brilliant young British economist, Frank Ramsey.

Ramsey was a member of an intellectual society—the Cambridge Apostles, dabbling in philosophy, maths, and economics. Remarkably, he made meaningful contributions to each before his untimely death from liver disease, age 26. At the urging of John Maynard Keynes, Ramsey wrote several papers on economics. For understanding the natural rate, the one that stands out is "A Mathematical Theory of Saving"—published in 1928.[6]

In the paper, Ramsey brings together Fisher's theory of choice between consuming now, or later, and Wicksell's link between the marginal product of capital and interest rates into one coherent model. Ramsey's model links the natural rate to trend growth as well as to households' saving preferences.

Ramsey's theory of saving may have been "one of the most remarkable contributions to mathematical economics ever made" as Keynes called it. At the time, though, it wasn't widely understood and failed to gain traction with other academics or policymakers. The pressing need to tackle the Great Depression, and then the turmoil of World War II, meant the focus of economics shifted elsewhere.

In the period after World War II, with memories of the Great Depression and the failures of laissez-faire economics fresh in the public imagination, it was Keynes' call for activist fiscal policy to manage the ups and downs of demand that dominated. Central banks were cast in a supporting role, charged with keeping borrowing costs for the government low and maintaining fixed exchange rates. The natural rate—never especially a hot topic—fell further out of fashion.

By the late 1970s, though, the combination of free spending by governments—including the United States for war in Vietnam—central banks more focused on keeping rates low than prices stable, and a major shock to oil prices as producers in the Middle East flexed their geopolitical muscles, meant inflation ran out of control. In the United States, the consumer price index entered the next decade with prices clocking close to a 15% annual gain.

That opened the door to a regime shift in economic policy and, belatedly, a shift to flexible exchange rates. Keynes' demand management was out. Monetarism—championed by Fisher's intellectual disciple Milton Friedman—was (temporarily) in. The initial strategy from Paul Volcker, the Fed chair that brought inflation under control, was straight out of Friedman's playbook. The Volcker Fed attempted to bring prices under control by setting a strict limit on the pace of growth in the money supply, crimping demand in the economy.

When that proved too difficult to implement, economists converged on short-term interest rates in money markets as the best way to control inflation. The final piece of the puzzle was insulating central banks from political influence—so interest rates could be set to win the fight against inflation,

[6] See Ramsey (1928).

not the next election. Formally, the Fed has been independent since 1951. It wasn't until the 1990s that reality caught up with the rules.

Somewhat circuitously, and almost a century after he proposed the idea, Wicksell's vision of a central bank pursuing price stability by setting interest rates became the standard operating framework for managing advanced economies. Not coincidentally, it was at the same moment that the natural rate of interest jumped nearly to the top of the economic research agenda.

Laubach and Williams: The Model of Neutral

Few economists have made as substantial a contribution to modern monetary policy as Columbia Professor Michael Woodford. His book, *Interest and Prices*—the same title as Wicksell's, also not a coincidence—further formalized the theories that underpin understanding of how interest rates affect the economy.

Woodford synthesized the monetarist and Keynesian schools of thought. The New Keynesian model he articulated came to define how many central banks think about monetary policy. While the natural rate plays a prominent role in Woodford's thinking, he did not attempt to explain in much detail what fundamental factors might determine it or try to estimate it.

Research by Thomas Laubach, an economist at the Fed, and John Williams—the same John Williams that debated the level of the neutral rate with Neel Kashkari—landed at around the same time as Woodford's book. It propelled Wicksell's theory to greater prominence.

Laubach and Williams used advanced econometric techniques to estimate variables that cannot be directly observed. For that they had Hungarian-American polymath Rudolf Kalman to thank. The statistical tool he designed in 1960—the Kalman filter—is used to make smart guesses about what's really going on in the world by combining noisy data with a model of the key relationships at work.

The Kalman filter is what keeps aircraft on the right trajectory, cruise missiles hitting their targets, satellites in orbit, and autonomous vehicles (mostly) from colliding with pedestrians. It also helps economists estimate the natural rate.

Using the Kalman filter, Laubach and Williams expressed their belief that the neutral real rate of interest follows the trend growth rate of the economy. They also relied on information about the business cycle to help infer where the neutral rates lies. Intuitively, when there's too much spending and the economy overheats, inflation will be above target. That suggests interest rates must have been below the natural rate. When there's too much saving, unemployment is high and inflation low – that implies interest rates must have been above the natural rate.

Trend growth is a loose anchor for the natural rate in the Laubach and Williams model and there is room for other drivers to have an impact. That's captured by a factor which they call "Z."

According to Laubach and Williams' estimates, the natural rate of interest has been falling for the past few decades. That's partly because trend growth has slowed but also because the mysterious Z factor has been pulling it down. They offered some possible explanations but nothing quantitative or complete on the drivers.

Bernanke and Summers: The Drivers of Neutral

With the natural rate now firmly back in the economics mainstream and central banks fully bought in, the focus of research has shifted to what might be driving it. One of the first big swings came in 2005 from then Fed Governor—and subsequently Chair—Ben Bernanke.

In the previous decade, and despite Fed rate hikes, long-term US borrowing costs (of which the path of expected policy rates is a key driver) had fallen, even in real (or inflation-adjusted) terms. In Bernanke's view, that was not primarily because of developments at home but rather because emerging markets—especially China and oil exporters, like Saudi Arabia—were recycling huge trade surpluses back into purchases of US Treasuries. Low US interest rates reflected the emergence of what Bernanke called a global savings glut.[7]

Former US Treasury Secretary Larry Summers saw things differently, with different drivers at play. In his view, interest rates stayed low because there was persistently insufficient demand in the economy. As evidence, he pointed to a wide—and widening—gap between projections for the level of GDP made before the Global Financial Crisis and reality.

When Summers ventured this theory in 2013, real GDP in G7 economies was almost 9% short of what might have been expected if 2000–07 growth rates had been sustained. In 2023, the shortfall reached around 13%.[8]

In Summers' view, the economy was in a downward spiral. Inadequate demand and insufficient space for stimulus meant weak growth. Weak growth

[7] See Bernanke (2005).
[8] See Summers (2013).

meant little incentive to invest, which meant a further blow to demand, lower natural rates, even less monetary policy space for stimulus, and even weaker prospects for the future. Reviving a term first coined in the 1930s, he called it secular stagnation.[9]

Divergent views from Bernanke and Summers—heavyweights of the economics profession—played out in 2015 in a public debate. Bernanke set out his skepticism of the secular stagnation hypothesis in a blog post, flagging a strong US labor market as counter evidence and the absence of a role for global savings in Summers' theory.[10]

Summers hit back, defending his theory and doubling down on his prescription that—with space for monetary stimulus constrained by the zero lower bound—fiscal policy had to do more to boost demand.[11] He also noted interest rates continued to decline even after emerging market current account surpluses shrank, and China stopped recycling its export earnings into US Treasuries, calling into question a key component of Bernanke's argument.

Who was right? Maybe everybody.

There is no contradiction between Bernanke's theory that the natural rate was pushed down by a global savings glut and Summers' view that demand was too weak to sustainably lift interest rates. The scale of the decline in long-term borrowing costs in recent decades means that both likely contributed, and there is still room left for other factors to play a role.

Bernanke and Summers identified some of the big forces dragging the natural rate down. The next step was to attempt to quantify their impact. Economists have taken three approaches.

The first is a summing up exercise. Lukasz Rachel and Thomas Smith—both economists at the Bank of England—contributed an early example.[12] They built an accounting framework to explain the 4.5 percentage point drop in global real interest rates between 1980 and 2015. They find that slower trend growth—which affects the return on capital—and demographics, which affect saving preferences, are the most important factors.

The second approach deploys sophisticated models to capture the age structure of the population and combines that with a simple model of how households make saving decisions. Because there is so much detail and so many variables involved, many of the parameters are specified based on other research rather than estimated from the data at hand.

[9] See Summers (2014).
[10] See Bernanke (2015).
[11] See Summers (2015).
[12] See Rachel and Smith (2015).

Ambrogio Cesa-Bianchi, Richard Harrison, and Rana Sajedi—all economists at the Bank of England—use a model in this spirit.[13] They found that slowing productivity growth and rising longevity explain the bulk of the decline in the natural rate since the mid-1970s.

The third approach uses what's known as a semi-structural model and lies somewhere in between the first two. Efforts in this direction posit that there is a relationship between the drivers and the natural rate and attempt to uncover their relative significance by estimating reduced-form models.

In this category we put Laubach and Williams (2003), Wynne and Zhang (2017), Caballero and Farhi (2018), and Del Negro et al. (2019). All tend to find a significant role for trend growth in determining the natural rate. The contributions of other drivers vary materially across different studies. This intermediate approach is the one we follow. We set out our model in the next chapter.

Rogoff, Rossi, and Schmelzing: The Challenge of History

As papers have proliferated, a parallel stream of research has called into question not just the models used to estimate the natural rate and its drivers but also the validity of the fundamental relationships on which they rely.

On the modeling, the oft-cited Laubach and Williams model has been criticized by former Riksbank economist Daniel Buncic. He questions whether econometric techniques can reliably extract estimates of the natural rate. He also shows that flexing the start of the sample period has significant implications for estimates of the level of the natural rate—a challenge to the robustness of the results.[14]

There's also the challenge posed by the historical data. The relationships between trend growth, demographics, and the natural rate—robust enough from the 1960s on—seem to evaporate when looking at a longer span of history. In fact, looking at data over centuries instead of decades, the relationship between growth and interest rates looks not just weak, but negative.

Kenneth Rogoff, Barbara Rossi, and Paul Schmelzing calculate global interest rates all the way back to the 14th century for advanced economies and assess the relationship with demographic and productivity factors, finding no causal role and divergences over long periods of time.[15] They also question

[13] See Cesa-Bianchi et al. (2022).
[14] See Buncic (2021).
[15] See Rogoff et al. (2022).

whether there is even an inflection point since 1981, conflicting with many other studies that look only at data from the past few decades.

Researchers at the Bank for International Settlements (BIS) pull the lens back to the 1870s.[16] Their results add to uncertainty over the robustness of the fundamental relationships assumed in much of the natural rate literature. BIS researchers also argue that monetary policy decisions, not structural forces like productivity and ageing, are the most important determinant of the natural rate.[17]

The implication of the BIS work is striking. It calls into question whether there is a single natural rate of interest determined by economic conditions and, indeed, whether the natural rate exists at all.

A Path Forward

The longer sweep of history certainly presents a challenge to conventional wisdom on the drivers of the natural rate. Still, 800 years is a long time. The modern world is very different from the medieval, and that raises questions about the extent to which data from past centuries should shape our view on current realities.

The data since World War II support the theory that underpins our understanding of the natural rate. Acknowledging the uncertainties and contrarian lessons from a longer history, it is in our view right to place much more weight on post-WWII data, and even more on data from the last half century, than earlier periods.

What about the other challenges? Could it be that the natural rate is simply a collective delusion of the economics profession? While it's possible that empirical support for the natural rate looks so bad in centuries past because economists have only recently willed it into existence, we think it is extremely unlikely.

Evidence of the importance of the deviations in actual interest rates from the natural rate to inflation outcomes isn't hard to find. Falling prices and high real rates deepened the Great Depression of the 1930s. In the 1970s, loose monetary policy contributed to spiraling prices. Equally, tight monetary policy from 1979 through the early 1980s under Volcker brought inflation back under control.

[16] See Borio et al. (2019).
[17] See Rungcharoenkitkul and Winkler (2021).

Turkey's experience offers a contemporary example. President Recep Tayyip Erdogan's belief that higher rates were not an effective way to bring inflation down contributed to price gains reaching 85% in 2022.[18]

None of that is definitive evidence on the level or drivers of the natural rate. But all of it is strong—in our view, decisive—evidence that there is a natural rate and understanding it is crucial to understanding how inflation, monetary policy, and the economy as a whole operate.

At the coal face of central banking, the day-to-day focus is on understanding and responding to the relentless sequence of shocks buffeting growth and inflation. Policymakers operating in an environment of extreme uncertainty feel their way to the right policy stance. As the Kashkari–Williams debate shows, estimates of the natural rate are an aid to that process. But a lack of real-time precision limits their relevance to finely balanced policy decisions.

By way of example, the confidence intervals surrounding the Holston-Laubach-Williams model were more than two percentage points wide during the late 2010s, even before the Covid-19 pandemic ripped through the world economy and deepened the challenges of estimating the neutral rate.[19] Estimates derived from different models, even those based on similar datasets, can differ by just as much.

So while inferring the natural rate from the temperature of the economy remains a useful exercise, given the uncertainties attached, we focus our attention on a longer view on the fundamental factors that have driven it over past decades and the outlook for the decades ahead.

Bibliography

Bernanke, B. (2005). "The Global Saving Glut and the U.S. Current Account Deficit." Federal Reserve Board. https://www.federalreserve.gov/boarddocs/speeches/2005/200503102/

Bernanke, B. (2015). "Why Are Interest Rates So Low, Part 2: Secular Stagnation." Brookings Commentary. https://www.brookings.edu/articles/why-are-interest-rates-so-low-part-2-secular-stagnation/

Bilgic, T., and Kandemir, A. (2022). "Erdogan Says Only Traitors or Illiterates Link Rate to Inflation." Bloomberg.com. https://www.bloomberg.com/news/articles/2022-05-27/erdogan-says-only-traitors-or-illiterates-link-rate-to-inflation

[18] See Bilgic and Kandemir (2022).
[19] See IMF (2023).

Borio, C., Disyatat, P., and Rungcharoenkitkul, P. (2019). "What Anchors for the Natural Rate of Interest?" Bank for International Settlements Working Paper, 777. Basel.

Buncic, D. (2021). "Econometric Issues with Laubach and Williams' Estimates of the Natural Rate of Interest." Sveriges Riksbank Working Paper No 397. Stockholm.

Caballero, R. J., and Farhi, E. (2018). "The Safety Trap." *The Review of Economic Studies*, 85(1): 223–274.

Cesa-Bianchi, A., Harrison, R., and Sajedi, R. (2023). "Global R" (No. 18518). CEPR Discussion Papers. London.

Del Negro, M., Giannone, D., Giannoni, M. P., and Tambalotti, A. (2019). "Global Trends in Interest Rates." *Journal of International Economics*, 118: 248–262.

Fisher, I. (1911). *The Purchasing Power of Money*. New York: Macmillan.

IMF (International Monetary Fund). (2023). *World Economic Outlook, April 2023*. Chapter 2. Washington DC.

Laubach, T., and Williams, J. C. (2003). "Measuring the Natural Rate of Interest." *Review of Economics and Statistics*, 85(4): 1063–1070.

Obstfeld, M. (2023). "Natural and neutral real interest rates: past and future." National Bureau of Economic Research Working Paper, 31949.

Rachel, L., and Smith, T. (2015). "Secular Drivers of the Global Real Interest Rate." Bank of England Staff Working Paper, 571.

Ramsey, F. P. (1928). "A Mathematical Theory of Saving." *The Economic Journal*, 38(152): 543. doi: https://doi.org/10.2307/2224098

Ricardo, D. (1809). *The Works and Correspondence of David Ricardo, Vol. 3 Pamphlets and Papers 1809–1811*. Online Library of Liberty. https://oll.libertyfund.org/titles/sraffa-the-works-and-correspondence-of-david-ricardo-vol-3-pamphlets-and-papers-1809-1811

Rogoff, K. S., Rossi, B., and Schmelzing, P. (2022). *Long-Run Trends in Long-Maturity Real Rates 1311–2021*. National Bureau of Economic Research. Cambridge, Massachusetts.

Rungcharoenkitkul, P., and Winkler, F. (2021). "The Natural Rate of Interest Through a Hall of Mirrors." BIS Working Paper, 974.

Summers, L. (2015). "On Secular Stagnation: A Response to Bernanke." Larry Summers Blog. http://larrysummers.com/2015/04/01/on-secular-stagnation-a-response-to-bernanke/

Summers, L. H. (2013). Remarks at IMF Economic Forum, Nov. 8. https://larrysummers.com/imf-fourteenth-annual-research-conference-in-honor-of-stanley-fischer/

Summers, L. H. (2014). "U.S. Economic Prospects: Secular Stagnation, Hysteresis, and the Zero Lower Bound." *Business Economics*, 49(2): 65–73.

Wicksell, K. (1898). *Geldzins und Güterpreise: Eine Studie über die den Tauschwert des Geldes bestimmenden Ursachen.* Jena: Gustav Fischer.

Wicksell, K. (1954). *Value, Capital and Rent.* New York: Augustus M. Kelley.

Wynne, M. A., and Zhang, R. (2017). "Measuring the World Natural Rate of Interest." *Economic Inquiry*, 56(1): 530–544. doi: https://doi.org/10.1111/ecin.12500

3

A New Model of the Natural Rate of Interest

Jamie Rush and Martin Ademmer

What is the natural rate of interest right now? How has it moved over time? What are the factors that drive it? The answers to those questions are not straightforward.

Economists agree on one thing—the natural rate of interest is that which is consistent with stable inflation and maximum employment. But they have different views on the specifics. Some imagine the natural rate that's needed to get inflation to target immediately, others over a longer time horizon. Some focus on the short-term interest rate, others on longer-term borrowing costs.

Then, there's the thorny issue of how to estimate it. That could be done top-down—taking the temperature of the economy and inferring the natural rate from that—or bottom up, assessing how factors like demographics and productivity growth are impacting borrowing costs. Some researchers assume the natural rate is determined locally; others allow for global factors to play a role.

In this chapter we attempt to steer a path through the complexity with a new model of the natural rate.[1]

The first step is to figure out which rate to measure. We settle on the rate on 10-year government bonds, which we think better captures the stance of monetary policy than the policy rate alone. From there, we combine a top-down model to estimate the level of the natural rate, and how it has evolved over time, with a bottom-up model to tease out the contributions of the drivers.

The results show that—adjusted for inflation—the natural rate on 10-year US Treasuries fell from nearly 5% in 1970 to below 2% in 2012, before rebounding slightly to 2.3% in 2022. The most important domestic determinants of the downward shift were slower trend growth and demographic

[1] See Ademmer and Rush (2024).

Jamie Rush and Martin Ademmer, *A New Model of the Natural Rate of Interest.* In: *The Price of Money.*
Edited by: Jamie Rush, Tom Orlik, and Stephanie Flanders, Oxford University Press. © Oxford University Press (2025).
DOI: 10.1093/9780197800942.003.0003

change. Our model also flags a significant role for global spillovers, inequality, and the falling cost of investment.

Our model isn't the only one in town. It's a good idea to consider our results alongside those from other analytical approaches—we share some of the main ones. It does use cutting edge econometric techniques and builds on existing wisdom. If economists are generally right about which factors have driven the natural rate lower, we think we have devised a good way of uncovering their relative importance.

Which Natural?

The stabilizing rate of interest, the short-term neutral interest rate, the long-term neutral rate, the short-term long-run neutral rate, and the natural rate: the basic belief that there's some rate of interest consistent with stable inflation and low unemployment is widely shared, the way to describe it is not. Economists use lots of different words to describe the natural rate, and often they have subtly different meanings.

Cutting through the terminological thicket, we see two important distinctions.

The first is the horizon over which inflation is seen as stabilizing. In the mind of Columbia Professor Michael Woodford—and it's his way of thinking that underpins central banks' Dynamic Stochastic General Equilibrium (DSGE) models of the economy—the neutral rate is the short-term interest rate consistent with getting inflation to target in the shortest possible time frame. In Woodford's world, the neutral rate moves around a lot, shifting with every shock that hits the economy.[2]

Fed economists Thomas Laubach and John Williams also focus on a short-term interest rate (the federal funds rate) but they have in mind a longer horizon for inflation stabilization.[3] They seek to uncover the policy rate that, if chosen, would keep inflation at target once all transitory shocks to the economy have worked their way through the system. This concept implies smoother, less volatile, estimates of the neutral rate.

The difference between these two concepts is simple—Woodford's neutral rate is what central banks should choose to get inflation back to target as quickly as possible. Laubach and Williams's neutral rate is the one that will prevail once inflation has already returned to target. Still, with the same name

[2] See Woodford (2003).
[3] See Laubach and Williams (2003).

for two overlapping but distinct concepts it's easy to see how confusion can creep in.

The second conceptual difference is the term of the interest rate—whether that's overnight rates in money markets or something longer term, like 10-year government bond yields.

Some studies consider neutral through the lens of longer-term interest rates. For Federal Reserve economist John Roberts in his 2018 paper, it's the 10-year Treasury yield that's the focus of attention, even as he attempts to estimate the rate consistent with getting inflation to target as quickly as possible.[4]

Completing the list of widely used definitions, a paper by Marco Del Negro and his Federal Reserve Bank of New York colleagues estimates both the short-term and long-term interest rate consistent with stable inflation, once all shocks have worked their way through the system.[5] As Table 3.1 shows, it's in the long-term, long-run corner of the literature that our own research resides.

The focus of our analysis is on estimating the level and drivers of the long-term interest rate required to stabilize inflation once all shocks have worked through the system. That focus is motivated by three considerations:

- Central banks have increasingly turned to unconventional measures like forward guidance and asset purchases to support the economy, the 10-year bond yield captures the stance of policy more completely than overnight rates.
- Households and businesses rarely borrow for a day at a time—they borrow for years and so it is long-term interest rates that should feature most

Table 3.1 Varieties of Neutral Rate

	Short-Term Interest Rates (Policy Rate)	Long-Term Interest Rates (10Y Treasury Yield)
Short-run inflation stabilization	Woodford (2003), DSGE models	Roberts (2018)
Long-run inflation stabilization	Laubach and Williams (2003), Del Negro (2017)	Our model, Roberts (2018), Del Negro (2017), derived from model

Source: Bloomberg Economics.

[4] See Roberts (2018).
[5] See Del Negro et al. (2017).

prominently in their decision-making and have the bigger impact on the economy.
- We are doubtful that econometric methods can calculate the rate required to bring inflation quickly back to target in real time with great precision—a viewpoint that's widely shared among policymakers.

With central bankers assessing the impact of so many shocks hitting the economy at any one time, and operating in an environment of elevated uncertainty, they feel their way toward the right policy stance by altering rates and monitoring the consequences—monetary policy is a live experiment.

Thinking about where interest rates may ultimately settle, once all shocks have worked their way through the system, is more consistent with our objective: identifying over a longer sweep of history why interest rates have fallen and forecasting where they are going. These motivations led us to the work of Del Negro et al., together with the theoretical exposition of Bank of England economists Lukasz Rachel and Thomas Smith.[6] Our econometric model builds on their work.

The centrality of 10-year borrowing costs for public finance choices, and as a benchmark for the valuation of other assets in financial markets, adds to the value of analyzing the natural rate through this lens.

Adjusting for Inflation

For many people in advanced economies, inflation has not been something that merits a lot of attention. Many of us have had the good fortune to live in a state of what central bankers call rational inattention—with inflation low and stable, it has simply not been worth spending too much time thinking about it.

That has also meant that for much of recent history it has been reasonable to assume that the difference between the nominal natural rate of interest and the real natural rate—the nominal rate adjusted for inflation—is roughly 2%. It is one reason we haven't so far spent much time distinguishing between the two.

But the difference between nominal and real can and often has mattered:

- During the Great Depression in the 1930s, nominal interest rates were low but plunging prices incentivized people to delay spending, worsening the slump—real interest rates were too high.

[6] See Rachel and Smith (2015).

- During the 1970s, when inflation was accelerating and uncertainty was extremely high, fear of rising prices brought spending plans forward, stimulating the economy and further exacerbating the inflation overshoot.
- And in the post-pandemic period of the 2020s, inflation in the United States and Europe rocketed toward 10%, with the impact of supply chain breakdowns compounded by massive fiscal stimulus in the United States and energy shortages (the result of Russia's invasion of Ukraine) in Europe.

Even in more normal times, businesses considering whether to embark on new investment projects compare expected profits (which depend on what price they think they will be able to get for their extra output) with the cost of the loan issued to finance that investment. Price expectations and inflation expectations do matter for decision-making in the economy.

Since the nominal interest rate we are using to capture the stance of monetary policy is a long-term concept, we use long-term inflation expectations to calculate the real rate of interest. Taking the United States as an example, that means the real rate is the 10-year Treasury yield less 10-year inflation expectations—based on survey data and extracted from FRB/US, the Fed's forecast model.

In what follows, our focus is the long-term natural rate of interest, by which we mean the 10-year real bond yield that is consistent with inflation at target and the economy operating at potential, once shocks have worked their way through the system. Where we use notation to describe this rate, that's R^*: upper case because it's the 10-year rate (not the policy rate) and a star because it's the natural rate (not the actual rate). The nominal rate equivalent is I^*.

Our Modeling Philosophy

Our model is underpinned by four beliefs:

1. *The natural rate is determined by fundamental economic drivers.*

We present our econometric model with a prior view and historical data for the variables that the literature suggests are the key drivers of the natural rate. For example, for the effect of trend growth we provide our model with the prior view—based on cautious reading of the academic literature—that every 1 ppt move in trend growth has a 0.5 ppt impact on the natural rate. Our model takes that as a starting point and combines it with the evidence from the historical data to get to a more precise estimate, ending in this case with a coefficient of 0.64.

2. *Actual interest rate data tell us something.*

Like Del Negro et al., we assume that borrowing costs can't have been too far away from the natural rate on average over the past half-century. If they were, then inflation would have exploded or the economy crumpled.

In practice, the way we take account of this is to build a model of the economic cycle, which includes interest rates, inflation, and GDP. It is a simple Vector Autoregression (VAR) model—a statistical approach which is largely atheoretical and assumes that the future path of interest rates is related to its previous values and the previous values of the other variables in the model.

The key assumption is that the VAR model is stationary. That means the gap between the variables and their trend values tends toward zero because all cycles eventually come to an end. That enables the model to act as a loose anchor, constraining estimates of the natural rate to be in the vicinity of actual borrowing costs. By getting rid of some uncertainty, this helps to raise the precision of our estimates of the effects of the drivers on the natural rate.

3. *The economics profession knows something.*

We also assume that forecasts of where 10-year bond yields will settle once the economic cycle is over (let's say five years ahead) tell us something about the natural rate. Economists use a lot of tools to think about such questions and so this is a way of shoehorning in wisdom drawn from a holistic set of research methods. The drawback is that economists have a frustrating tendency to get it wrong. So, while we place some weight on this anchor, we allow plenty of room for fallibility.

The purpose is to further disentangle the long-term interest rate trend from the vicissitudes of the short-term cycle, sharpening our estimates of the impact of the drivers. It is common practice in the academic literature to use survey measures of expectations in this way. Del Negro et al., for example, used inflation forecasts in their 2017 paper.

4. *The natural rate is globally determined.*

The natural rate of interest is determined by the balance between saving and investment. Because capital flows across borders, chasing the best returns, developments abroad will have an impact on domestic borrowing costs. To some extent, every country faces the global natural interest rate, but for several reasons we should expect to see variation between countries.

Most low-income countries do not have developed financial markets, meaning capital does not flow freely between them and the developed world. Africa, for example, accounts for about a fifth of the global population but only about 3% of GDP and a tiny fraction of financial assets. That means that, important as they are for other reasons, demographic factors in Africa only have a modest impact on the natural rate in advanced economies like the United States.

China offers another example. A country of 1.4 billion people with an economy similar in size to the United States ought to have a bearing on global markets. But access to Chinese capital markets is restricted, meaning—till now at least—the impact of developments in China on borrowing costs in the rest of the world has been determined more by government policy—especially management of the exchange rate and foreign exchange reserves—than by fundamentals.

Investors also tend to understand their local market better than foreign markets and prefer returns in their own currency. That creates a home bias, which raises the prominence of local drivers in determining the local natural rate, and can drive a wedge between that and the global rate.

In Del Negro's (2017) work, the model is focused on the United States. His (2019) paper takes a top-down global view. We settle somewhere in between, estimating the model for 12 advanced economies that are deeply integrated into global capital markets. This allows global determinants to have an impact on the United States, but also permits the United States to have an influence on the rest of the world.

Our results give us a path for the natural 10-year real interest and a set of coefficients that link its evolution between 1970 and 2022 to a set of fundamental drivers. Once we have estimated how the drivers affect borrowing costs, we don't need to rely on VAR models, hard data, or survey data to project the path of the natural rate forward. Projections for the drivers are all we need.

The Drivers

We have tried to be comprehensive in our model, including many drivers that have been identified in the literature.

Trend GDP growth—the economy's potential growth rate is a function of productivity gains and labor force growth. Both are likely to affect the natural rate of interest.

As the labor force expands workers must be equipped with the tools they need to be productive, and that lifts demand for capital. The other source of growth—improvements in the efficiency with which labor and capital are combined—also raises the natural rate. Because technology and know-how complement the stock of physical capital, faster productivity growth tends to raise the return on capital.

We use historical trend growth rates published by the Organisation for Economic Co-operation and Development to estimate our model, and Bloomberg Economics' long-term forecasts to project forward and conduct scenario analysis.

The dependency ratio—most people rely on their parents to support them when they are children, save during their prime working years, and spend down their pensions in retirement. As the ratio of dependents to workers goes up, the supply of savings goes down, and the natural rate of interest rises. We define the dependency ratio as the number of people aged below 22 and above 55, relative to the number of prime-age workers. We rely on the United Nations for historical data, forecasts, and scenarios.

Income inequality—higher earners tend to save a larger proportion of their incomes. So as income inequality rises, saving goes up, and the natural rate falls. The data we use come from the World Inequality Database. We define income inequality as the proportion of post-tax income going to earners in the top 10% of the distribution. Where those data are unavailable, we plug the gaps with pre-tax data.

The relative price of investment goods—as computers have become cheaper, the cost to businesses of upgrading their technology has declined. That's reduced nominal investment demand and dragged down the natural rate. We have used data from national accounts to calculate the ratio of the business investment deflator to the consumption deflator.

Net safe asset supply—the supply of safe assets, which we take to be US, UK, French, and German debt, has climbed in recent decades as the Global Financial Crisis (GFC) and Covid-19 pandemic drove up borrowing. In the first part of the 21st century, demand for safe assets from China and oil exporters also rose, absorbing the increase in supply. In the years ahead, the concern is that advanced economy borrowing needs will stay high, but demand for their debt will not. The net safe asset data are calculated from Bloomberg, the International Monetary Fund (IMF), and national sources.[7]

Debt issuance—higher domestic indebtedness raises default risks, pushing up on the country-specific premium on bonds and lifting the rate of interest.

[7] See Ferreira and Shousha (2020) for more on the impact of safe asset supply on the natural rate of interest

For some countries this is likely to matter more than others. The debt-GDP ratio data we use are from Bloomberg, the IMF, and national sources.

Inflation risk—with the oil price shock of the 1970s, uncertainty over the medium-term path of inflation spiked, as did uncertainty over how interest rates would evolve. The post-pandemic spike in inflation in the early 2020s introduced a similar but less pronounced dynamic. Fear of inflation reduces the attractiveness of locking money away for years at a time, raising the natural rate of interest on longer-dated securities. We can't measure this directly, so we use our own estimates of trend inflation as a proxy.

Convenience yield—investors are usually willing to accept a lower return for the convenience of holding safe and liquid government bonds. If this premium for safety and liquidity goes up, it will depress the natural rate. We capture this using Bloomberg data on corporate and public bond yields.

Key Findings

As Figure 3.1 shows, in nominal terms the natural rate for 10-year US Treasuries (I*) fell from a peak of about 12% in the early 1980s to a bit less than 4% in 2015—marking the end of a more than three-decade-long decline. The natural rate has climbed a little since 2020, mainly because governments have piled on debt since the pandemic, raising the supply of safe assets and increasing fiscal risk.

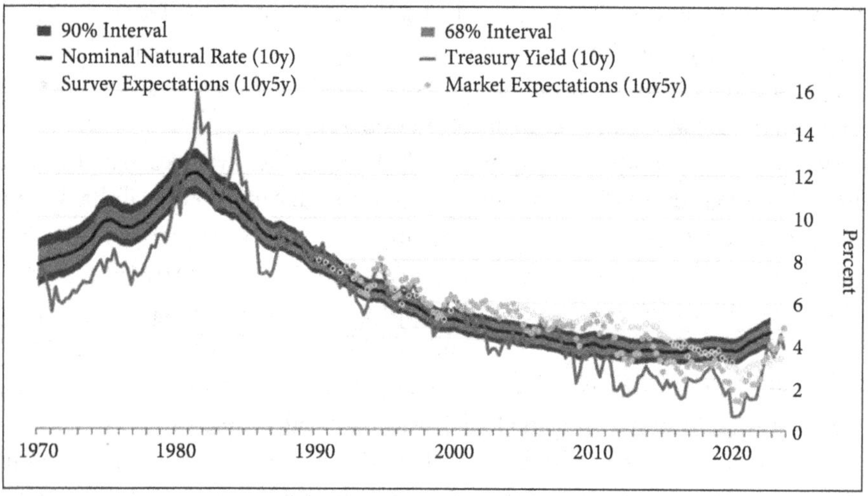

Figure 3.1 Long Decline in the Natural Rate Is at an End.
Source: Ademmer and Rush (2024).

A lot of the decline in nominal interest rates since the early 1980s is down to inflation having been squeezed out of the system. We estimate that lower long-run inflation expectations directly subtracted more than 4 ppt from yields since then.

In our full sample, we estimate the real long-term natural rate of interest fell by a bit more than 3 ppt. That might sound like a small drop in the return on safe assets, but consider the rule of 72—division of that number by your rate of return tells you roughly how long it takes for an investment to double in value.

In 1970 with real rates of return at almost 5%, it would take just over 14 years to double the value of your investment. At the 1.7% trough in the mid-2010s, it would take 42 years. That's a big difference.

As Figure 3.2 shows, one of the most important reasons for the drop in the real natural rate was weaker growth. In the 1960s and 70s, a swelling workforce and, in the first part of the period, rapid productivity gains meant average annual GDP growth was close to 4%. Strong growth created a powerful incentive to invest—lifting the cost of borrowing.

By the 2000s, those drivers were running out of steam. In the wake of the GFC of 2007–08, average annual GDP growth slumped to around 2%. A more sluggish US economy meant the attractiveness of investing for the future was weaker. We estimate this dragged the natural rate lower by about 1 ppt.

Shifting demographics also contributed through a second channel. From the 1980s onward, as the baby boom generation started squirrelling away

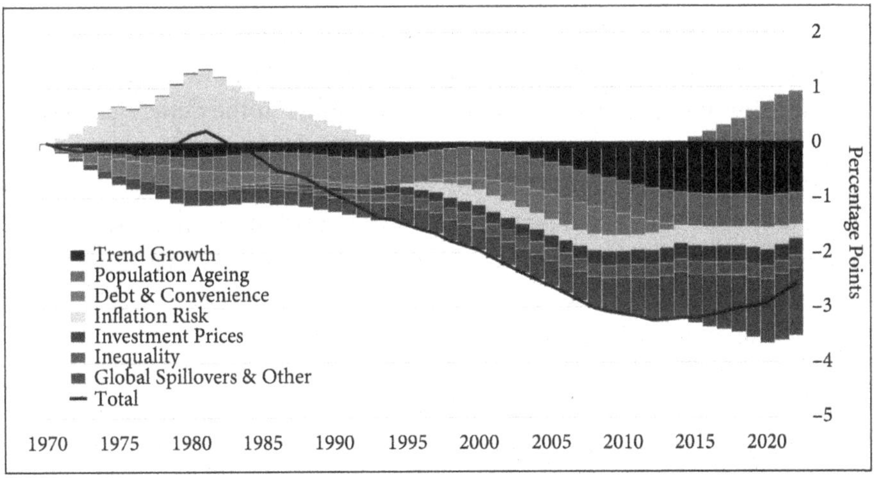

Figure 3.2 Decomposing the Fall in the Real Natural Rate of Interest

Source: Ademmer and Rush (2024).

more funds for retirement, the supply of savings went up, adding more downward pressure on the natural rate. We estimate shifts in the dependency ratio created about a 0.6 ppt drag.

Other factors also played a role:

- On the saving side, China was running large current account surpluses and recycling them into US government bonds. Federal debt issuance was also low. Before the GFC, these factors pushed down the natural rate by 0.5 ppt. By 2022, with debt up and Chinese demand down, these influences had begun pushing the natural rate up.
- In the United States, income inequality went up—high earners tuck away a higher share of their income, which further increased the supply of savings, subtracting 0.25 ppt from the natural rate.
- On the investment side, computers got cheaper and more powerful, meaning companies didn't have to spend so much upgrading their technology—lowering investment demand for capital and dragging the natural rate lower by around 0.3 ppt.

For the United States, we estimate that domestic drivers are by far the most important in determining the natural rate, with a weight of two-thirds. Spillovers from the rest of the world have a weight of only about a third. But because the slowdown in trend growth, for example, has been much more pronounced in other advanced economies than in the United States, global spillovers have also been an important driver of the decline in US borrowing costs.

We estimate the global spillovers have subtracted more than 1.2 ppt from the US natural rate of interest between 1970 and 2022. Slower global growth accounts for about 0.8 ppt of that total, with shifts in the dependency ratio, inequality, and investment prices accounting for the remainder.

For the other 11 countries in our model, domestic variables play a less important role, and global factors are more important. In the UK, the split is roughly 50–50. US drivers, in other words, have a bigger impact on the natural rate in other advanced economies than their drivers have on the United States. That shouldn't be surprising, given America's dominant position in global capital markets.

As Figure 3.3 shows, the real natural rate has moved in similar ways across advanced economies, with more variation in the 1970s and 80s—when country-specific risks varied wildly—than in the period since. The GDP-weighted average natural rate for the 12 countries in our model dropped from around 5.3% to 1.4%, following a similar trajectory to the United States.

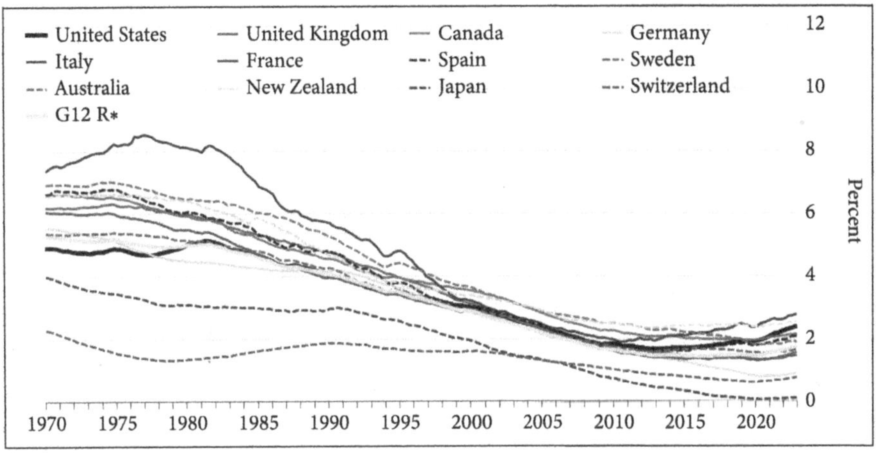

Figure 3.3 Comparing the Natural Rate of Interest in Advanced Economies
Source: Ademmer and Rush (2024).

As Figure 3.4 shows, slower trend growth was the biggest drag. Demographics also dragged, though there were some big differences between countries. Canada's dependency ratio plunged between 1970 and 2022, while Sweden's barely budged. There is also substantial variation in the contributions of domestic fiscal policy and inflation risk, given different levels of indebtedness and varying experiences during the high inflation period at the start of the sample.

Comparisons With Other Estimates

How do the findings from our model stack up against those from others? There aren't a huge number of studies that assess long-term borrowing costs. The closest comparators come from economists at the Fed. We estimate the natural rate declined by about 3.3 ppt between 1970 and 2015. As Figure 3.5 shows, that's similar to the 3 ppt drop that Federal Reserve economist John Roberts reports but quite a bit more than the 1.2 ppt Del Negro and his colleagues find.

Part of the difference may be varying interpretations of the natural rate during the high inflation period. We directly include an inflation risk premium, which raises our natural rate in that period. Del Negro et al. do not. If we compare the drop since 1990 (when inflation had generally settled down), we and Del Negro et al. both find a decline of about 2 ppt. Roberts shows a decline of about 2.9 ppt.

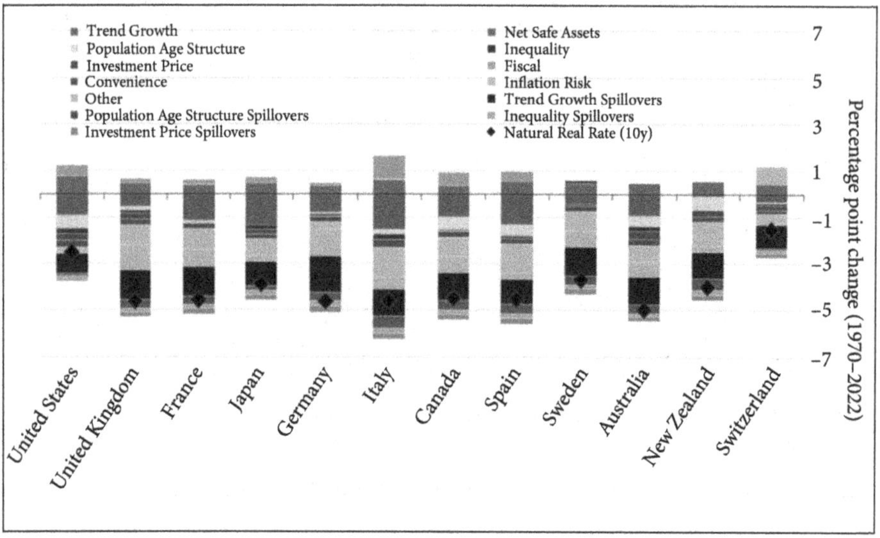

Figure 3.4 The Drivers of Lower Borrowing Costs

Source: Ademmer and Rush (2024).

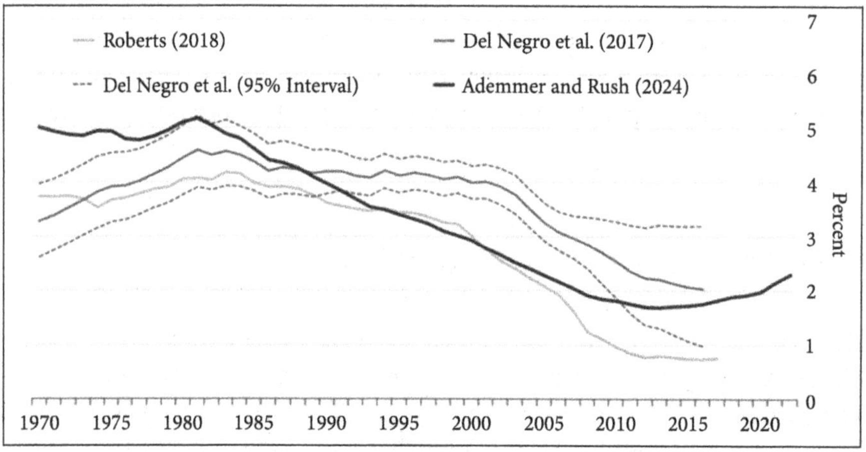

Figure 3.5 Long-Term Natural Rates Compared

Source: Ademmer and Rush (2024); Del Negro et al. (2017); Roberts (2018).

When it comes to the explanation for the drop, the Roberts' model relies only on taking the economy's temperature to infer the natural rate, so no comparison is possible. Del Negro et al. attribute more of the decline to movements in convenience yields—the hit investors are willing to take in exchange for greater liquidity. We include more drivers than Del Negro, so it is perhaps

Table 3.2 Contribution to the Change in the Real Natural Rate of Interest, 1980–2015

	Our Model (US)	Rachel and Smith (Global)
Total	−3.3	−4.5
Growth	−1.1	−1
Demographics	−0.5	−0.9
Inequality	−0.4	−0.45
EM Saving	−0.3	−0.25
Relative Investment Prices	−0.4	−0.5
Convenience Yield	−0.3	−0.7
Others*	−0.4	−0.7

*Includes some variables which do not overlap between models
Source: Ademmer and Rush (2024). Rachel and Smith (2015)

not surprising that we find the reasons for the decline are more spread out across them.

A direct comparison with Rachel and Smith's findings isn't possible because their group of advanced economies differs from ours. But it's close enough to allow some assessment of the similarities and differences. In Table 3.2 we compare their numbers on the drop in the neutral rate in the United States and the contribution of different drivers with our own. They are in the same ballpark, increasing our confidence in the robustness of our results.

Our main contribution to the literature is to combine the theory behind the key factors driving the natural rate from Rachel and Smith's calibrated approach with the econometric rigor applied by Del Negro and his coauthors. We're satisfied that the results are broadly consistent with both papers on the key drivers and reflect our best understanding of the drivers of interest rates over the past half-century.

Uncertainty

It's important to keep in mind that we are not able to pin down the natural rate with high precision. The credible interval bands surrounding the natural rate in Figure 3.1 only reflect uncertainty about the parameters we have estimated; they do not take into account that the theory or the model could be wrong. We have no way of incorporating that uncertainty.

To get an impression of the scale of model uncertainty, in Figure 3.6 we plot a selection of short-term natural rate estimates. To make our own numbers for the natural rate on 10-year bonds broadly comparable, we have subtracted an estimate of the trend term premium—the difference in the yield on short- and long-dated US debt, adjusting for the effect of the economic cycle.[8]

Our estimates are often in the center of the pack. At the same time, the range of results using different types of models is wide, ranging between 0% and 4% in the 1970s, and 0% and just over 2% in the early 2020s.

While we may not be able to say where the natural rate lies with precision, the broad trends identified by the different models are similar. Whether we look at short- or long-term estimates, they point to a significant move downward over the past half-century.

We think there is value in linking that shift to economic fundamentals. After all, without those links it is not possible to make any plausible assessment of where rates may be heading. That enterprise is the focus of the following chapters.

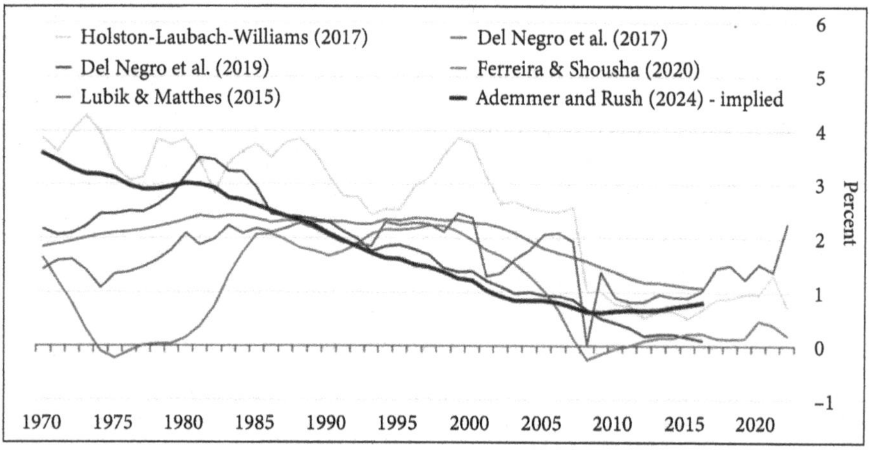

Figure 3.6 Short-Term Real Natural Rates Compared

Source: Ademmer and Rush (2024); Del Negro et al. (2017); Del Negro et al. (2019); Ferreira and Shousha (2020); Holsten, Laubach, and Williams (2017); Lubik and Matthes (2015).

[8] Note, that our model is only intended to uncover the impact of the drivers on long-term yields; it is not possible in our framework to cleanly disentangle their effects on the short-term neutral policy rate and the trend term premium for the countries we assess. For an estimate of the latter, we have relied on Del Negro et al. (2017).

Bibliography

Ademmer, M., and Rush, J. (2024). "Drivers of the Natural Long-Term Rate of Interest (and Why the Economy Hasn't Tanked)." *Oxford Open Economics*, 3, odae012. https://doi.org/10.1093/ooec/odae012

Del Negro, M., Giannone, D., Giannoni, M. P., and Tambalotti, A. (2017). "Safety, Liquidity, and the Natural Rate of Interest." *Brookings Papers on Economic Activity*, 2017(1):235–316.

Del Negro, M., Giannone, D., Giannoni, M. P., and Tambalotti, A. (2019). "Global Trends in Interest Rates." *Journal of International Economics*, 118:248–262.

Ferreira, T. R. T., and Shousha, S. (2020). "Scarcity of Safe Assets and Global Neutral Interest Rates." International Finance Discussion Papers No. 1293. Washington DC: Board of Governors of the Federal Reserve System.

Holston, K., Laubach, T., and Williams, J. C. (2017). "Measuring the Natural Rate of Interest: International Trends and Determinants." *Journal of International Economics*, 108:S59–S75.

Laubach, T., and Williams, J. C. (2003). "Measuring the Natural Rate of Interest." *Review of Economics and Statistics*, 85(4):1063–1070.

Lubik, T., and Matthes, C. (2015). "Calculating the Natural Rate of Interest: A Comparison of Two Alternative Approaches." Richmond Fed Economic Brief No. 15-10. Federal Reserve Bank of Richmond.

Rachel, L., and Smith, T. (2015). "Secular Drivers of the Global Real Interest Rate." Bank of England Staff Working Paper, No. 571. https://www.bankofengland.co.uk/working-paper/2015/secular-drivers-of-the-global-real-interest-rate

Roberts, J. M. (2018). "An Estimate of the Long-Term Neutral Rate of Interest." *FEDS Notes*, 2018 (2227).

Woodford, M. (2003). *Interest and Prices: Foundations of a Theory of Monetary Prices.* Princeton: Princeton University Press.

4

Hard Times, Happy Days, and Electric Sheep

How Slowing Productivity Growth Dragged Down the Natural Rate of Interest, and the Fourth Industrial Revolution May Push It Up Again

Ana Andrade

To understand the importance of productivity in economics, consider life depicted in a 19th-century novel, a 20th-century TV show, and a science fiction film.

Hard Times, the novel by Charles Dickens published in 1854, depicts the grinding poverty and brutal working conditions of factory workers in Britain during the first industrial revolution. Steam power has increased output and made factory owners rich. But by replacing rather than augmenting labor, it has immiserated workers.

Fast forward to the 1950s, and life, as shown in the TV show "Happy Days," has changed beyond recognition. At the center of the show, the Cunningham family are the beneficiaries of the second industrial revolution. Electrification, the internal combustion engine, and mass production were game changers for productivity. And because the new technologies tended to be labor-augmenting rather than replacing, the gains were broadly shared.

Blade Runner, the 1982 film based on the Philip K. Dick novel *Do Androids Dream of Electric Sheep*, portrays a future society where technology has leaped forward again, but standards of living have not. The plot centers on a group of superhuman replicants—robots that look and act like people—that have turned on their human masters. Once again, the question of whether advances in technology are labor-augmenting or labor-replacing comes to the fore. The replicants fall into the latter category.

Increasing productivity—getting more outputs from the same set of inputs—is something of a holy grail in economics. After all, it's raising

Ana Andrade, *Hard Times, Happy Days, and Electric Sheep*. In: *The Price of Money*. Edited by: Jamie Rush, Tom Orlik, and Stephanie Flanders, Oxford University Press. © Oxford University Press (2025).
DOI: 10.1093/9780197800942.003.0004

incomes that has the most material and direct impact on well-being. "Once you start thinking about economic growth," said Nobel Prize-winning MIT Professor Robert Lucas, "it's hard to think about anything else." As *Hard Times* and *Blade Runner* show, what matters for welfare is not just the increase in productivity, but how it is shared out.

Shifts in productivity, and who benefits from them, are also one of the main factors impacting the natural rate of interest. If labor-augmenting technologies boost productivity, that means growth is faster. That, in turn, means more incentive to invest, and so a higher natural rate. If productivity decreases, or labor-replacing technologies result in lower growth, that dynamic spins into reverse and the natural rate falls.

In the last 40 years, the pace of productivity increases has—in general—been muted. The information and communication technology revolution delivered a significant boost in the 1990s and 2000s. But relative to the game-changing technologies of the early 20th century—like electrification—the impact was limited. Advances in technology that replaced rather than supported workers—industrial robots for example—further blunted the boost to growth. And on either side of the computer revolution were the stagflation hangover of the 1980s and the post Global Financial Crisis funk of the 2010s.

In general, then, in the last half-century weak productivity gains have been a contributing factor to the slowdown in growth and the fall in the natural rate—which we estimate has drifted down from about 5% in 1970 to around 2% in 2022. Looking forward:

- Optimists see game-changing potential in technologies like artificial intelligence, betting they will deliver productivity gains comparable to those of the late 1990s and early 2000s—a return to Happy Days.
- Pessimists view the same technologies as offering only peripheral improvements.
- The dystopian view is that AI will be a game changer, but, by replacing workers rather than increasing their output, will result more in wider inequality than stronger growth—the Blade Runner outcome of super-advanced technology combined with limited improvements in welfare.

For the natural rate, those optimistic, pessimistic, and dystopian pathways flag the possibility of pressure for rates to rise, hold broadly steady, or resume their downward path. We explore all three scenarios, placing a somewhat greater probability on the view that AI won't represent a step-change in growth.

From Hard Times to Happy Days: A History of US Productivity Growth

Robert Gordon, a professor at Northwestern University and author of *The Rise and Fall of American Growth*, a sweeping analysis of productivity trends over the last two centuries, offers a framework for thinking about how different technologies have shaped the path of human progress.[1] He identifies three industrial revolutions.

The first came with the advent of steam power, commercialized by James Watt in the late 18th century. Steam power revolutionized the production of textiles, drove the first railway trains, and opened the door to the creation of the modern factory. Those were game-changing technologies, but it took a while for them to translate into a meaningful pick-up in growth.

Instead of increasing output, in the early years, the new machines ended up replacing labor. As a result, the economic pie grew a little, but the way it was shared out changed a lot. Factory owners—like Josiah Bounderby in Dickens' *Hard Times*—got more. Workers—like the hapless employees in Bounderby's factory—got less. Social upheaval followed.

It wasn't till the second industrial revolution—which began in the late 19th century—that workers began to enjoy the benefits of gains from new technology. By the 1920s, mass transport by railway and underground, electric lighting and household appliances, the telephone, running water and the internal combustion engine were all widely used.

As a result, the drudgery of tasks like carrying water was eliminated, working days were lengthened, and transportation and communication became faster and safer. An additional benefit—the streets of major cities were free of the manure that had been an unfortunate by-product of the horse-based transport system. It was a period of unparalleled progress, with benefits stretching far into the 20th century.

Annual labor productivity gains in the United States from 1891 to 1972 averaged close to 2.5%, catalyzing an extraordinary period of rising prosperity. By the 1950s, the comfortable home, automobile in the driveway, and Saturday night movies (enjoyed by the Cunninghams in Happy Days) were not aspirational luxuries but firmly within grasp for middle-class American families.

The third revolution came with widespread adoption of information and communication technologies (ICT) and industrial robots in the 1990s and early 2000s. Adoption of personal computers, software for word processing

[1] See Gordon (2012).

and managing data, and the birth of the internet didn't have the same impact as electrification and the internal combustion engine. Neither were the benefits so widely shared. Factory workers found themselves replaced by robots, and advances in software meant many clerical workers found themselves out of a job.

Still, as Figure 4.1 shows, there were definite gains, with annual average productivity growth in the United States during 1996–2004 bouncing back to a little above 3%.

From 2004 on, the pace of productivity gains has slowed again. A number of plausible—and not mutually exclusive—explanations suggest themselves.

- Stanford's Nicholas Bloom says ideas have become harder and costlier to dream up—slowing the pace of innovation.[2]
- According to analysts at the OECD, innovation is taking place, but the benefits are captured by superstar firms like Alphabet and Amazon, not diffused through the economy.[3]
- Economists at the IMF have made the case that barriers to trade and technology transfer slow productivity gains, raising the stakes as the United States and China become more suspicious of each other.[4]

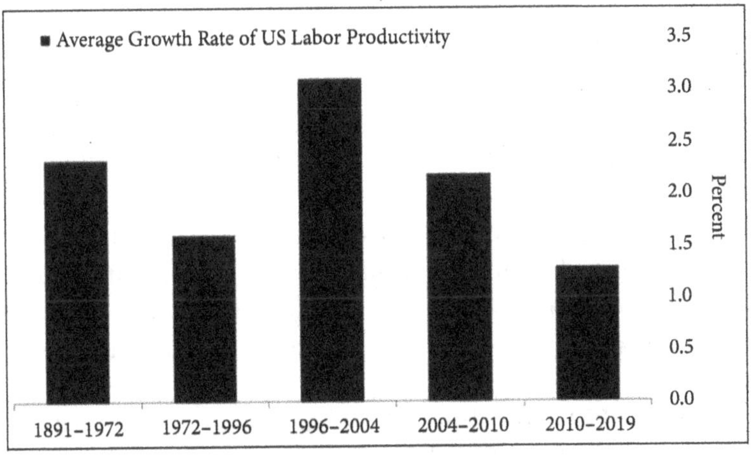

Figure 4.1 History of US Productivity Growth

Source: 1891–1972 average growth rates are from Gordon (2012). Other periods are from US nonfarm business labor productivity from the Fed database.

[2] See Bloom et al. (2020).
[3] See Berlingieri et al. (2020).
[4] See Adler et al. (2017).

- Former US Treasury Secretary Larry Summers argues the Global Financial Crisis had a long running impact,[5] with tight funding conditions, damaged balance sheets, and uncertainty stifling the animal spirits of innovators and entrepreneurs.[6]
- Stanford's Erik Brynjolfsson argues there have been substantial productivity gains, but they are not showing up in the economic data.[7] Google Maps, for example, makes it hard to get lost, but those benefits don't always register in gross domestic product (GDP).

Whatever the reason, in the period from 2004, when the ICT revolution ran out of steam, to the eve of the Covid pandemic in 2019, the pace of productivity growth in the United States slumped back to around 1.5%. Worse, with some of those advances coming more from labor-replacing than -augmenting technology, what gains there were got captured by the top 1%, and real incomes for middle class Americans actually fell.

It's possible the Covid pandemic—which raged around the world in 2020 and 2021—might have been the trigger for a fresh surge in productivity growth. A brief but deep recession, with workers and customers stuck at home, forced low-productivity brick and mortar firms—local cinemas, for example—into bankruptcy. High-productivity digital firms—like Netflix—took a larger market share.

On top of that, by forcing a transition to remote working, lockdowns triggered accelerated adoption of new technologies—Zoom for meetings, for example—while also pushing businesses to rethink their operations. It's possible that the digital leap forward will ultimately be a catalyst for efficiency gains.

So far, though, there's little evidence of that showing up at the macro level. Micro-level surveys also showed mixed results. Evidence from a study of call center workers, for example, pointed to 13% gains from remote working.[8] But a study of graduate employees in an IT services company found productivity dropped by up to 20% when they stayed home.[9]

Gains from the ICT revolution took a while to show up in the data. It's possible the same will be true of accelerated digitization of work forced upon the world by Covid lockdowns. So far, though, the idea of a pandemic-driven renaissance in productivity growth remains an intriguing but unproven hypothesis.

[5] See Blanchard, Cerutti, and Summers (2015).
[6] See Duval, Hong, and Timmer (2017) and Bloom (2014).
[7] See Brynjolfsson and McAfee (2011, 2014).
[8] See Bloom et al. (2015).
[9] See Gibbs, Mengel, and Siemroth (2022).

Blade Runner or Tech-Utopia?

What does the future hold? We consider three scenarios.

First and, in our view, more likely is that the future looks broadly similar to the recent past. Perhaps AI and other new technologies won't live up to the hype. Or perhaps they will, but fading gains from the ICT revolution will mean an offsetting drag. Either way, our conservative base case—which aligns with that of Northwestern's Gordon—is that we are not on the cusp of a sudden leap in productivity growth and that annual gains in the years ahead will be around 1.2% in the United States—broadly in line with the decade before the Covid pandemic.

What if that is too pessimistic? After all, the decade before the pandemic was also the decade after the Global Financial Crisis—which may have had a protracted negative impact on productivity. It was also a period before large language models like ChatGPT demonstrated the potentially game-changing impact of AI. In our second scenario, we align with optimists, like Stanford's Brynjolfsson, and assume that the world is on the brink of a fourth industrial revolution.[10]

How big could the boost to productivity be? In a study leveraging the 2019 Annual Business Survey—a detailed census of the business landscape in the United States—MIT professor Daron Acemoglu made the case that the use of AI alone was associated with a boost to labor productivity of 2%, but users of any two of a broader set of technologies might expect gains of around 12% on average.[11]

Following the template of the ICT revolution,[12] we assume that 12% gain would take a while to show up at all and would be fully realized over the course of a decade. That takes US annual productivity gains in the 2030s up to 2.4%, markedly higher than 1.2% in our baseline scenario. Taken together with our forecasts for labor supply, that suggests trend growth in the United States could accelerate to 2.7% over that period.

Not all countries are as good at rolling out innovations as the United States. To capture cross-country differences, we scale the boost to productivity from new technology by each country's adoption of mobile broadband (defined as subscriptions per capita) relative to the United States. That's a crude metric. Still, the degree of success that different economies enjoyed at adopting one of the bigger innovations of the recent decades provides a reasonable benchmark for their ability to do so with the coming wave of advances.

[10] See Brynjolfsson, Mitchell, and Rock (2018).
[11] See Acemoglu et al. (2022).
[12] See Hatzius and Briggs (2023).

That exercise suggests other advanced economies will benefit from the roll-out of AI and other innovations, but not to the same extent as the United States. In general other advanced economies would see annual productivity gains of about 0.7%—a bit more than half the 1.2% annual gains our exercise suggests for the United States. As Figure 4.2 shows, for the group of twelve advanced economies we include in our study of the natural rate, that would take annual trend growth in the 2030s up to an average of around 2%, compared to around 1% in our baseline.

So far, we have assumed that any AI-driven innovation wave won't lead to significant job losses. In other words, AI helps people to be more productive in their existing roles, and anyone that gets replaced by an algorithm finds a new job doing something else. That's a big assumption, but it's not without foundation.

MIT Professor David Autor[13] finds that 60% of employment in 2018 was in job titles that didn't exist in 1940. Advances in technology certainly destroy specific jobs—few people today are managing company accounts with a pen and paper. But the optimistic conclusion from Autor's work—and the fact that the ICT revolution has not driven a permanent rise in unemployment—is that new opportunities are created as well.

What if things don't play out that way? In their book *Power and Progress*, MIT's Acemoglu and his colleague Simon Johnson make the case for the

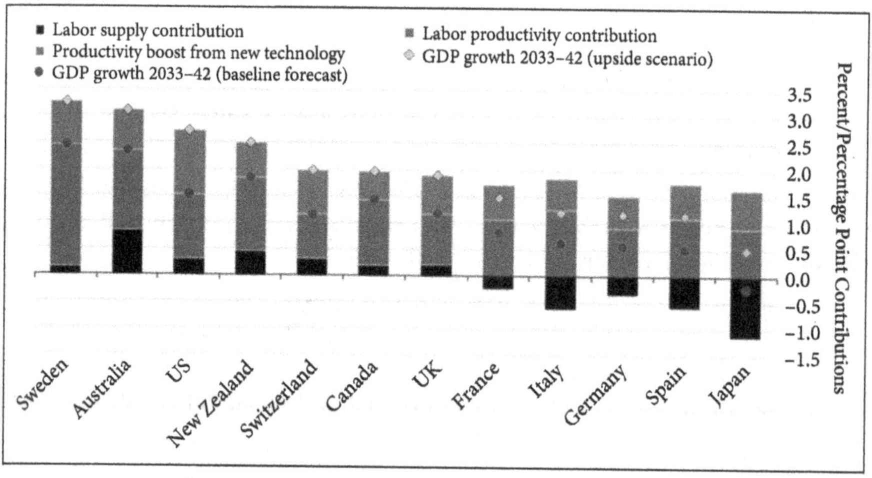

Figure 4.2 Optimistic Scenario: Future Productivity Gains
Source: Bloomberg Economics

[13] See Autor et al. (2022).

pessimists, showing that innovation and prosperity don't always go hand in hand.

From the Neolithic agricultural revolution to the information age, Acemoglu and Johnson show how new technologies that replace workers rather than augmenting their output can result in higher unemployment and widening inequality rather than stronger growth and rising prosperity.

Developments in manufacturing over the last 40 years support the labor-replacing thesis. The rise of industrial robots, largely a labor-replacing technology, has driven a fall in prime-age male participation across advanced economies.[14] Rust belt unemployment in the United States, and all the social blight that has brought with it, is a counter argument to the thesis that new job opportunities will spring up for those displaced by advances in technology.

With that in mind, we consider a scenario where looming technological advances are mainly labor-replacing. To see how this would impact long-term growth and interest rates, we need to have an idea about the percentage of jobs that can be automated. Oxford University researchers Carl Frey and Michael Osborne kicked-off the discussion in 2013, claiming that 47% of US jobs were at risk of being replaced by AI.[15]

Since then, the consensus has moved significantly downward. One OECD study[16] that looks at the degree of substitution of job tasks rather than occupations, and covers a range of countries, puts the share of workers at risk of being replaced at around 9% for the United States.

As Figure 4.3 shows, once we take potential job losses into account, the boost to growth from new technologies is materially reduced. For the United States, for instance, the 12% boost from new technologies over the adoption period is reduced to a net impact of 3% in total—a mere 0.3% on annual growth. For other advanced economies, the increase in annual growth would fall to around 0.2%.

The implications of mass adoption of labor-replacing technology go beyond the impact on trend growth. If our negative scenario played out, there would also be a significant adverse impact on inequality. The owners of capital would capture most of the benefits from advances in productivity. Workers would lose out. Widening inequality would also have implications for the neutral rate—a question we explore in Chapter 12.

[14] See Grigoli, Koczan and Topalova (2018) and Acemoglu and Restrepo (2020).
[15] See Frey and Osborne (2017).
[16] See Arntz, Gregory and Zierahn (2016).

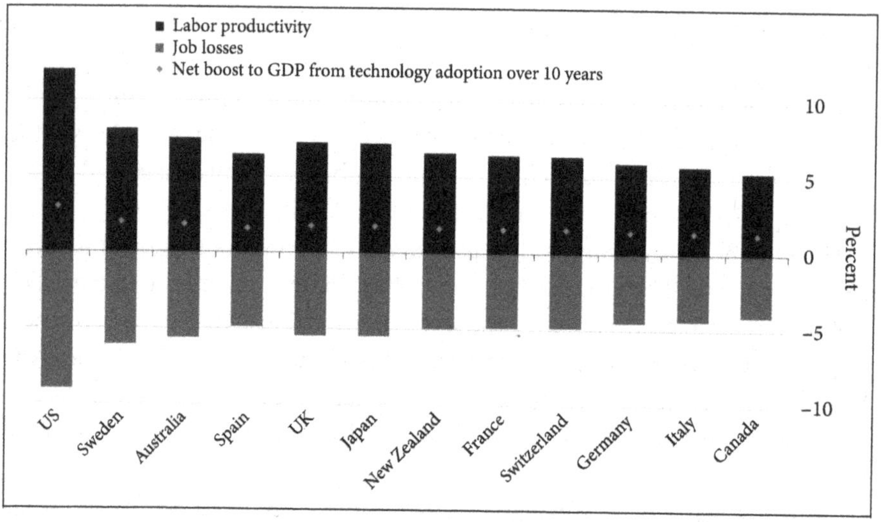

Figure 4.3 Pessimistic Scenario: Productivity Gains Offset by Job Losses
Source: Bloomberg Economics

Productivity and the Natural Rate

How do changes in trend growth impact the natural rate? Whether it's due to the workforce expanding or productivity gains accelerating, the influence on demand for capital is in the same direction:

- A bigger labor force must be equipped with the tools they need to be productive, which lifts demand for capital. Or, flipping that around and arriving at the same conclusion—a faster growing population means the stock of machinery per person goes down, raising the return on investing in new equipment.
- Technology and know-how complement the stock of physical capital. If technology improves at a faster pace, that raises the return on capital because more can be produced with the same inputs.

The traditional way to think about economic growth is through the lens of MIT professor Robert Solow's Nobel Prize-winning model, introduced in 1957.[17] Solow's model shows how growth accelerates when labor inputs go up, the capital stock expands, or technology progresses. Assuming that the amount of saving does not change, stronger demand for capital due to

[17] See Solow (1957).

accelerating population growth or faster technological progress will push up the natural rate.

This is the bedrock underpinning the famous model of Fed economists Thomas Laubach and John Williams. The Laubach and Williams model says the natural rate depends on productivity growth, population growth, and how much consumers prefer to consume now rather than later. Higher productivity and population growth raise the return on capital and create more demand for investment, pushing the rate up.

So far, so straightforward. But theory is only part of the story. There is also the empirical record to confront. Bank for International Settlements economist Claudio Borio conducted a series of simple, statistical tests on the link between interest rates and trend growth for a period starting in 1870.[18] He found that a strong and positive link only holds from the 1980s onwards, with all periods prior to that showing a statistically weak, and at times even negative, relationship.

Research assessing an even longer span of history casts further doubt on the relationship.[19] Trawling the archives, Schmelzing constructs a long-run interest rate series going back to the 14th century. He shows that rates have been falling across centuries—suggesting there are longer-run structural forces at work and cutting against the argument that it's the recent slowdown in growth that's behind the decline in the neutral rate.[20]

Those long-run studies are intriguing. At the same time, the economy of the late 20th and early 21st centuries is very different from that of the late 19th—and even further removed from that of the Middle Ages. It's reasonable to answer questions about what has driven rates down in the last 50 years, and where they are headed in the decades ahead, with reference to recent—as opposed to ancient—history.

For the last 50 years, there's little empirical controversy around the tight link between growth and interest rates. Borio himself finds both a positive and statistically significant relationship between trend growth, productivity, and neutral rates in his baseline estimates for the United States between 1985 and 2016. The link is even tighter at the global level and over a longer period from 1950.

Other studies corroborate the link. Laubach and William's work estimates a one-for-one relationship between trend growth and interest rates in the United States from 1961 onwards. The Bank of England's Lukasz Rachel finds

[18] See Borio, Disyatat, and Rungcharoenkitkul (2019).

[19] See Rogoff, Rossi, and Schmelzing (2022).

[20] Other studies looking at the lack of a significant or even positive relationship between growth and interest rates can be found in Hamilton et al. (2016) and Hartzmark (2016).

slower growth accounts for more than one-fifth of the decline in interest rates in the 30 years to 2013.[21] At the Federal Reserve, Marco del Negro shows slower growth accounts for 40% of the decline in the natural rate in the period from 1960 to 2016.[22]

The bottom line: extensive theoretical work and strong evidence of an empirical relationship over recent decades mean it is reasonable to assume there is a link between growth and the natural rate, but there is room for doubt about how strong that link is. That's the starting point for our own model.

Our Model

Our model—set out in detail in Chapter 3—requires a starting assumption for what the relationship between growth and the natural rate might be. We assume a coefficient of 0.5—meaning a one percentage point decrease in trend growth would drive a 0.5 ppt decline in the natural rate. That 0.5 assumption is between the roughly one-to-one relationship in the Laubach and Williams model and the no-relationship result suggested by Borio and Schmelzing's investigations of the longer span of history.

With that agnostic starting assumption, in the period from 1970 onward, the data turn us toward a coefficient of 0.64 for the United States—meaning every one percentage point drop in trend GDP or labor productivity growth results in a 0.64 ppt drop in the natural rate. Domestic drivers have a weight of about two-thirds in determining the natural rate of interest for the United States, with foreign variables accounting for about a third.

We estimate that trend growth in the United States has slowed to about 1.8% in 2022, from 3.6% in 1970. That adds up to a drag of about 1 percentage point on the natural rate of interest, of which around 30 basis points was because of lower labor productivity growth. As Figure 4.4 shows, the even more pronounced slowdown in trend growth among other advanced economies trimmed a further 80 basis points from the natural rate.

Looking forward, in our central scenario, with growth in advanced economies slowing from about 1.4% in 2022 to 1.1% by 2050, our model points to a downward drag on the natural rate of close to 20 basis points in the next 30 years. The drag on the natural rate from slowing growth will remain, but will be far less pronounced in the decades ahead than those behind.

21 See Rachel and Smith (2015).
22 See del Negro et al. (2017).

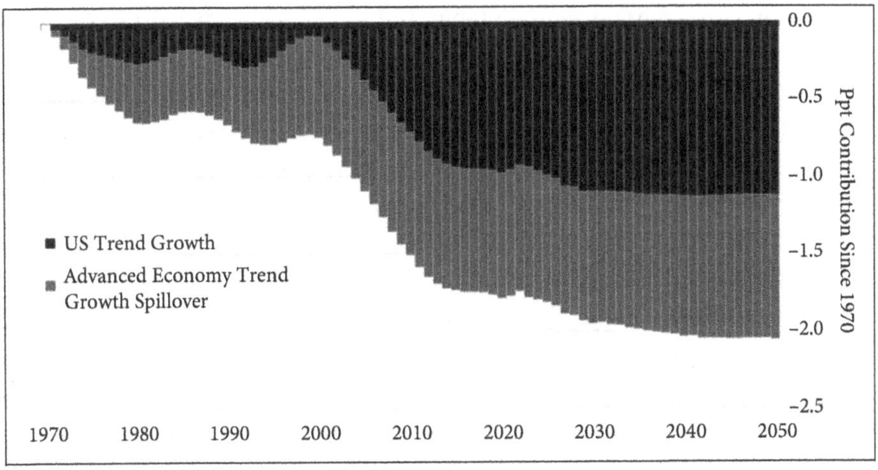

Figure 4.4 Growth Will Drag on Rates, But Less So than in the Past

Source: Ademmer and Rush (2024), Bloomberg Economics

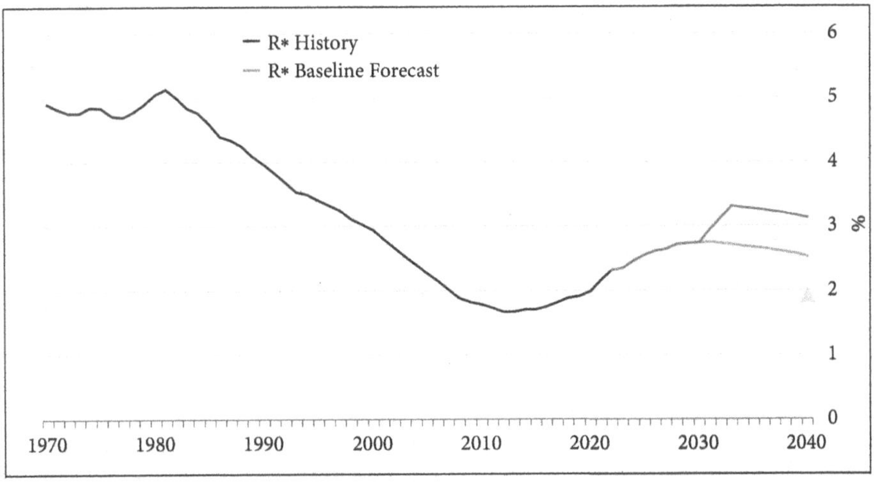

Figure 4.5 Impact of Faster Trend Growth on the Natural Rate

Source: Ademmer and Rush (2024), Bloomberg Economics

How about in our upside scenario for productivity growth, where AI and other innovations deliver a decade-long boost to trend growth without resulting in an offsetting surge in unemployment? As Figure 4.5 shows, that could lift the natural rate by between 50 and 60 basis points.

One important implication of our analysis is that countries outside the United States are substantially exposed to US borrowing costs because it's the deepest financial market on the planet. But they may not benefit to the same extent from the application of advanced technologies.

Take Italy. Should the AI revolution deliver in the United States but pass Italy by, its trend growth rate won't be much higher than in the baseline forecast. But global spillovers could raise borrowing costs for the government in Rome by around 0.5 ppt. Higher borrowing costs would not be matched by stronger growth—compounding Italy's debt distress. Missing out on revolutions in technology could turn out to be a costly mistake.

In the dystopian *Blade Runner* future, the boost to growth from strong productivity gains is offset by a drag from sweeping job losses. That would mean a more modest positive impact on trend growth and therefore the natural rate. Inequality, the subject of Chapter 12, would also leap as the benefits of next-frontier technologies accrue mainly to the wealthy. This scenario is consistent with a drag on the natural rate of about 60 basis points by 2040.

Conclusion

Summing up, there's a link between productivity growth and the natural rate of interest. Faster productivity growth means more opportunities for investment, pushing the natural rate up.

Reviewing the grand sweep of history, there's room for doubt about the strength of that relationship. In the period from the second half of the 20th century on, both the theory and the evidence point in the same direction—a decline in productivity growth has been one of the main factors dragging the natural rate down.

Our model shows the natural real rate on 10-year US Treasuries falling from 5% in 1970 to around 2% in 2022. A decline in trend growth in the United States—the result of both slower growth in the labor force and weaker productivity gains—explains about 1 ppt of the drop. Slower trend growth in other advanced economies explains a further 0.8 ppt.

Looking forward, our baseline assumption is that productivity gains will continue on the trend seen in the years before the Covid pandemic. If that happens, slowing trend growth will remain a drag on the natural rate, but markedly diminished. It will push down by a further 20 basis points by the mid-2030s. With offsetting pressure from other factors, that would leave the natural rate at around 2.8%.

We also consider a risk scenario where AI and other technologies drive an acceleration in productivity gains. If that happens, annual productivity gains could pick up to 2.4%, taking the natural rate to around 3.3% in the 2030s. Finally, we consider an extreme scenario in which productivity gains are completely offset by job losses. In that case, the impact on trend growth would be modest, and rising inequality would weigh on the natural rate.

Bibliography

Acemoglu, D., and Restrepo, P. (2020). "Robots and Jobs: Evidence from US Labor Markets." *Journal of Political Economy*, 128(6): 2188–2244.

Acemoglu, D., Anderson, G. W., Beede, D. N., Buffington, C., Childress, E. E., Dinlersoz, E., Foster, L. S., Goldschlag, N., Haltiwanger, J. C., Kroff, Z., Restrepo, P., and Zolas, N. (2022). *Automation and the Workforce: A Firm-Level View from the 2019 Annual Business Survey.* Cambridge, Massachusetts: National Bureau of Economic Research.

Ademmer, M., and Rush, J. (2024). "Drivers of the Natural Long-Term Rate of Interest (and Why the Economy Hasn't Tanked)." *Oxford Open Economics*, 3, odae012. https://doi.org/10.1093/ooec/odae012

Adler, G., Duval, R., Furceri, D., Çelik, S., Koloskova, K. and Ribeiro, M. (2017) "Gone with the Headwinds: Global Productivity." IMF's Staff Discussion Notes No. 2017/004, 98. https://www.imf.org/en/Publications/Staff-Discussion-Notes/Issues/2017/04/03/Gone-with-the-Headwinds-Global-Productivity-44758

Arntz, M., Gregory, T., and Zierahn, U. (2016). "The Risk of Automation for Jobs in OECD Countries." *OECD Social, Employment and Migration Working Papers*, 189(189): 12–15. https://www.oecd.org/en/publications/the-risk-of-automation-for-jobs-in-oecd-countries_5jlz9h56dvq7-en.html

Autor, D., Chin, C., Salomons, A. M., and Seegmiller, B. (2022). *New Frontiers: The Origins and Content of New Work, 1940–2018.* Cambridge, Massachusetts: National Bureau of Economic Research.

Berlingieri, G., Calligaris, S., Criscuolo, C., and Verlhac, R. (2020). "Laggard Firms, Technology Diffusion and Its Structural and Policy Determinants." OECD Science, Technology and Industry Policy Papers, No. 86, OECD Publishing, Paris, https://www.oecd.org/en/publications/laggard-firms-technology-diffusion-and-its-structural-and-policy-determinants_281bd7a9-en.html

Blanchard, O. (2023). *Fiscal Policy under Low Interest Rates.* Cambridge: MIT Press.

Blanchard, O., Cerutti, E., and Summers, L. (2015). "Inflation and Activity: Two Explorations and Their Monetary Policy Implications." *IMF Working Papers*, 15(230): 1.

Bloom, N. (2014). "Fluctuations in Uncertainty." *Journal of Economic Perspectives*, 28(2): 153–176.

Bloom, N., Liang, J., Roberts, J., and Ying, Z. J. (2015). "Does Working from Home Work? Evidence from a Chinese Experiment." *Quarterly Journal of Economics*, 130(1): 165–218.

Bloom, N., Jones, C. I., Van Reenen, J., and Webb, M. (2020). "Are Ideas Getting Harder to Find?" *American Economic Review*, 110(4): 1104–1144.

Borio, C., Disyatat, P., and Rungcharoenkitkul, P. (2019). "What Anchors for the Natural Rate of Interest?" Bank for International Settlements Working Paper, 777. https://www.bis.org/publ/work777.htm

Brynjolfsson, E., and McAfee, A. (2012). *Race Against the Machine: How the Revolution is Accelerating Innovation, Driving Productivity, and Irreversibly Transforming Employment and the Economy*. Lexington: Digital Frontier Press.

Brynjolfsson, E., and McAfee, A. (2014). *The Second Machine Age: Work, Progress, and Prosperity in a Time of Brilliant Technologies*. New York: W. W. Norton.

Brynjolfsson, E., Mitchell, T., and Rock, D. (2018). "What Can Machines Learn, and What Does It Mean for Occupations and the Economy?" *AEA Papers and Proceedings*, 108(108): 43–47.

Del Negro, M., Giannone, D., Giannoni, M. P., and Tambalotti, A. (2017). "Safety, Liquidity, and the Natural Rate of Interest." *Brookings Papers on Economic Activity*, 2017(1): 235–316.

Frey, C. B., and Osborne, M. A. (2017). "The Future of Employment: How Susceptible Are Jobs to Computerisation?" *Technological Forecasting and Social Change*, 114(1): 254–280.

Gibbs, M., Mengel, F., and Siemroth, C. (2022). "Work from Home & Productivity: Evidence from Personnel & Analytics Data on IT Professionals." *Journal of Political Economy Microeconomics*, 1(1), 7–41.

Hatzius, J. and Briggs, J. (2023). "The Potentially Large Effects of Artificial Intelligence on Economic Growth", Goldman Sachs. https://www.gspublishing.com/content/research/en/reports/2023/03/27/d64e052b-0f6e-45d7-967b-d7be35fabd16.html

Gordon, R. J. (2012). *Is US Economic Growth Over? Faltering Innovation Confronts the Six Headwinds*. (No. w18315). Cambridge, Massachusetts: National Bureau of Economic Research.

Hamilton, J. D., Harris, E. S., Hatzius, J., and West, K. D. (2016). "The Equilibrium Real Funds Rate: Past, Present, and Future." *IMF Economic Review*, 64(4): 660–707.

Hartzmark, S. M. (2016). "Economic Uncertainty and Interest Rates." *Review of Asset Pricing Studies*, 6(2): 179–220.

Duval, R., Hong, G., and Timmer, Y. (2017). "Financial Frictions and the Great Productivity Slowdown." IMF's Working Paper No. 2017/129, 32. https://www.imf.org/en/Publications/WP/Issues/2017/05/31/Financial-Frictions-and-the-Great-Productivity-Slowdown-44917

Grigoli, F., Koczan, Z. and Topalova, P. (2018). "Drivers of Labor Force Participation in Advanced Economies: Macro and Micro Evidence." IMF's Working Paper No. 2018/150, 40. https://www.imf.org/en/Publications/WP/Issues/2018/06/25/Drivers-of-Labor-Force-Participation-in-Advanced-Economies-Macro-and-Micro-Evidence-45977

Rachel, L., and Smith, T. (2015). "Secular Drivers of the Global Real Interest Rate." Bank of England Staff Working Paper, 571. https://www.bankofengland.co.uk/-/media/boe/files/working-paper/2015/secular-drivers-of-the-global-real-interest-rate.pdf

Rogoff, K., Rossi, B., and Schmelzing, P. (2022). *Long-Run Trends in Long-Maturity Real Rates 1311–2021*. Cambridge, Massachusetts: National Bureau of Economic Research.

Solow, R. M. (1957). "Technical Change and the Aggregate Production Function." *Review of Economics and Statistics*, 39(3): 312–320.

5

Demographic Destiny

How Baby Boom Savers Drove the Fall of the Natural Rate and Will Drive the Rise

Stuart Paul and David Wilcox

In 1960, the average American was 28 years old, the working age population was expanding rapidly, and there were 1.15 dependent children, young adults, or retirees for every working age adult. By 2010, the average age had increased to 36, the working age population was close to a peak, and the number of dependents for every working age adult had fallen to 0.89. Fast forward to 2060 and the average age will have increased to 43 and there will be 1.05 dependents per working age adult.

Shifting demographics have significant implications for the economy. An expanding workforce means faster growth and more opportunities for profitable investment. Working age adults are typically savers—stashing away a portion of their income in stocks, bonds, real estate, and saving accounts as insurance against a rainy day and for income in retirement. Children and old people, in contrast, tend to be spenders. Children need food, shelter, education, and healthcare. Older people typically get along by spending down their retirement savings.

The balance between spending and saving—and the shifts in that balance caused by changes in the demographic profile of the population—are important for the natural rate. Factors that increase the demand for savings—like rising potential growth as the working age population expands—tend to push the natural rate up. Factors that increase the supply of savings—like a falling dependency ratio increasing the share of savers in the population—tend to push it down.

From 1970 to 2022—when the annual growth rate of the working age population in the United States fell from 2.0% to 0.1%—the dependency ratio dropped from 1.24 to 0.93. We estimate that the natural rate, which we define as the long-term real interest rate consistent with stable inflation in

Stuart Paul and David Wilcox, *Demographic Destiny*. In: *The Price of Money*. Edited by: Jamie Rush, Tom Orlik, and Stephanie Flanders, Oxford University Press.
DOI: 10.1093/9780197800942.003.0005

the medium term, declined by about 2.5 ppt, with demographic influences accounting for about half the drop. In the years ahead—with the working age population set to plateau and the dependency ratio to rise—demographic pressure on the natural rate will swing from significant downward drag to modest upward boost.

Demographic Trends: History and Outlook

As Figure 5.1 illustrates, a chart of the US fertility rate from 1900 to the present day looks like a "W" written by a penman who, perhaps because of advancing age, lacked the energy to finish the final upward stroke.

- The fertility rate entered the 20th century on a pronounced downward trend, as rapid social change and adoption of basic methods of birth control pushed the average family size down.
- During the Great Depression, the US unemployment rate soared to a high of almost 25%, children became a luxury many could ill afford, and the fertility rate dropped even more quickly. Through most of the 1930s, it would hover around 2, slightly below the "replacement rate" required to offset deaths and maintain steady population size.
- It wasn't until the end of World War II, with the depression over, the troops back home, and the mood jubilant, that the birth rate rebounded. The Baby Boom, as it is called, ran from 1946 through 1964, with the

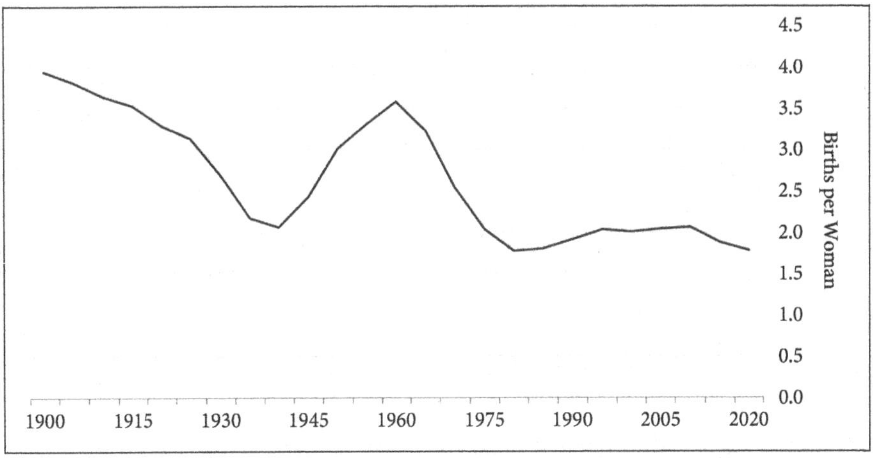

Figure 5.1 US Fertility Rate, 1900–2020

Source: United Nations World Population Prospects, Bloomberg Economics.

birth rate peaking in the late 1950s at 3.7—a level that had not been seen for 50 years.

- The factors that caused the boom to turn to bust are not well settled. Higher labor force participation by women, a larger share of the population attending college, wider availability of contraception, and increased costs of raising a child all likely contributed. Whatever the reasons, by the 1970s the US fertility rate had fallen back to around 2, a level where it has stayed ever since.

Our model of drivers of the natural rate includes two demographic variables. First, growth of the working age population—defined as people aged 15–64. Second, the dependency ratio—defined as the number of people aged 0–24 plus the number of people aged 65 and older, divided by the number of people aged 25 to 64.

In the United States and other advanced economies the decline in fertility since the 1960s has translated into a marked slowdown in population growth.

- As Figure 5.2 shows, growth of the US working age population peaked at 2% per year in the early 1970s. Since then, it has trended down to zero in the early 2020s. Based on the medium fertility scenario from the United Nations, in the decades ahead, it is expected to hover around zero.
- In other advanced economies, growth in the working age population started lower, got to zero earlier, and has been negative for most of the

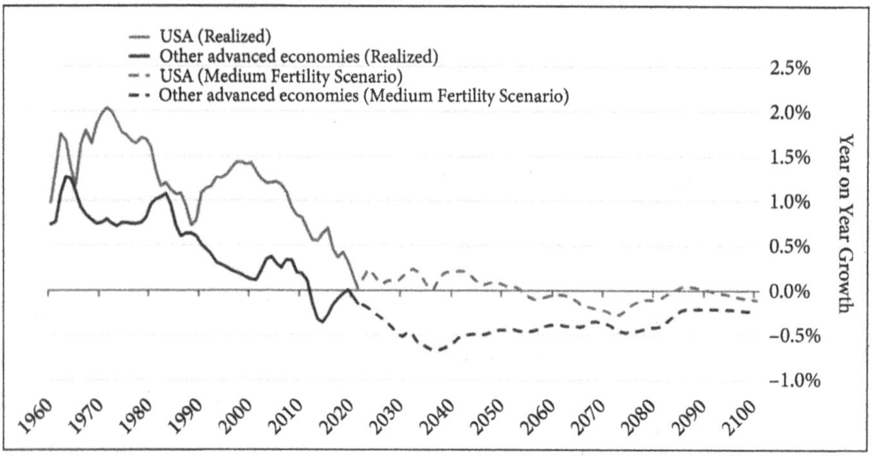

Figure 5.2 Advanced Economy Population Growth

Source: United Nations World Population Prospects, Bloomberg Economics.

period since the early 2010s. In the years ahead, the UN medium-fertility scenario points to the working age population declining at a more rapid pace until the late-2030s, at which point the pace of decline slows into the end of the century.

The dependency ratio fell from the mid-1970s to around 2010 in the United States and other advanced economies. Since then, it has leveled off in the United States and started to climb elsewhere. In the years ahead, with the retirement of the baby boomers, that upward trend is set to extend to the United States and continue in other advanced economies.

- As Figure 5.3 shows, the US dependency ratio peaked at 1.25 in the late 1960s when the boomers were still children. Over the final decades of the 20th century, as they entered the workforce, it declined markedly. In the first two decades of the 21st century, it has been flat at around 0.9. In the years ahead, with the boomers continuing to retire, it is set to climb, reaching 1.0 in 2050.
- In the other advanced economies, the dependency ratio started at a lower level, followed a similar downward trajectory, and has rebounded earlier. That divergence with the United States is explained by a combination of differing trends in life expectancy, fertility rates, and migration flows.

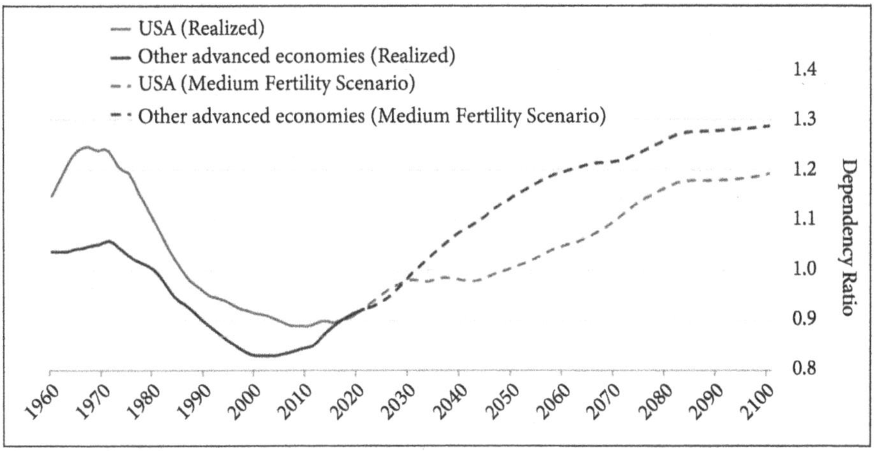

Figure 5.3 Advanced Economy Dependency Ratio

Source: United Nations World Population Prospects, Bloomberg Economics.

Population and the Natural Rate: A Contentious Debate

The literature assessing the influence of demographics on the natural interest rate is fractious and inconclusive.

Demographics were implicitly present in the Laubach-Williams model.[1] They impose that the natural rate moves one-for-one with changes in trend gross domestic product (GDP) growth. Trend growth equals the sum of growth in hours worked and productivity, and the growth in hours worked depends substantially on that of the working age population.

Laubach and Williams' research planted the presumption that demographics should matter for the natural rate. Despite that, researchers continue to dispute whether—and to what extent—demographics actually play a role.

Subsequent investigations have mostly taken one of two broad approaches. One strand of work has focused on developing elaborate representations of the age structure of the population, using what are known in the trade as "overlapping generations models."

- This approach formed the centerpiece of a recent analysis by economists from the International Monetary Fund. The authors conclude that demographic factors pushed down short-term borrowing costs by 0.4 to 1.5 ppt between the late 1970s and the late 2010s in the eight countries they examined.[2] The UK and the United States were among the countries encountering a drop at the smaller end of that range.
- Another example of this style of analysis was reported in a paper by researchers at the Bank of England.[3] They estimate that global r* (the short-term real interest rate consistent with stable inflation) declined a particularly large amount—from about 2.75% in the mid-1970s to -0.25% in 2015—a decline they attribute mostly to "falling productivity growth and increased longevity."

The other main style of analysis takes a strictly empirical approach and abstains from imposing a theoretical framework. The findings are decidedly mixed.

- An important example comes from Kurt Lunsford—a staffer at the Federal Reserve Bank of Cleveland, and Kenneth West—professor at the University of Wisconsin. Lunsford and West use data reaching back to

[1] See Laubach and Williams (2003).
[2] See IMF (2023): 54, Figure 2.7.
[3] See Cesa-Bianchi, Harrison, and Sajedi (2023).

1890.[4] They test more than 30 variables, and conclude that the growth of hours worked and the dependency ratio are both positively correlated with r^*.

- Claudio Borio of the Bank for International Settlements examines data from 1870 to 2016 across 19 countries, concluding that the relationship between demographics and the natural rate holds in recent decades but not earlier periods.[5] Harvard professor Ken Rogoff, CEPR fellow Barbara Rossi, and Paul Schmelzing of Boston College assemble an even longer data set and draw broadly the same conclusion.[6]

A more fundamental argument—advanced by Olivier Blanchard of the Peterson Institute—is that the presumption of a link between real interest rates and the growth rate of the economy was misguided from the outset.[7]

Blanchard notes that such a link *does* figure prominently in standard theoretical models of how *individual* consumers optimally choose the pattern of consumption over their lifetimes. However, there is no presumption that the same relation should manifest in data for the overall economy.[8] This may help explain why the relationship between r^* and various presumed drivers, such as trend growth, is so fragile in the data.

While Blanchard sees no reason to anticipate a reliable link between real interest rates and aggregate economic growth, he *does* see a causal role for demographics in the formation of r^*. In particular, an increase in longevity will probably be associated with an increase in the ratio of years in retirement to years working and, therefore, an increase in saving.[9] The increase in saving will drive r^* down. With life expectancy likely to continue increasing—even if at a reduced pace in the wealthiest economies—Blanchard anticipates that r^* will remain low and may move lower.

We conclude that the question of whether demographics matter for r^*—and if so, how much and through what channels—is not yet settled. Our model, described in the next section, attempts to cut through the confusion by taking a pragmatic approach.

[4] See Lunsford and West (2019).

[5] See Borio et al. (2019).

[6] See Rogoff et al. (2022).

[7] See Blanchard (2023).

[8] Blanchard gives an example of a theoretical economy in which the real interest rate exceeds the rate of time preference of individual consumers. As a result, every individual optimally chooses an upward-sloping trajectory of consumption over their lifetime. However, because the population is stable over time and productivity is—by assumption—flat, consumption in the aggregate is also flat.

[9] If the ratio of years in retirement to years working remains constant, then, at least in simple models, saving will likewise remain constant.

A New Model of R*

Demographic factors impact our model, set out in detail in Chapter 3—through two channels:[10] Indirectly through potential growth, which is driven in large part by the growth of the working age population. And directly through the dependency ratio. Our model is estimated on long-term borrowing costs, and we denote the natural rate on longer maturity bonds as "R*."

We find that trend growth has a coefficient of about 0.64, meaning every 1 ppt increase in growth pushes up the natural rate by 0.64 ppt. That's lower than the one-for-one relationship Laubach and Williams assume but higher than the long-term historical record suggests. For the dependency ratio, we find that every one-point increase raises R* by about 2.5 basis points.

We allow the US natural rate to be determined by both domestic and foreign influences, where spillovers from other countries are captured by including a GDP-weighted average of their drivers. We find that US drivers are the dominant determinant of the US natural rate. They also play an important role in determining other countries' borrowing costs, likely reflecting the central position of the US financial system in global capital markets.

In the United States, the growth rate of the working age population declined from 2% in 1970 to basically zero in the early 2020s—a material drop in an important determinant of the natural rate. Over the same period, our model shows R∗ dropped from about 5% to closer to 2% with the declining growth rate of the working age population accounting for about 55 basis points of the decline. Slowing population growth in other advanced economies accounted for a further 15 basis points.

The decline in the dependency ratio has played a similarly important role, trimming about 55 basis points from the US natural rate between 1970 and 2022. The decline in the dependency ratio in other advanced economies subtracted about a further 10 basis points.

As Figure 5.4 shows, slower population growth and a falling dependency ratio reduced the US natural real rate by about 135 basis points between 1970 and 2022. That's about a half of the total fall over that period.

For other advanced economies, the picture looks broadly similar. Demographic factors at home, and spillovers from shifts abroad, dragged the natural rate down by about 115 basis points between 1970 and 2022.

[10] Also see Ademmer and Rush (2024).

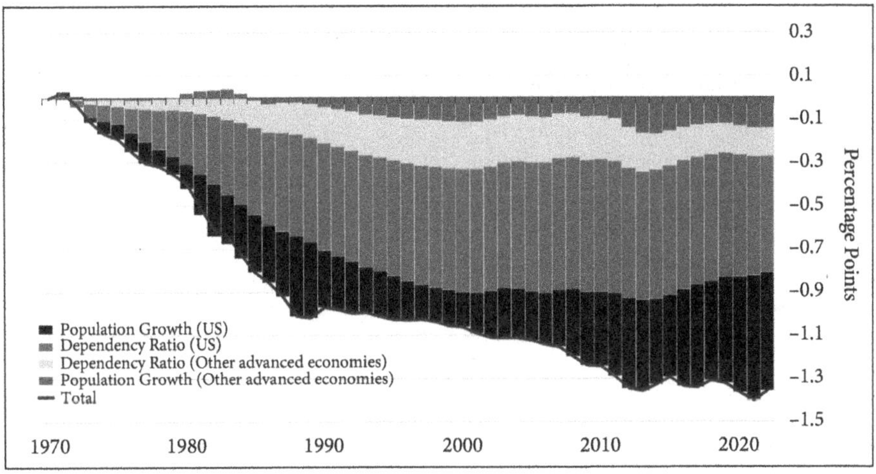

Figure 5.4 Impact of Demographics on Natural Rate in the United States: History
Source: Ademmer and Rush (2024).

Looking forward, the main impact of demographics on potential growth looks to be over. In the decades ahead, growth in the US working age population is set to hover around zero. Population growth will slow by more in other advanced economies, but spillovers to the United States will be modest. Our model suggests that domestic and foreign population growth will trim just 5 basis points from the US natural rate by 2050.

The US dependency ratio is set to climb as baby boomers move into retirement, and fertility rates stay low. Our model suggests an increase in the ratio from 0.93 in 2022 to around 1 in 2050 is set to add a little over 10 basis points to the natural rate of interest by 2050. Outside the United States, the ratio is set to climb rapidly, especially in Europe. Open international capital markets mean the wave of dissaving caused by aging populations will likely spill over to the United States.

As Figure 5.5 illustrates, our model suggests this will be the dominant demographic shift impacting the US natural rate in the years ahead, contributing a boost of approaching 20 basis points by 2050.

Putting it all together, our model suggests demographic change was one of the main reasons the natural rate fell from the 1970s into the 2010s. In the years ahead, though, we expect population aging to lift the US natural rate by about 25 basis points by 2050. Looking even further ahead to 2100, when low fertility rates have fed through more completely to the demographic structure of the population, the boost to the natural rate could be more like 70 basis points.

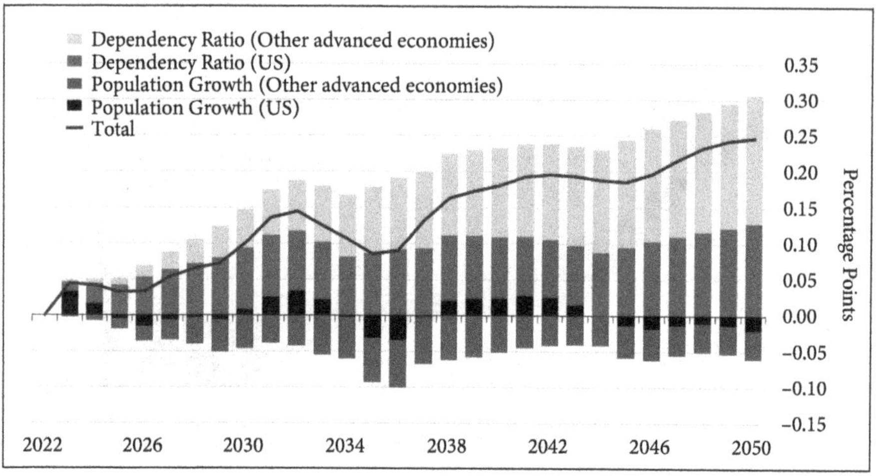

Figure 5.5 Impact of Demographics on Natural Rate in the United States: Forecast
Source: Ademmer and Rush (2024), Bloomberg Economics.

In addition to our baseline forecast, we consider two scenarios linked to the high- and low-fertility variants of the UN population projections. The immediate impact of higher fertility is more children and a higher dependency ratio—which means a lower savings rate and so a higher natural rate. In the long term, it also means faster population growth, which means more opportunities for profitable investment and so also a higher natural rate.

Those dynamics are evident in Figure 5.6 which shows that if the shape of the population in the United States and other advanced economies follows the UN high-fertility scenario, demographic factors will push the US natural rate up 80 basis points by 2050. In the low-fertility scenario, those dynamics swing into reverse, and first a lower dependency ratio, then a slower pace of population growth subtract 35 basis points from the natural rate.

Demographics aren't destiny, but for long-term trends in economic growth, savings, and the natural rate of interest they are close. From the 1970s to the 2010s, as the Baby Boom generation worked and fertility rates stayed low, growth in the US working age population slowed to zero and the dependency ratio fell. With slower trend growth reducing the incentive to invest, and a lower dependency ratio raising the saving rate, the result was a lower natural rate.

In the years ahead, as the baby boomers retire, growth in the working age population is set to stay around zero, and the dependency ratio will halt its decline and start to climb higher again. Our model suggests that this will raise the natural rate by about 25 basis points by 2050.

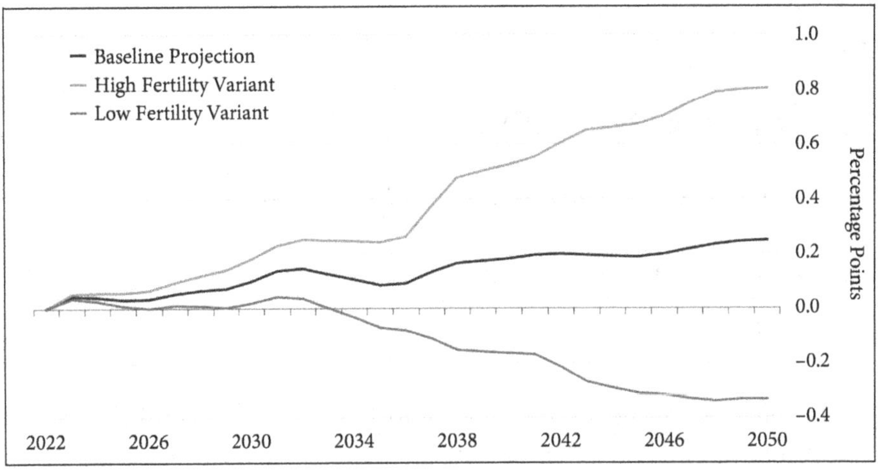

Figure 5.6 Impact of Demographics on Natural Rate in the United States: Forecast Scenarios
Source: Ademmer and Rush (2024), Bloomberg Economics, United Nations.

Bibliography

Ademmer, M., and Rush, J. (2024). "Drivers of the Natural Long-Term Rate of Interest (and Why the Economy Hasn't Tanked)." *Oxford Open Economics*, 3, odae012. https://doi.org/10.1093/ooec/odae012

Blanchard, O. (2023). *Fiscal Policy under Low Interest Rates*. Cambridge: MIT Press.

Borio, C., Disyatat, P., and Rungcharoenkitkul, P. (2019). "What Anchors for the Natural Rate of Interest?" Bank for International Settlements Working Paper, 777. https://www.bis.org/publ/work777.htm

Cesa-Bianchi, A., Harrison, R., and Sajedi, R. (2023). "Global R*." CEPR Discussion Papers. https://cepr.org/publications/dp18518

IMF. (2023). "World Economic Outlook, April 2023." Chapter 2. https://www.imf.org/-/media/Files/Publications/WEO/2023/April/English/ch2.ashx

Laubach, T., and Williams, J. C. (2003). "Measuring the Natural Rate of Interest." *Review of Economics and Statistics*, 85(4): 1063–1070.

Lunsford, K. G., and West, K. D. (2019). "Some Evidence on Secular Drivers of US Safe Real Rates." *American Economic Journal: Macroeconomics*, 11(4): 113–139.

Rogoff, K. S., Rossi, B., and Schmelzing, P. (2022). *Long-Run Trends in Long-Maturity Real Rates 1311-2021*. Cambridge, Massachusetts: National Bureau of Economic Research.

6

No More Free Lunch

Rising Debt Will Push Borrowing Costs Higher

Maeva Cousin and Jamie Rush

In the four decades before the 2008 Global Financial Crisis (GFC), debt in major advanced economies was not—in general—a cause for concern. US government borrowing was low and stable. Rising demand for Treasuries—especially from China—helped soak up what issuance there was, and interest costs were low. At the turn of the century, President Bill Clinton went so far as to declare the United States, "on track to eliminate public debt by the end of the decade."[1]

That's not what happened. When Lehman Brothers collapsed, the ensuing market mayhem ripped through the global economy. Activity slumped, tax receipts dwindled, spending went up, stimulus fell short, and, in the years that followed, fiscal consolidations failed. The result was soaring debt-to-GDP ratios. Then, when the Covid-19 pandemic erupted, governments embarked on a fresh round of stimulus, piling on more debt.

To put some numbers on it, in 2007 US debt stood at roughly 35% of GDP. By 2022, it had reached 95% of GDP, and Congressional Budget Office (CBO) forecasts show it on a path to exceed 105% in 2028. Debt in some other advanced economies is even higher. Italy's ratio in 2022 was close to 140%. Japan's was north of 250%.

Rising debt is having a substantial impact on the natural rate of interest, especially at the 10-year maturity, which is the focus of our study. We identify two main channels:

- Net global safe asset supply—more debt issued by historically safe sovereigns with deep bond markets (including the United States, UK, Germany, and France)—relative to the size of global GDP puts upward pressure on the natural rate across all countries.

[1] See Clinton (2000).

Maeva Cousin and Jamie Rush, *No More Free Lunch*. In: *The Price of Money*. Edited by: Jamie Rush, Tom Orlik, and Stephanie Flanders, Oxford University Press. © Oxford University Press (2025).
DOI: 10.1093/9780197800942.003.0006

- Domestic sovereign debt—higher government debt relative to the size of the economy—raises competition for domestic savings. It also increases the likelihood of default and the possibility that debt will be inflated away. Those are risks for which investors require compensation.

We estimate that rising US government debt added more than a percentage point to the natural rate between 2008 and 2022. For the other advanced economies in our study, the combination of increased global supply of safe assets and rising domestic debt pushed the natural rate up by an average of 60 bps.

What comes next depends on governments' ability to put debt on a sustainable path. In our baseline, we use the CBO forecasts for debt-to-GDP for the United States and the International Monetary Fund (IMF) forecasts for other countries out to 2028, and assume fiscal consolidation stabilizes the ratio in the years after that.[2] Our model suggests the rise in US debt projected by the CBO could push the natural rate up by another 50 bps by the late 2020s.

Risks are squarely to the upside. We also consider a scenario where governments take another five years to bring budget deficits under control as nominal GDP growth slows, borrowing costs stay high, and finance ministries fail to make the required adjustments. If that happens, US government debt could be close to 130% of GDP in 2035, driving the natural rate higher by 130 bps in total.

Prodigal governments aren't the only villains in the rising natural rate story:

- Higher investment, in particular the estimated $30 trillion cost to finance the transition to net zero carbon emissions (see Chapter 7), will likely add to the challenge of balancing the books.
- Geopolitical tensions and changes to investment patterns by emerging economies—China in particular and perhaps also Saudi Arabia and other oil exporters—will likely lower the global demand for safe assets (see Chapters 9 and 10).
- There's also the danger of a vicious circle, as higher debt pushes up interest rates, and higher interest rates make debt servicing more expensive.

Public Debt: A Brief History in Two Acts

The history of government borrowing across most advanced economies since the 1970s can be split into two periods: the 40 years before the GFC and the

[2] See CBO (2023) and IMF (2023).

15 years since. In the first period, debt ratios were generally low and stable. In the second, they were not.

In the United States, the decades before the GFC saw strong nominal growth (averaging close to 7.5% a year), fiscal prudence (primary balances not far from zero), and a low stock of debt that helped contain interest costs. As a result, in 2007, US federal debt held by the public was a modest and manageable 35% of GDP.

Other advanced economies also kept borrowing under control. By 2007, most of the other 11 in our study had debt below or only slightly above the 60% of GDP threshold beyond which risk premiums might start to climb.[3] Italy and Japan, where public debt reached 103% and 173%, respectively, were the two exceptions.

The GFC that began to unfold at the end of 2007 came with a huge fiscal price tag attached. GDP plummeted, tax revenues fell, benefit spending increased, and governments opened the stimulus spigots.

All of that resulted in blowout budget deficits. In the 2010s, as low nominal growth crimped tax revenue, it became increasingly difficult to balance the books. In some countries, particularly in Southern Europe, austerity proved self-defeating, as falling activity added to the pressure on the public finances, and debt ratios marched higher.

By 2019, on the eve of the Covid-19 pandemic, debt as a share of GDP was generally well above 2007 levels. As Figure 6.1 shows, it had risen to 79% of GDP in the United States, 134% in Italy, and 236% in Japan.

The pandemic was the trigger for another shift higher. Shuttered economies meant GDP plunged, and tax revenue dried up. Huge income support packages and other stimulus meant spending ballooned. The result was a huge increase in debt-to-GDP ratios, with double-digit jumps common.

The rise in government debt in the United States, UK, Germany, and France pushed up the supply of safe assets relative to the size of the global economy. As Figure 6.2 shows, total public debt of the United States, UK, France, and Germany jumped from 18% of global GDP, in 2007, to nearly 23% in 2009, and 35% in 2020.

Demand for safe assets didn't rise enough to match the increase in supply. China, in particular, had transitioned its growth model away from dependence on a managed exchange rate and strong exports, meaning its purchases of US government debt had effectively ended. As a result, the net supply of safe assets increased significantly.

[3] See Alcidi and Gros (2018).

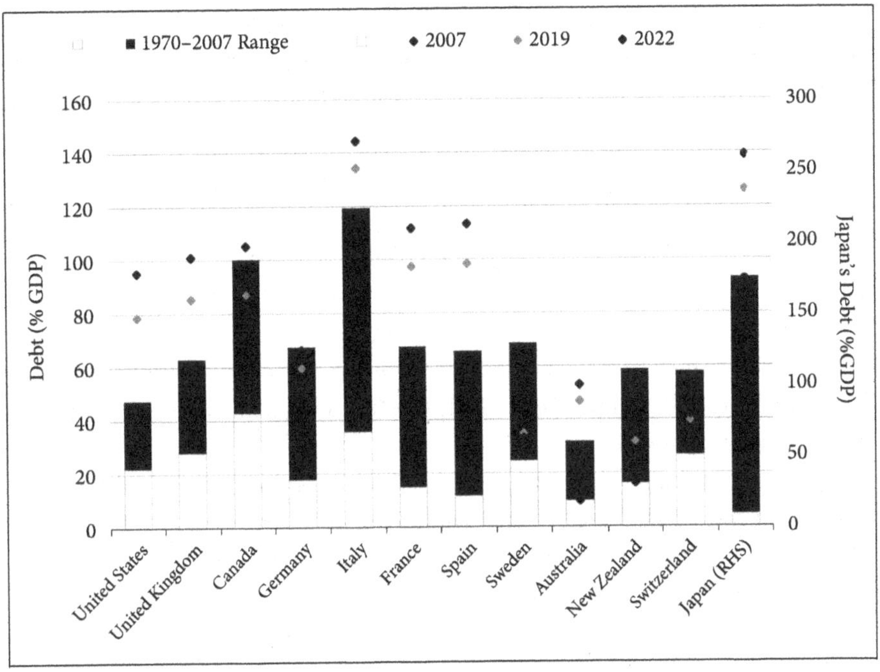

Figure 6.1 Global Financial Crisis, Covid Pandemic, Were Triggers for Rising Debt

Source: US: Federal Debt Held by the Public (Congressional Budget Office); Other Countries: General Government Debt, IMF.

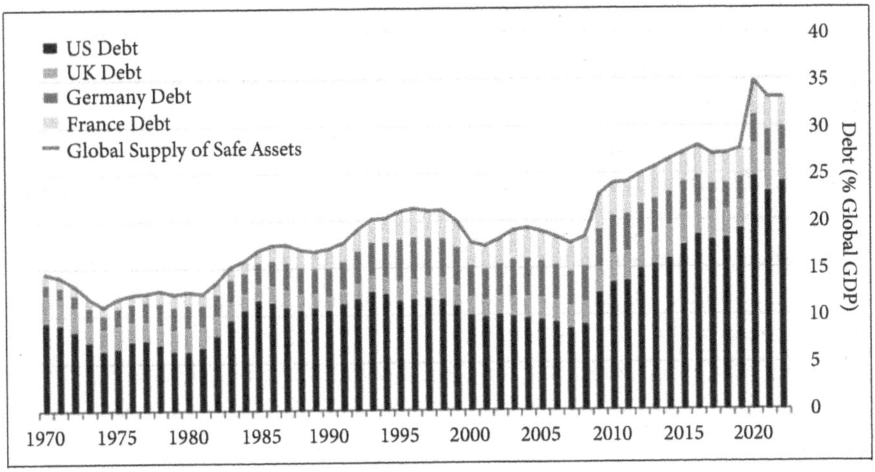

Figure 6.2 Global Supply of Safe Assets Leapt

Source: Bloomberg Economics.

We define the net supply of safe assets as the sum of US, UK, French, and German sovereign debt, less foreign governments' exchange reserve holdings—similar to the definition used by Fed economists Thiago Ferreira and Samer Shousha.[4]

From Rising Debt to a Higher Natural Rate

To assess the impact of rising indebtedness on the natural rate, we consider two main channels. First is via the contribution to global saving imbalances. Second is through competition for domestic savings and the perceptions of default and inflation risk.

A key contribution to our understanding is former Fed Chair Ben Bernanke's view that a global savings glut pushed down the sustainable rate of interest in the United States in the period before the GFC.

Back then, the yuan was weak, helping to supercharge Chinese exports and damping imports. To prevent the resulting trade surplus driving up the value of the currency, China's central bank bought exporters' dollar earnings at a fixed rate, recycling them into US Treasuries. Oil exporters in the Middle East were awash with cash and, with little desire to spend it at home, did the same.

The Bernanke hypothesis is that foreign demand for safe assets outstripped supply, creating an imbalance between investment and saving on a global scale and pushing down the natural rate. The corollary is that when issuers of safe assets open the spending taps and raise debt, then we should expect supply to outstrip demand and the natural rate to rise.

Reflecting Bernanke's contribution, other studies of the natural rate also include the net supply of safe assets as an explanatory variable or appeal to his hypothesis to underpin their analysis. Work in that vein—including by Ferreira and Shousha and Del Negro and colleagues—has influenced the design of our model.[5]

Because we are estimating the natural rate of interest for long-term sovereign bonds, we also need to take into account the impact of higher indebtedness on a country-specific basis. That's because high government spending creates competition for local savings. Combined with barriers to cross-border capital flows, that creates country-specific impacts on the natural rate.

[4] See Ferreira and Shousha (2020).
[5] See Ferreira and Shousha (2020) and Del Negro et al. (2017).

It's also important because high debt burdens are more likely to result in default or inflation—both of which erode the value of debt. With investors demanding compensation for that risk, the country-specific risk premium on sovereign bonds rises as debt climbs.

The political economy of macroeconomic management is complex, and any single measure of fiscal sustainability is unlikely to capture the full picture.

- It wasn't an increase in debt that prompted the UK's borrowing costs to blow out during the short-lived administration of Prime Minister Liz Truss in 2022. Rather, it was expectations of further profligacy and the sidelining of the budget watchdog that did the damage.
- Italy provides an example in the opposite direction, benefiting from a long track record of covering its interest bill by running wide primary surpluses, even if it rarely manages to push debt down.

The UK and Italy—and all other countries—are judged on whether the future path of borrowing looks sustainable in the context of past experience, not based on a single debt sustainability metric.

That said, as a summary metric, we think the debt-to-GDP ratio is a reasonable choice. Others agree. Debt to GDP plays a key role in assessments of fiscal sustainability by the IMF and the European Commission—outlined in a paper by Centre for European Policy Studies economists Cinzia Alcidi and Daniel Gros.[6]

How much do bond yields tend to go up as debt increases? It's hard to say with certainty. In their stress tests, the European Commission and the IMF assume that bond yields climb by between 3 and 4 bps for each percentage point increase in the debt ratio above a threshold. Looking at the empirical literature, several studies document statistically significant impacts of debt on borrowing costs.

- Using data from a panel of 16 OECD countries, former Harvard economist Silvia Ardagna and colleagues find only a modest increase of 0.6 bps for a 1 ppt increase in the debt ratio in their baseline specification.[7] But when they allow for a nonlinear relationship, they find low debt countries experience an increase of 2.4 bps and high debt countries see their borrowing costs jump by 3.8 bps.
- Relying on data from a panel of 31 countries, IMF economists find that a percentage point increase in the debt ratio might be expected to add

[6] See Alcidi and Gros (2018).
[7] See Ardagna, Caselli, and Lane (2007).

5 bps to 10-year borrowing costs.[8] The impact depends on the initial fiscal conditions, with bigger increases possible for countries with wide budget deficits or high debt.
- For the United States, Federal Reserve veteran Thomas Laubach found that a percentage point increase in the projected debt-to-GDP ratio raises long-term borrowing costs by 3–4 bps.[9] Fed economist Eric Engen and Columbia professor Glen Hubbard found an increase of about 3 bps.[10]

Our Model

In line with the empirical evidence, debt in our model—described in detail in Chapter 3—drives the natural rate through both global safe asset supply and domestic borrowing costs.[11]

- Our model results suggest that a 1-ppt increase in net safe asset supply relative to global GDP pushes up the natural rate by 4 bps on average across the 12 advanced economies we cover. At a country level, the impact ranges from a high of 7 bps in the United States to a low of 3 bps in Switzerland.
- Our results also show that, on average, every 1-ppt increase in domestic debt above a 60% of GDP threshold pushes the natural rate up by 1.1 bps. Country coefficients range from a high of 1.8 bps in the United States to just 0.1 bps in Japan, where high demand for government bonds from domestic investors results in a unique dynamic.

Pulling those two threads together gives us the aggregate impacts of higher debt on the natural rate:

- The United States accounts for about a fourth of global GDP—meaning that, a 1-ppt increase in the US debt-to-GDP ratio raises the net supply of safe assets as a share of global GDP by 0.25 ppt.
- A sensitivity of 7 bps means that should push up the natural rate in the United States by about 1.8 bps.
- The direct effect from domestic debt, where the coefficient is 1.8, adds another 1.8 bps to this effect.
- Overall then, our model suggests a 1-ppt increase in the US debt-to-GDP ratio is expected to lift the natural rate by 3.6 bps in the United States.

[8] See Kumar and Baldacci (2010).
[9] See Laubach (2009).
[10] See Engen and Hubbard (2004).
[11] For more detail on our model see Ademmer and Rush (2024).

That's broadly consistent with the empirical literature on the impact of debt on bond yields.

- The increase in US debt would also be expected to raise the natural rate in other advanced economies in our analysis by an average of just over 1 bps, as the increased supply of safe assets spills over to assets that are substitutes.

Taking those results to the historical data, we can tell a story about how changes in debt have affected the natural rate.

In the 40 years before the GFC, a downward trend in the net global supply of safe assets meant a downward influence on the natural rate. The amount of debt issued by the United States, UK, France, and Germany was contained, and—in the 1990s and 2000s—purchases by China and petrostates like Saudi Arabia meant plenty of demand for safe assets.

As Figure 6.3 shows, between the mid-1990s and 2007, net safe asset supply subtracted 20 bps from the natural rate, on average, across the advanced economies in our analysis and 30 bps in the United States.

For most advanced economies, low debt-to-GDP ratios also helped limit upward pressure in local markets. Italy and Japan stand out as bigger borrowers but faced different market consequences.

- In Italy, debt rose to nearly 105% of GDP in 2007 from around 35% in 1970, adding more than 0.5 ppt to its natural rate.

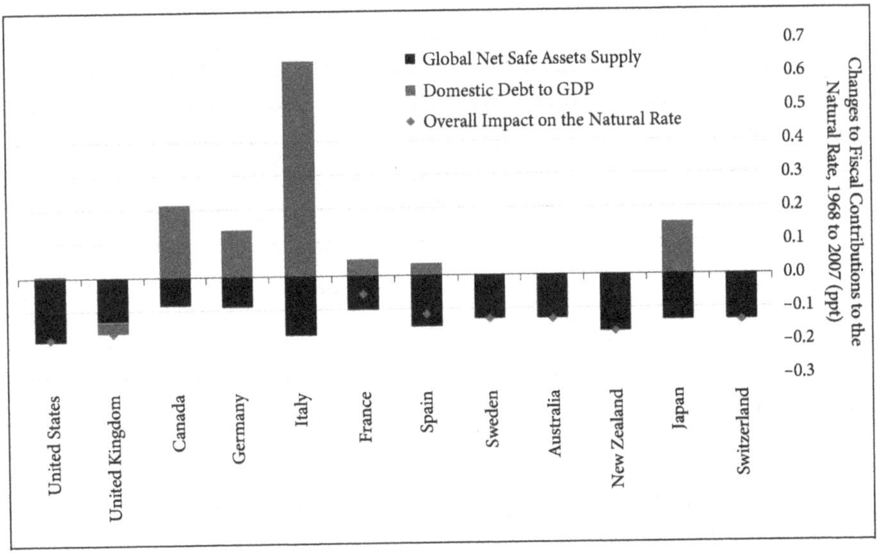

Figure 6.3 Before the Global Financial Crisis, Debt Impact on Rates Was Modest

Source: Ademmer and Rush (2024).

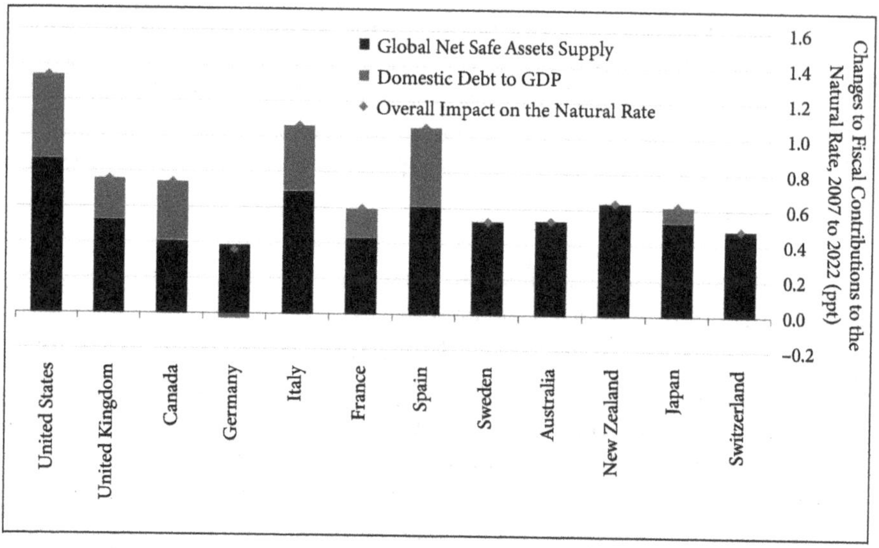

Figure 6.4 Post Global Financial Crisis, Higher Debt Lifted Natural Rate
Source: Ademmer and Rush (2024).

- In Japan, debt surged to about 170% of GDP from around 10%. Despite that, the rise in Japan's natural rate remained very limited, pointing to a much lower sensitivity to shifts in domestic debt than in other advanced economies.

The 15 years since the GFC have been tougher on government balance sheets. The surge in advanced economy debt, and the failure of safe asset demand from China and other big savers to keep pace, has lifted the net supply of safe assets as a share of global GDP. We estimate that has added 50 bps to the natural rate of interest on average across the 12 countries in our sample. The rise in domestic debt has added to the upward pressure.

In the United States, as Figure 6.4 shows, the increase in debt at home and abroad has added more than 1.3 ppt to the natural rate between 2007 and 2022, of which nearly 0.9 ppt came from the increase in the net supply of safe assets and 0.4 ppt from the rise in domestic debt.

Central Banks to the Rescue

Faced with a surprisingly sluggish recovery from the GFC, weak underlying inflation and policy rates bumping against the zero lower bound, central banks have engaged in round after round of quantitative easing (QE) - printing money to buy government bonds.

So as debt issuance rocketed, a new buyer stepped into the market, and that helped keep interest rates low. The pandemic period saw a repeat performance. Huge debt issuance was mopped up by central banks and parked on their balance sheets.

Between the GFC and 2022, US debt rose by more than $19 trillion. The Fed's balance sheet expanded, with Treasury holdings increasing by around $5 trillion dollars.[12] And China's FX reserves—which are substantially invested in US Treasuries—swelled from just over $1 trillion to close to $4 trillion before falling back to just over $3 trillion. In other words, the Fed was a more important buyer of Treasury debt than China.

A number of academic studies document the impact of quantitative easing on 10-year borrowing costs.[13] All find the impact to be material. Most also find them to be persistent: it follows that the stock of assets parked on central bank balance sheets is still depressing long-term yields and providing stimulus to some extent, even as short-term policy rates have increased.

Should we include central banks in our measure of safe asset demand? In our view, the answer is no. For most central banks, the plan has always been to sell down a large portion of the assets they have accumulated. In the end, QE is cyclical, even if it operates at a different cadence from conventional monetary policy.

Thinking of it another way, our view is that central banks are not themselves able to determine the natural rate. Rather, they respond to the state of the economy - sometimes in unconventional ways.

That said, the persistent impact of QE does complicate the way we estimate the impact of fiscal drivers on the natural rate. We address this in two ways:

- First, we appeal to the academic literature on the durable impact of higher indebtedness on long-term borrowing costs and feed this into our model as priors that inform the results.
- Second, we use data for long-run expectations of interest rates, as well as actual 10-year borrowing costs, to inform our estimate of the natural rate and therefore the relationship with the drivers.

To see the importance of long-run expectations, consider this example. In early 2019, 10-year US Treasury yields were about 2.65%. Looking further ahead to a time when quantitative tightening could reasonably be expected to be well advanced, the picture was different. Market expectations for the 10-year yield in five years' time were higher at 3.25%, while survey expectations were for long-term borrowing costs to settle higher still at about 3.75%.

[12] See Board of Governors (2002).
[13] See Kim Laubach, and Wei (2020), Weale and Wieladek (2016), and Swanson (2021).

During the pandemic, the gap between actual 10-year yields and long-run expectations was even wider, at about 2 ppt. By utilizing this information in our model, we are able to look beyond some of the cyclical influences of unconventional monetary policy and sharpen our estimates of long-run determinants of the natural rate.

The Path Ahead: Rising and Higher Rates

What comes next for rates depends on governments' ability to get public borrowing under control. In its October 2023 Fiscal Monitor, the IMF projected that 2020–21 was the peak for debt-to-GDP in many advanced economies, with the ratio set to gradually fall or at least stabilize between 2022 and 2028.

The United States is the most noteworthy exception. A political logic that makes it easy to cut taxes but hard to reduce spending is expected to drive the debt-to-GDP ratio higher in the years ahead. The February 2023 forecasts from the CBO showed US federal debt reaching more than 105% of GDP in the late 2020s, up from around 95% in 2022.

Our baseline assumes that the US debt-to-GDP ratio follows the CBO projection out to 2028. Debt for the other 11 countries in our sample follows the IMF forecast. After 2028, we assume governments do what's needed to stabilize their debt ratios. The implication for debt ratios are illustrated in Figure 6.5.

A rising debt trajectory in the United States, combined with the end of incremental purchases of US government debt by China, will continue to increase the net global supply of safe assets through the 2020s. As Figure 6.6 shows, combined with the direct impact from a higher debt-to-GDP ratio domestically, we expect it could add another 0.5 ppt to the US natural rate of interest by 2035.

For other countries where the IMF projects the debt-to-GDP ratio to stay broadly stable or even decline by 2028, the impact is expected to be more modest. In Canada and Germany, where debt is projected to decline rapidly as a share of GDP, the decrease in domestic pressures could more than offset the upside impact from the US-led rise in global supply of safe assets.

What if Governments Don't Tackle Their Deficits?

Our baseline forecast assumes that governments will eventually get serious about bringing borrowing under control. Political intransigence means that is not a safe bet. From failed austerity in Britain, to pension strikes in France,

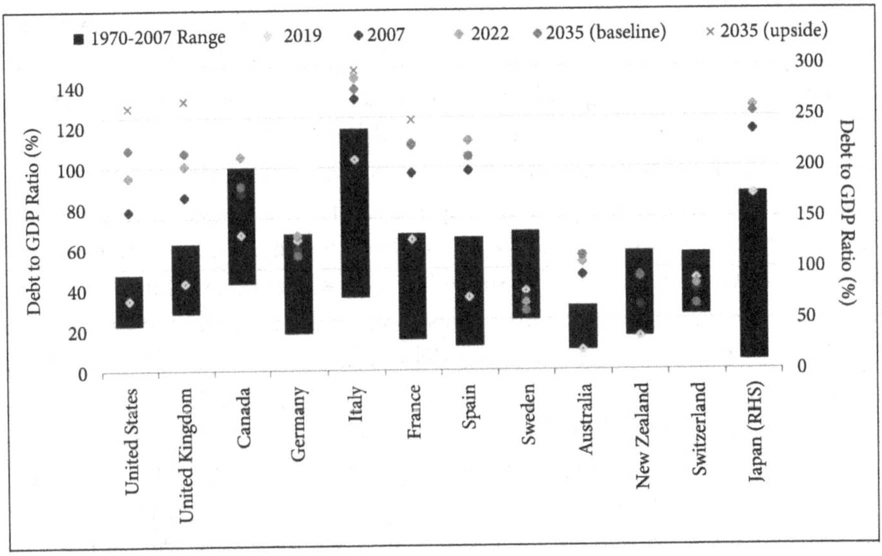

Figure 6.5 Forecasting Debt-to-GDP Ratios
Source: Bloomberg Economics.

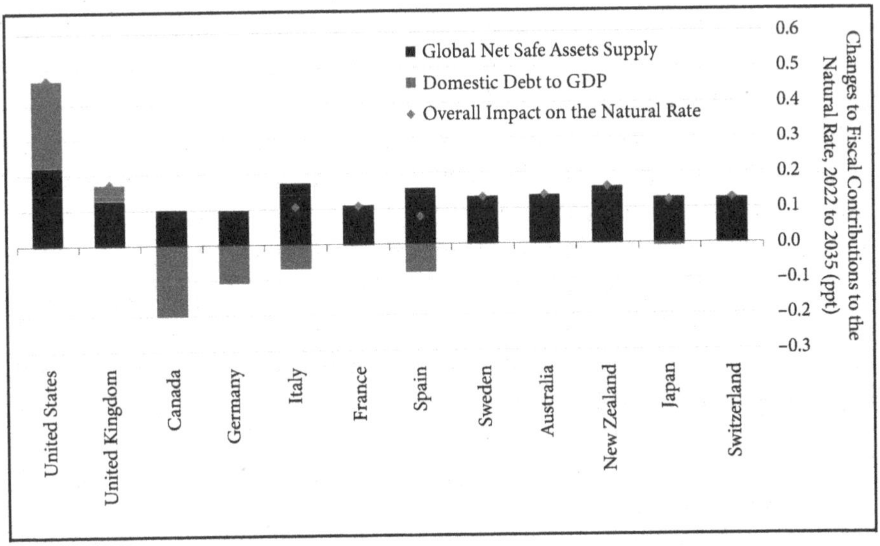

Figure 6.6 Rising Debt Set to Push Rates Higher
Source: Ademmer and Rush (2024), Bloomberg Economics.

and frequent flirtations with the debt ceiling in the United States, the lesson of recent history is that cutting back on already strained public services is tough, and raising taxes even tougher.

There's also an unhelpful self-reinforcing dynamic at work, where higher debt pushes interest rates higher, and higher interest rates add to the cost of debt servicing, forcing budget deficits wider. Long-term interest rates that rose materially following the end of the pandemic threaten to add to the strain.

To assess the risks, we rely on a Bloomberg Economics model of debt sustainability that combines our long-term forecasts for growth, debt, and inflation with a bond-by-bond treatment of debt dynamics. That allows us to assess how debt and servicing costs will evolve as the outstanding stock rolls over to higher prevailing interest rates than at the time of issue. Using this model, we find that US government debt could be above 110% of GDP, by 2028, and 130% by 2033.

The situation in the United States underscores just how big a challenge balancing the books is going to be. Steadying debt at below 110% of GDP would require the primary deficit (the gap between noninterest spending and tax revenues) to turn consistently positive from 2029 and reach 0.8% of GDP by the late 2030s.

Between 2015 and 2019, the United States ran a primary deficit of 2.0% of GDP. Relative even to that norm, that means a consolidation of about 3% of GDP is required—and at a time when an ageing population will add to spending pressure. The UK and France could also see their debt-to-GDP ratios climb rapidly.

In an untamed deficits scenario, by the 2030s additional upward pressure on the net global supply of safe assets and domestic debt-to-GDP ratios would leave US borrowing costs about 80 bps higher than in our baseline. As Figure 6.7 shows, that would bring the total upward impact to 130 bps.

Pressure on the global supply of safe assets would also push up rates for other sovereigns. Italy is in a particularly vulnerable position. By 2035, it could face an increase of 35 bps, which could reinforce upside risks arising from its own domestic debt position.

Free Lunch is Over

The GFC marked a turning point in government finances. Debt ballooned. The Covid crisis saw borrowing rise even higher. Increased supply of safe assets and governments competing for domestic savings meant that rise in debt has pushed the natural rate higher.

Looking forward, political intransigence over deficits, financing the green transition, and the high price of defense in a more dangerous world mean debt could rise higher. The end of China's Treasury purchases and quantitative

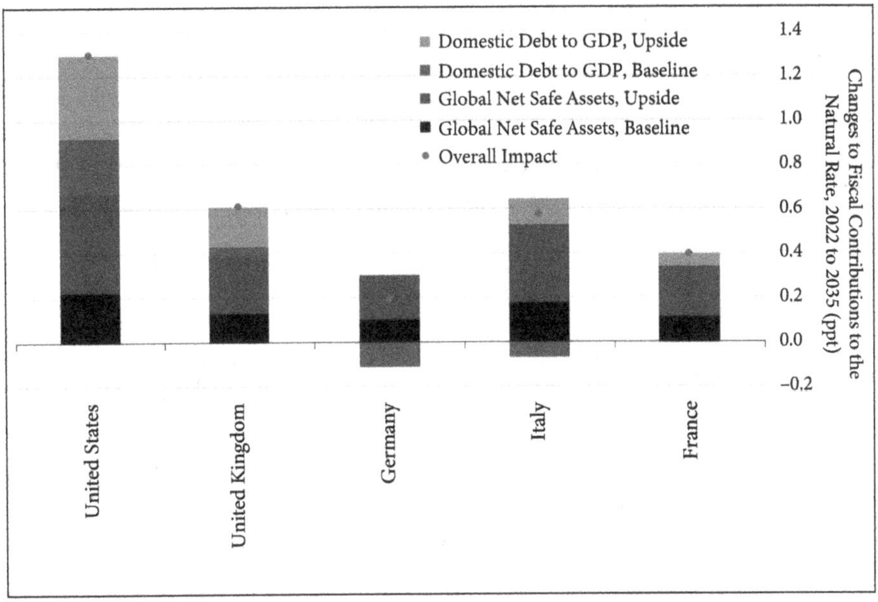

Figure 6.7 Baseline and Upside Scenario for Debt Contributions to Natural Rate
Source: Ademmer and Rush (2024), Bloomberg Economics.

tightening by the Fed and other major central banks mean major buyers are exiting the market.

The bottom line is that governments got lucky in recent decades. The impact of higher borrowing on debt servicing costs was tempered by ever-declining long-term interest rates. The free lunch is now over. The bill is about to arrive.

Bibliography

Ademmer, M., and Rush, J. (2024). "Drivers of the Natural Long-Term Rate of Interest (and Why the Economy Hasn't Tanked)." *Oxford Open Economics*, 3, odae012. https://doi.org/10.1093/ooec/odae012

Alcidi, C.. and Gros, D. (2018). Debt Sustainability Assessments: The State of the Art. Brussels: European Parliament.

Ardagna, S., Caselli, F., and Lane, T. (2007). "Fiscal Discipline and the Cost of Public Debt Service: Some Estimates for OECD Countries." *B.E. Journal of Macroeconomics*, 7(1): 1–35.

Board of Governors of the Federal Reserve System. (2002). Assets: Securities Held Outright: U.S. Treasury Securities: All: Wednesday Level. FRED, Federal Reserve Bank of St. Louis.

Clinton, W. (2000). *The United States on Track to Pay Off the Debt by End of the Decade*. Washington, DC: Clinton Whitehouse Archives.

Congressional Budget Office (2023). "The Budget and Economic Outlook: 2023 to 2033"

Del Negro, M. D., Giannone, D., Giannoni, M. P., and Tambalotti, A. (2017). "Safety, Liquidity, and the Natural Rate of Interest." *Brookings Papers on Economic Activity*, 2017(1): 235–316.

Engen, E. M., and Hubbard, R. G. (2004). "Federal Government Debt and Interest Rates." *NBER Macroeconomics Annual*, 19: 83–138.

Ferreira, T. R. T., and Shousha, S. (2020). "Scarcity of Safe Assets and Global Neutral Interest Rates." International Finance Discussion Papers 1293." Washington, DC: Board of Governors of the Federal Reserve System (US).

IMF (International Monetary Fund). (2023). "Fiscal Monitor, October 2023"

Kim, K., Laubach, T., and Wei, M. (2020). "Macroeconomic Effects of Large-Scale Asset Purchases: New Evidence." *Finance and Economics Discussion Series*, Washington, DC: Board of Governors of the Federal Reserve System (US). 2020(047).

Kumar, M. S., and Baldacci, E. (2010). "Fiscal Deficits, Public Debt, and Sovereign Bond Yields." *IMF Working Papers*, 10(184)

Laubach, T. (2009). "New Evidence on the Interest Rate Effects of Budget Deficits and Debt." *Journal of the European Economic Association*, 7(4): 858–885.

Swanson, E. T. (2021). "Measuring the Effects of Federal Reserve Forward Guidance and Asset Purchases on Financial Markets." *Journal of Monetary Economics*, 118: 32–53.

Weale, M., and Wieladek, T. (2016). "What Are the Macroeconomic Effects of Asset Purchases?" *Journal of Monetary Economics*, 79: 81–93.

7

Temperature Rising

How Global Heating Will Drag the Natural Rate of Interest Down, and Investment in Net Zero Will Push It Up

Maeva Cousin and Jamie Rush

2024 was the hottest year on record. The mean global temperature exceeded the preindustrial average by almost 1.5 degrees.[1] On the current trajectory, global heating is on track to exceed 2 degrees by 2050. Much worse outcomes are possible if the planet crashes through tipping points that accelerate warming.

Capping the rise in global temperatures at two degrees or below might still be achievable if economies transition rapidly to net-zero carbon emissions, but that will require huge structural change and massive investment. Relative to the scale of the challenge, current efforts are inadequate. The early days of the second Donald Trump presidency suggest that for the world's biggest economy tackling climate change is no longer a priority.

For the global economy, the implications of global heating and the net-zero paths are extreme and divergent:

- From the farm, to the factory, to the office, higher temperatures will weigh on output. Some sectors, including electricity production, transportation, and tourism, face a future where frequent disruptions are the new normal.
- Rising temperatures will increase the frequency and severity of extreme events, like the floods, tornadoes, and wildfires that have hit economies around the world in recent years. This will add to downside risks to growth and raise the incentives for saving to insure against disasters.
- Adding it up, projections from the Network for Greening the Financial System (NGFS)—an international central bank initiative to track the economic and financial impact of climate change—suggest the cost of

[1] See Copernicus (2024).

Maeva Cousin and Jamie Rush, *Temperature Rising*. In: *The Price of Money*. Edited by: Jamie Rush, Tom Orlik, and Stephanie Flanders, Oxford University Press. © Oxford University Press (2025).
DOI: 10.1093/9780197800942.003.0007

global heating could reach 6% of global gross domestic product (GDP) by 2050.

- Decarbonizing the economy to prevent a catastrophic rise in temperatures will come with its own challenges, as taxes on emitting greenhouse gas and regulations needed to spur change weigh on growth. The costs will be up front. The benefits will take decades to be fully realized.
- Transforming the energy system to achieve net zero will require massive investment. BloombergNEF estimates that the United States will need to spend an extra $10 trillion on its energy infrastructure by 2050. This will be tough to finance without adding to already-elevated debt.

For the natural rate of interest, those forces impact in different directions. Lower growth reduces the incentive to invest, pulling the natural rate down. Heightened risk from extreme weather adds to incentives for cautionary saving, pulling in the same direction. The massive investment needed to green the energy system and achieve net-zero emissions, in contrast, will push it up.

In this chapter, we bring together projections for growth impacts of rising temperatures and investment requirements to get to net zero to estimate the consequences for the natural rate. We consider scenarios where policy—and temperature increases—continue on the current trajectory, and where a major shift catalyzes the investments required to get to net zero and cap temperature gains at two degrees.

The results for the United States show that on the current trajectory, slower growth will drag the natural rate on 10-year Treasury bonds down by a modest 10 bps by the late 2040s. In the net-zero scenario, it's higher investment that dominates, pushing the natural rate up by about 35 bps.

We estimate the nominal 10-year natural rate on US Treasuries was around 4.5% in 2022. If climate change was the only vector impacting the natural rate, our policy continuity scenario would see it fall to about 4.4% in 2040, and our net-zero scenario see it rise to 4.7%. In reality, other forces—notably sovereign debt issuance—have a larger impact. Taking account of those other forces, we see the natural rate reaching 4.7% in 2040 in the continuity scenario, and 5% in the net-zero scenario.

The dynamics of climate change, and the battle against it, are complex and uncertain. The natural rate of interest has its own mysteries. Bringing the two sets of uncertainties together compounds the problem and means that our results should be taken as estimates with a wide band of uncertainty around them. We have more certainty on our broad conclusions: left unchecked, climate change will lower the natural rate; the investments needed to get to net zero would push it up.

Climate Change, the Green Transition, and the Economy

Current Policies Scenario

If governments don't take action to move to a low carbon economy, greenhouse gas emissions will stay high, triggering a damaging increase in temperatures and rising physical costs. To estimate the price of inaction, we rely primarily on the Phase III results from the NGFS.[2]

The NGFS assesses climate change scenarios in a two-step process:

- First, it uses integrated assessment models (here we rely on the results from the Remind-Magpie model) to understand how energy systems adjust to changes in the prices of different technologies and in carbon prices, how that impacts economic activity, and how that affects the path of greenhouse gas emissions.
- Second, it uses that emissions forecast to project global mean temperatures using the Model for the Assessment of Greenhouse-gas Induced Climate Change (MAGICC).

There is a lot of uncertainty surrounding the link between emissions and temperatures. An important reason for that: the risk of reaching climate tipping points—thresholds beyond which climate change becomes a self-sustaining and accelerating process.

This also means that risks to temperature projections are skewed to the upside, and that this skew is more pronounced in high-emission scenarios, as the risk of reaching tipping points increases. To account for this, we follow the NGFS approach and base our own assessment on the 95th percentile of the temperature distribution in the current policies scenario, and the median path for the transition scenario.

Under these assumptions, as Figure 7.1 shows, current policies put global mean temperatures on a path to exceed their preindustrial level by 2.7 degrees in 2050 and 4.7 degrees by 2100.

For a given path of temperature increases, economic losses are estimated using a damage function developed by researchers at the Mercator Research Institute on Global Commons and Climate Change, which maps the impact of temperature increases to growth.[3] Given the modeled increase in temperatures to 2.7 degrees above their preindustrial level, global GDP is projected to be about 6% smaller by 2050 than it would have been without global warming.

[2] See NGFS (2022).
[3] See Kalkuhl and Wenz (2020).

Kalkuhl and Wenz's analysis shows that the higher the initial temperature, the worse the impact of further heating. Among the 12 mostly temperate economies considered in our analysis, this means that the estimated impact is slightly more moderate, averaging 4.2% on a GDP-weighted basis rather than 6% at the global level.

As Figure 7.2 shows, US GDP in 2050 is 5% smaller than if temperatures didn't rise. The drag on annual growth builds up gradually from about 0.15

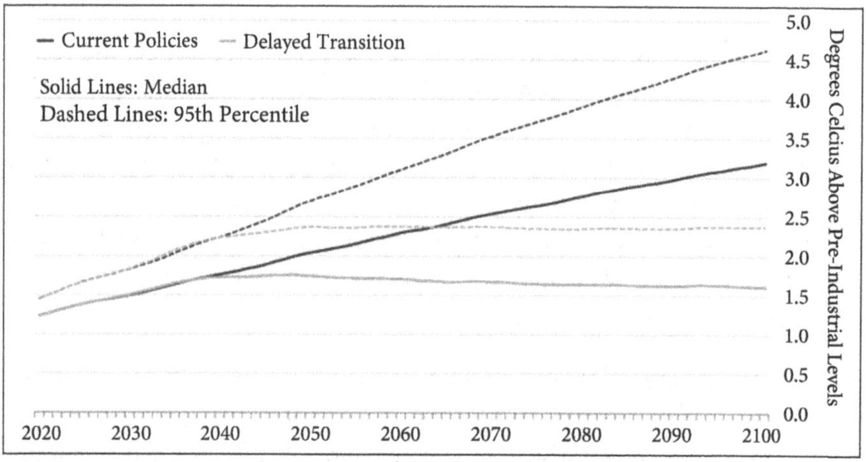

Figure 7.1 Temperature Projections Under Different Climate Scenarios
Source: Phase III NGFS, MAGICC, Remind-Magpie.

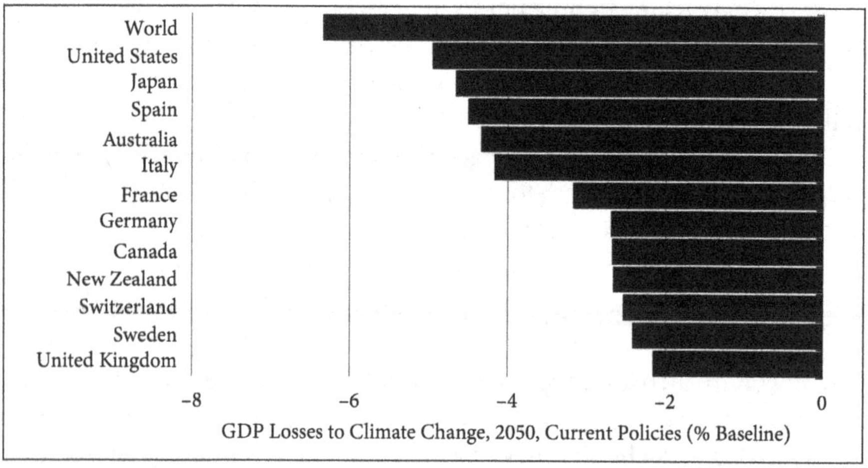

Figure 7.2 GDP Losses to Climate Change Under Current Policies
Source: Phase III NGFS, Remind-Magpie.

ppt in 2030, rising to close to 0.2 ppt by the late 2040s and higher still in the following decades.

For the natural rate, a slower pace of growth means fewer opportunities for profitable investment, meaning less demand for savings and lower borrowing costs. Higher precautionary saving as insurance against extreme weather events would likely add to this drag.

The Kalkuhl and Wenz estimates only capture the chronic impact of higher temperatures on labor and agricultural productivity and the depreciation of the stock of capital—more rapid erosion of the value of utilities, factories, and housing. Effects from extreme weather events, like wildfires, storms, and hurricanes, as well as rising sea levels, are not included. We consider their possible implications for the natural rate later in this chapter through a different lens.

Low Carbon Transition Scenario

What if the world gets serious about achieving net zero?

As the world moves further into the 2020s, a smooth, rapid, and coordinated transition to reach net zero by 2050 and keep the rise in global temperatures below 1.5 degrees—the assumption underpinning the NGFS's Net Zero scenario—appears far-fetched. Limited progress at COP29 in 2024 is a reminder that governments have not yet committed to a credible path. Indeed—emissions were still going up in 2023.[4] Climate change is not reversing, it's accelerating.

A belated effort to move the world onto a low carbon path and limit the rise in temperatures to 2 degrees—along the lines of the NGFS' Delayed Transition scenario—remains possible and forms the basis of our scenario analysis.

In this scenario, policies are little changed in the 2020s, with major progress delayed until the 2030s. In the Remind-Magpie model, this is achieved by raising global carbon prices to $200/ton (2010 prices) by 2040 and close to $400/tonne by 2050, with advanced economies and China leading the change. Prices in the rest of the world increase more gradually, reaching $150/tonne in 2050.

In this scenario the median projection is for temperatures to peak at 1.75 degrees above their preindustrial average over the 2040s before gradually receding to around 1.6 degrees above by 2100. Plugging those numbers into

[4] See European Commission (2023).

the Kalkuhl and Wenz damage function shows physical costs of about 3% of GDP globally in 2050. As Figure 7.3 shows, for our group of advanced economies, the cost is about 2%—roughly half the costs projected in the current policy scenario.

In addition to the physical impacts of climate change on GDP, the cost of the transition to net zero has to be considered. In the model, tackling carbon emissions is equivalent to a supply shock that raises the cost of energy—similar to what happens if supply disruptions push up the price of a barrel of oil. Overall, the NGFS estimates that transition costs could reach nearly 2% of global GDP by 2050.

Pivoting again from the impact on the level of GDP to the drag on growth, transition costs are expected to build up rapidly over the first half of the 2030s, when carbon prices begin to rise and the economy struggles to adjust. This is when the impact on growth is expected to be felt most keenly. We estimate it could shave up to 0.3 ppt off annual US growth in the early 2030s.

As investment in green technologies progresses and the structure of the economy adapts, transition costs are expected to increase less rapidly and then unwind slightly. In the United States, NGFS results show the drag on growth from the transition easing from 2035 before turning into a modest boost to growth in the 2040s.

Adding up the physical and transition costs, as Figure 7.4 shows, the drag on US growth peaks around 0.4 ppt in the early 2030s, before tailing off to close to zero in the 2040s as temperatures plateau. As in the business-as-usual

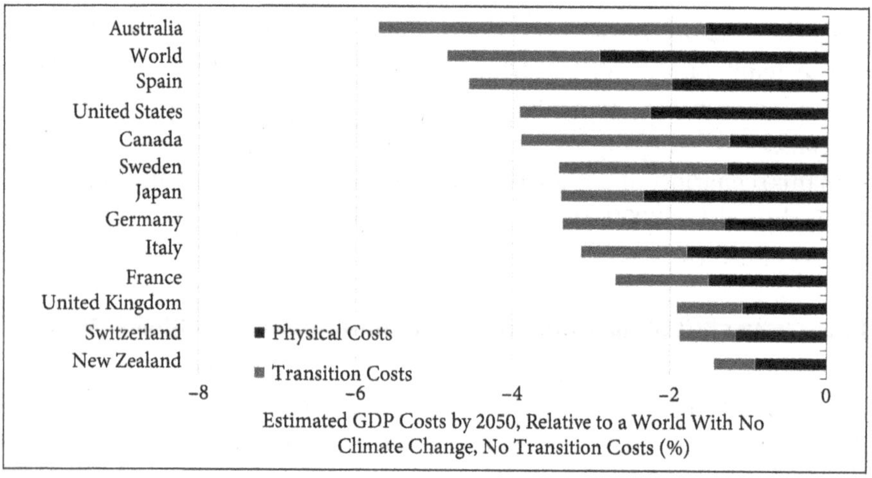

Figure 7.3 Physical and Transition Costs in a Low Carbon Transition Scenario

Source: Phase III NGFS, Remind-Magpie.

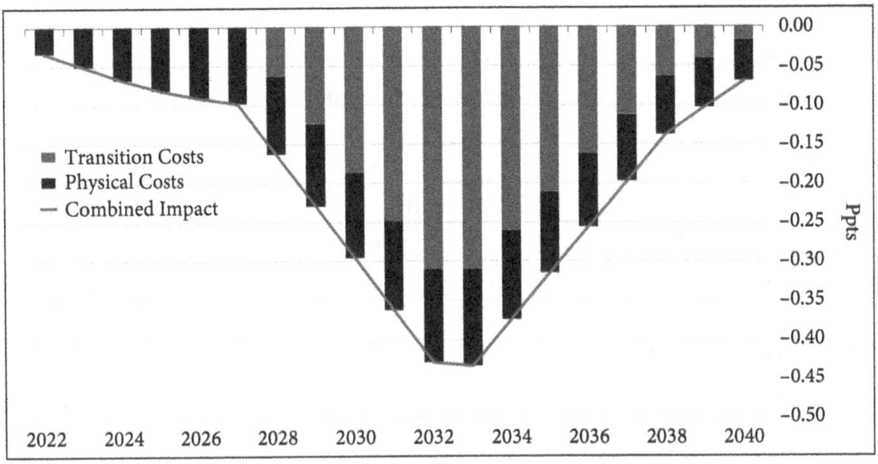

Figure 7.4 Low Carbon Transition Drag on US Growth to Peak in Mid-30s
Source: Bloomberg Economics using NGFS Phase III (Remind-Magpie, Nigem).

scenario, slower growth means fewer opportunities for profitable investment and a drag on the natural rate.

Just as the impacts of global heating could be more pronounced than assumed because of the potential for conflict and mass migration, it's possible that Project-Apollo-scale investment in the green transition could result in technologies that have wider applications, lifting productivity. The models we rely on have no mechanism for capturing those potential spillovers. Conceivably, they could add a boost to growth.

How the Low Carbon Transition Will Affect Sovereign Debt

Achieving net zero is going to be costly. The initial hit to output as the economy adjusts to higher energy costs will be expensive. Investments to reconfigure the energy system will add to the bill. This could have a sizable impact on debt, as governments may end up bearing the costs. This could affect the natural rate through two channels:

- Deficit-funded investment in the United States, Germany, France, and the UK—the sovereigns that we consider as safe-assets issuers—will raise the global supply of safe assets. At the same time, shrinking revenue from fossil fuel exports could dent demand for safe assets from Saudi Arabia and other petrostates.

- The United States and other advanced economies are likely to face additional pressures on government investment and sovereign debt, which could also affect perceptions of credit-worthiness, compete for savings domestically, and lift borrowing costs.

To understand how green investment under our low carbon transition scenario might affect the trajectory for sovereign debt, we use detailed green investment projections from BloombergNEF's long-term energy outlook.[5]

BloombergNEF estimates that the world will need to invest about 2% of global GDP each year in energy supply—including power plants, electricity grids, hydrogen production and distribution, carbon capture and storage, and residual fossil extraction—to reach net zero by 2050. This compares with about 1.3% projected under current policies. Major policy shifts don't happen overnight. As Figure 7.5 illustrates, we assume a delay in the additional investment to 2030.

Combining these investment projections with our long-term GDP forecasts, we estimate that additional investment in energy supply will add up to nearly 11% of GDP globally by 2050. Disaggregated BloombergNEF estimates show that investment needs differ substantially between regions, depending on the structure of their economy and energy systems.

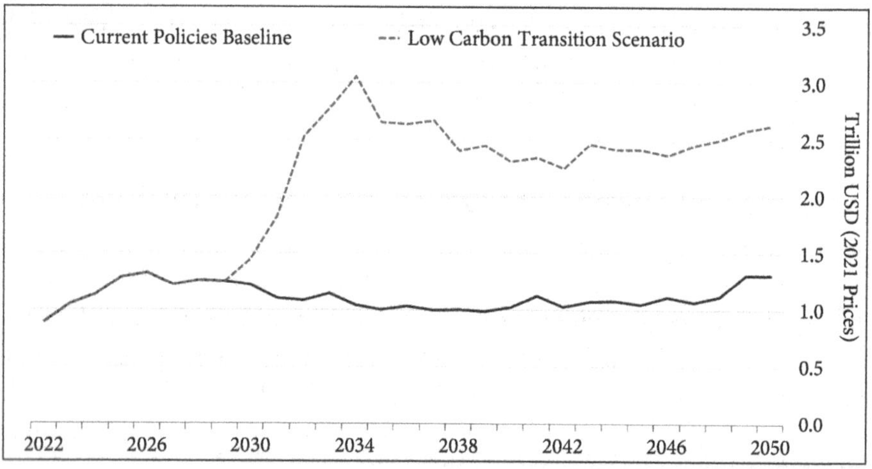

Figure 7.5 Global Energy Supply Investment Over the Next Three Decades

Source: BloombergNEF, New Energy Outlook 2022 (Current Policies: BNEF's Economic Transition Scenario; Low Carbon: BNEF's Net-Zero Scenario, delayed by 10 years).

[5] See BNEF (2022).

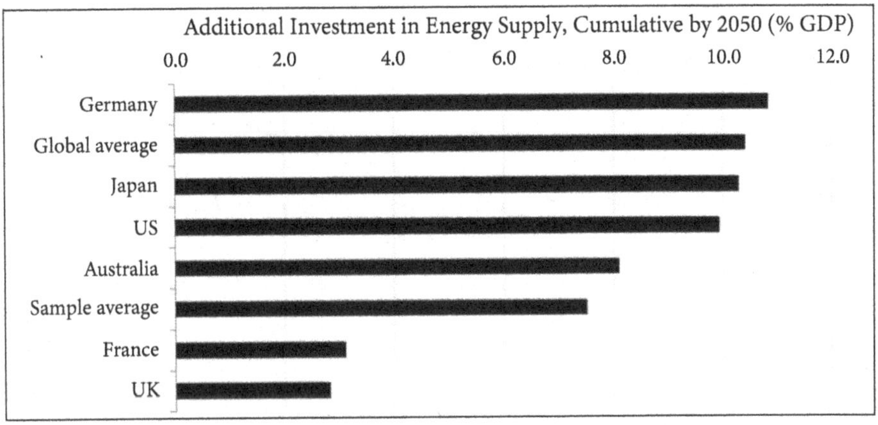

Figure 7.6 Additional Investment Needed By 2050 in a Low Carbon Transition Scenario
Source: BloombergNEF (2022 New Energy Outlook), Bloomberg Economics.

Across our sample of advanced economies, additional investment-to-GDP ratios are projected to average a slightly less eye-popping 7.5% by 2050. As Figure 7.6 shows, behind that average is a range from more than 10% for the industrial, carbon-intensive Germany, to around 3% for more services-oriented, coal-lite France and the UK.

BloombergNEF doesn't project investment in Canada, New Zealand, Italy, Spain, Sweden, and Switzerland, specifically. Given low coal use and high renewable share in the current electricity mix of these countries, we expect their additional investment ratios would be close to those for the UK and France.

Upside Risks to Sovereign Debt

There are substantial upside risks to governments' debt-to-GDP ratios—as debt accumulated during the Global Financial Crisis and pandemic gets refinanced at higher interest rates, raising servicing costs. Adding to that, ageing populations will put pressure on health and pension spending, while growing geopolitical tensions may bulge military budgets.

It is not clear where the required additional investment in energy infrastructure will come from, but it is likely that some of the burden will be borne by governments. Depending on how this extra public spending is financed—and whether revenues from carbon taxation are used to fund part of it—this creates additional upside risks to governments' debt, as well as the supply of safe assets.

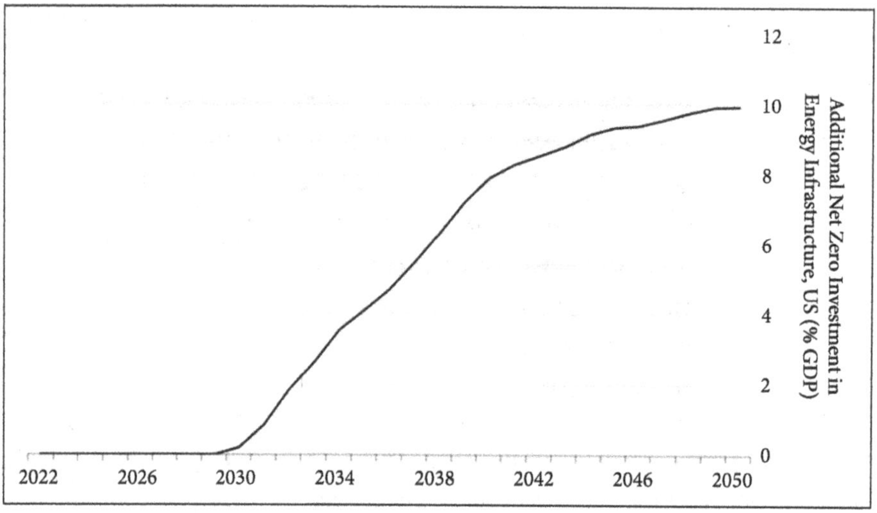

Figure 7.7 Low Carbon Transition Investment Could Add to US Sovereign Debt
Source: Bloomberg Economics, using BNEF NZS Investment Estimates.

To assess the risk, we assume that all additional investment is covered by governments and financed by borrowing. If that happens, we estimate that the supply of safe assets could be 2 ppt of global GDP higher by 2050. As Figure 7.7 shows, the US debt-to-GDP ratio could be about 10 ppt higher than it would have been had the government not financed any investment in the green transition.

In the low carbon transition scenario, then, there are two major forces pulling the natural rate of interest in opposite directions. Slower growth means fewer opportunities for profitable investment, dragging the natural rate down. Reconfiguring energy supply requires massive investment, likely financed in substantial part by borrowing—pulling the natural rate up.

Climate Change and the Natural Rate – Other Estimates

The macroeconomic implications of climate change are a major focus of attention for economists. Research on the impact on interest rates is still in its infancy.

The European Central Bank and Bank of England have published assessments of how climate change may affect the economy and the conduct of monetary policy.[6] Both included qualitative assessments of the possible effects of the physical risks of climate change and the climate transition on

[6] See European Central Bank (2021) and Bank of England (2022).

Table 7.1 Central Bank Views on How Climate Change Impacts Natural Rate

	Physical Risks	Transition Risks
Trend productivity growth	Negative: Hotter temperatures and diversion of capital toward abatement rather than productivity-enhancing investment, lower trend growth and R*.	Ambiguous: increase in carbon prices needed to spur transition lowers productivity. Orderly transition may only have a small impact and could foster faster growth long-term
Volatility, uncertainty, and risk aversion	Negative: increased probability of disasters and greater output volatility raises risk aversion and precautionary saving and, so, raises the risk premium and lowers the risk-free rate and R*.	Small negative, particularly in a disorderly transition: uncertainty over future policies and risks of investing in future "stranded assets" could increase risk aversion and lower R*.
Investment, including government investment	Ambiguous: reconstruction and abatement could raise investment needs and create upward pressure on R*. Overall, this may be offset by lower investment in other forms of capital, although state-financed spending may still need to rise.	Positive: the transition will require a sizable increase in investment into green capital, including capital financed by the state (infrastructure), some of which may be debt-financed (though this might be lowered by spending revenue from carbon taxation).

Source: Bloomberg Economics, European Central Bank, Bank of England.

the natural rate of interest. Table 7.1 summarizes the key channels identified in their analysis.

To our knowledge, there have been very few quantitative estimates of these effects. A European Central Bank (ECB) working paper, building on work by economists at the Riksbank focused on physical risks in the standard Ramsey framework underpinning some models of the natural rate.[7] They find that lower trend growth and a higher probability of more costly disasters would be the dominating forces dragging on the natural rate—perhaps by a staggering 8 ppt.

In 2023, the International Monetary Fund (IMF) used G-Cubed—a multi-country, multi-sector model of the global economy—to assess how climate mitigation policies could affect the natural rate over the next 30 years.[8]

[7] See Bylund and Jonsson (2020).
[8] See IMF (2023) and Liu et al. (2020).

Under an orderly transition scenario, they find that the drag on growth from carbon taxation would dominate—lowering the neutral rate by around 0.4 ppt initially, and around 0.75 ppt by 2040.

Additional demand for investment has only a marginal positive impact on their neutral rate estimates in a budget-neutral package (where additional government spending is financed by revenues from carbon taxation). Our view is that significant fiscal giveaways would be required to build political support for higher carbon taxes. Taking into account investment needs, we think budget neutrality is implausible.

The IMF does consider a front-loaded, debt-financed investment effort. In that scenario, the lift to borrowing costs from higher spending more than offsets the drag from lower growth in the first 10 years of the transition. That results in an overall small but positive shock to the neutral rate.

Probability of Disasters, Risk Aversion, and the Neutral Rate

In addition to downside risks to long-term growth, climate change increases the chances of disasters. Higher temperatures raise both the probability and severity of extreme events like fires, floods, storms, and droughts. Greater tensions surrounding access to essential resources, including water, may also raise the risk of conflict in what is already a fractious geopolitical environment.

Using the experience of wars and crises in the 20th century (pointing to an annual probability of economic disaster of 1.7% with an average loss in GDP per capita of about 30%), Harvard Professor Robert Barro shows that adjusting standard models to account for the potential for disasters helps explain some key asset pricing puzzles—notably the higher-than-expected equity premium and lower-than-expected risk-free rate.[9]

As a specific application, he explores the "mystery" that real interest rates on US government bonds tend to fall during wars, when most macroeconomic models would have projected a rise, given the sharp increase in sovereign issuance. Barro suggests the drop may be explained by an increase in the perceived probability of future disasters, prompting an increase in precautionary saving.

[9] See Barro (2006).

Estimating how much the probability of disasters and the magnitude of associated losses are expected to increase is tough to do. Applying this analysis to look at the possible implications of climate change, Bylund and Jonsson simply use Barro's estimates for the 20th century to show how, as perceptions of risks readjust to a new environment, the impact on the neutral rate could be substantial. Figure 7.8 illustrates the relationship.

Given the deep uncertainty around this transmission channel, we haven't explicitly taken it into account in our central forecasts of the natural rate. As climate change skews risks to the downside, it's reasonable to expect some additional downward pressure on borrowing costs as precautionary saving rises.

Climate Change and the Natural Rate: Bringing the Key Channels Together

In this chapter we have focused on the impact of climate and the green transition on two fundamental drivers of the natural rate of interest: trend growth and government borrowing. This final section brings together those channels, using the model introduced in Chapter 3. Other risks, including the upside risks to inflation from higher energy prices, are considered elsewhere.

In our current policy scenario, there's no transition to finance, so the only impact on the natural rate comes from slower trend growth. That

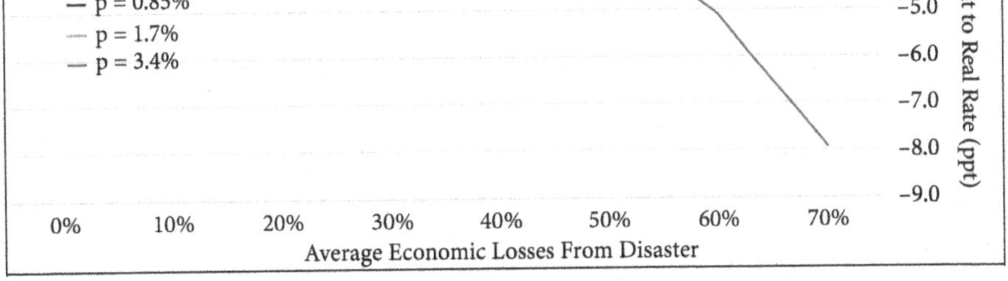

Figure 7.8 Stylized View of Economic Disasters Impact on Risk-Free Rates

Source: Barro (2006), Bylund and Jonsson (2020), and Bloomberg Economics.

lies unambiguously to the downside because global heating slows growth, pushing borrowing costs down.

While the expected hit to GDP of higher temperatures is significant, the effect builds up gradually and the impact on annual growth (and hence the natural rate) is relatively small. For the United States, the impact is a drag on the natural rate of around 0.1 ppt in 2040. Not included in our model, but likely a factor: an increase in precautionary saving that could mean the drag is larger.

Among the economies covered in our study, US growth is expected to be among the most negatively impacted, alongside Southern Europe, Australia, and Japan, reflecting a hotter starting point and so more damage from climate change. The UK and Sweden are expected to face lower economic costs, but spillovers from a weaker US economy would still lower their natural rate.

If the world succeeds in transitioning to a low carbon economy, there's still a drag on growth; but as the rise in temperatures is reduced, the drag is smaller. And there's more investment spending—which we assume is financed by government borrowing—pushing the natural rate up. It's the latter of those two dynamics that dominates—with a higher supply of safe assets and a larger stock of government debt likely to lift borrowing costs.

For the United States, as Figure 7.9 shows, our low carbon transition scenario adds more than 0.3 ppt to the natural rate by the 2040s. As higher US deficits push up the global supply of safe assets, this would also raise rates in other countries, reinforcing domestic pressures from financing their own green investment. There's also a shift in the trajectory over time, with the natural rate initially falling as the slower growth impact dominates, before beginning the climb in the mid-2030s as higher investment kicks in.

Summing up, research on the impact of climate change on the natural rate is still in its infancy. Significant uncertainties about the major dynamics—from climate change itself to the government response, the impact on the economy, and the drivers of the natural rate—mean results should be viewed as indicative estimates, not precise forecasts.

That said, the big picture is clear: left unchecked, rising temperatures would hit growth, reducing incentives to invest, and lowering the natural rate. Increased risk of extreme weather events would increase precautionary saving, dragging it further down. If, on the other hand, governments around the world make concerted efforts to get to net zero, massive investment required to reconfigure the energy system would add significantly to borrowing. In that scenario, it's the higher investment that dominates, and the natural rate rises.

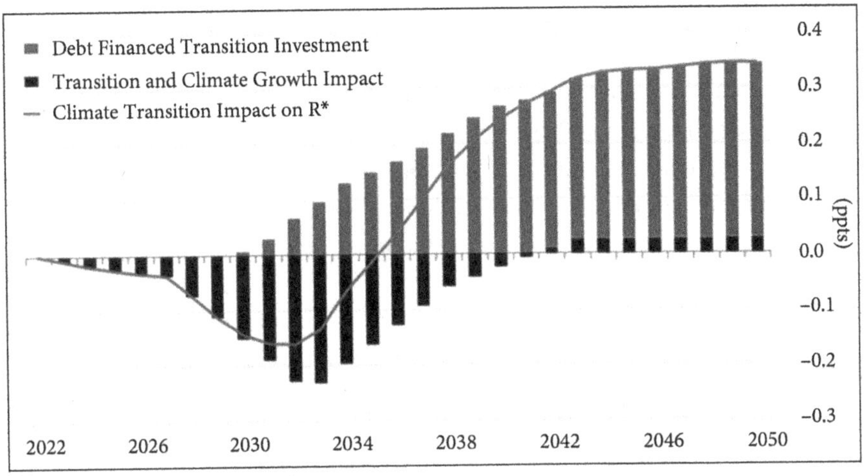

Figure 7.9 Higher Investment Needs Could Leave US Natural Rate Higher
Source: Ademmer and Rush (2024), Bloomberg Economics.

Bibliography

Ademmer, M., and Rush, J. (2024). "Drivers of the Natural Long-Term Rate of Interest (and Why the Economy Hasn't Tanked)." *Oxford Open Economics*, 3:odae012. https://doi.org/10.1093/ooec/odae012

Bank of England. (2022). "Climate Change: Possible Macroeconomic Implications." *Bank of England Quarterly Bulletin*, 2022(Q4).

Barro, R. J. (2006). "Rare Disasters and Asset Markets in the Twentieth Century." *Quarterly Journal of Economics*, 121(3): 823–866.

BNEF (2022). "New Energy Outlook 2022." https://about.bnef.com/new-energy-outlook-series/

Bylund, E., and Jonsson, M. (2020). "How Does Climate Change Affect the Long-Run Real Interest Rate?" Sveriges Riksbank Economic Commentary No.11 2020. https://www.riksbank.se/globalassets/media/rapporter/ekonomiska-kommentarer/engelska/2020/how-does-climate-change-affect-the-long-run-real-interest-rate.pdf

Copernicus. (2024). "Copernicus Global Climate Report 2024 confirms last year as the warmest on record, first ever above 1.5°C annual average temperature." climate.copernicus.eu.

European Central Bank. (2021). "Climate Change and Monetary Policy in the Euro Area." Occasional Paper No 271. https://www.ecb.europa.eu/pub/pdf/scpops/ecb.op271~36775d43c8.en.pdf

European Central Bank (2022). “The Effects of Climate Change on the Natural Rate of Interest: A Critical Survey.” Working Paper No 2744. https://www.ecb.europa.eu/pub/pdf/scpwps/ecb.wp2744~9c3a54be4f.en.pdf

European Commission. (2023). “EDGAR – The Emissions Database for Global Atmospheric Research.” edgar.jrc.ec.europa.eu.

IMF (International Monetary Fund) (2023). “World Economic Outlook: A Rocky Recovery.” Chapter 2. https://www.imf.org/-/media/Files/Publications/WEO/2023/April/English/ch2.ashx

Kalkuhl, M., and Wenz, L. (2020). “The Impact of Climate Conditions on Economic Production. Evidence from a Global Panel of Regions.” *Journal of Environmental Economics and Management*, 103: 102360.

Liu, W., McKibbin, W. J., Morris, A. C., and Wilcoxen, P. J. (2020). “Global Economic and Environmental Outcomes of the Paris Agreement.” *Energy Economics*, 90: 104838.

NGFS (Network for Greening the Financial System). (2022). “NGFS Scenarios for Central Banks and Supervisors.” https://www.ngfs.net/system/files/import/ngfs/medias/documents/ngfs_climate_scenarios_for_central_banks_and_supervisors_.pdf

8

The Return of History

How A Second Cold War Could Drive the Natural Rate Higher

Maeva Cousin, Dan Hanson, Eleonora Mavroeidi, Tom Orlik, Jamie Rush, Bhargavi Sakthivel, and Jennifer Welch

In 1989, anticipating the end of the Cold War and the final triumph of free-market democracies, political scientist Francis Fukuyama proclaimed, "The End of History."[1] With the benefit of more than three decades hindsight, it's fair to say Fukuyama was a little premature. Authoritarianism is on the rise, democracy in decline. State intervention is back in vogue, and free-market fundamentalism out of fashion.

History, it appears, is back. What happened? A lot.

Near the top of the list—the rise of China. In 1990, China's GDP was a tiny 6.7% of that of the United States, its military was still in the early stages of modernization, and its leadership—following Deng Xiaoping's famous dictum—were hiding their strength and biding their time. Perhaps that's why, despite its enormous population, rapid growth, and single-party political system, China didn't loom large in the US assessment of future threats.

Fast forward to 2016, and China's GDP had risen to 60% that of the United States, the People's Liberation Army (PLA) had grown into a formidable fighting force—especially in their Asia-Pacific backyard, and President Xi Jinping's Belt and Road Initiative had announced China's arrival on the world stage. Small wonder, then, that the Pentagon had come to regard the PLA as the pacing challenge for the US military, or that Presidential hopeful Donald Trump's promise to "beat China" resonated with US voters.

Trump's election to the White House proved a pivot point. Since 2016, the United States and China have imposed tariffs on hundreds of billions of dollars of bilateral trade. The United States has used export controls to block China's access to advanced semiconductors. Capital flows have

[1] See Fukuyama (1989).

Maeva Cousin et al., *The Return of History*. In: *The Price of Money*. Edited by: Jamie Rush, Tom Orlik, and Stephanie Flanders, Oxford University Press. © Oxford University Press (2025). DOI: 10.1093/9780197800942.003.0008

changed direction, with foreign investment exiting China. And new connector economies—Mexico, Morocco, Vietnam, and others - have moved to fill the gap created by the United States–China rift.

The broader geopolitical landscape has also been transformed.

Washington DC and Beijing are barely talking. Moscow and Beijing are talking a lot. On the eve of Russia's February 2022 invasion of Ukraine, Xi and Putin declared a "partnership without limits." Read across to Taiwan suggested an invasion by mainland China was a live risk. In 2023, Gaza provided another reminder of how long-simmering tensions could erupt into bloody conflict. The Covid pandemic underscored that dependence on foreign suppliers for crucial goods was a vulnerability.

For the global economy and markets, that matters:

- In the go-go years for globalization, ever-increasing cross-border flows of goods, services, capital, workers, and ideas contributed to higher growth. With those flows reduced and rerouted, that dynamic risks swinging into reverse, dragging growth lower.
- In the past, imports of Made-in-China goods and competition from low-wage workers helped keep inflation low and stable. Now, tariffs are pushing up import prices, and Russia's invasion of Ukraine demonstrated how supply shortages can drive inflation sharply higher.
- Globalization—in particular the tightly-integrated electronics supply chain—significantly reduced the relative price of investment goods. Looking forward, the relative price of computers and other investment goods has already stopped falling. If supply chains fracture, they could rise.
- The end of the Cold War was the trigger for payment of a peace dividend, with US spending on defense falling from 6% of GDP in 1989 to 3% in 2023. In a more dangerous world, defense spending—and pressure for government borrowing—is rising again.

For the natural rate of interest, those are potentially consequential shifts. With the exception of lower trend growth, they all point upward:

- Reduced and redirected flows of commerce would mean slower global growth and fewer opportunities for productive investment, dragging the natural rate down.
- More expensive capital goods would increase investment spending pushing the natural rate up.
- Lower inequality, if businesses reshore jobs and workers are protected from foreign competition, will mean less money in the hands of high-income savers, pushing the natural rate up.

- Geopolitical fractures are also reflected in capital markets - fewer savings from China and some other countries flowing into the United States will also push the natural rate up.
- Higher defense spending, if it's not offset by higher taxes or reduced outlays elsewhere in the budget, would mean increased government borrowing—adding more upward pressure on the natural rate.
- Persistently higher inflation as tariffs are ramped up and access to a cheaper global workforce becomes more difficult could also mean a higher natural rate.

There is a debate underway about how severe the ruptures are and what the future holds.

At one end of the spectrum, "slowbalization"—a term coined by Dutch writer Adjiedj Bakas—captures the idea that global ties continue to increase but at a slower pace. At the other end, "Thucydides trap"—a term coined by Harvard Professor Graham Allison—posits a high probability of war between the United States, as the world's established power, and China, as the rising challenger. Somewhere in between is the idea of a Cold War II, with the world dividing into rival geopolitical blocs.

In this chapter, we assess how the period of go-go globalization impacted the natural rate. We then consider a baseline forecast for the years ahead—basically a continuation of the current slowbalization trend. And we map out a Cold War II scenario where global trade barriers return to a level last seen in the 1990s—before China joined the World Trade Organization—and defense spending rises sharply.

We focus on the influence of trade, finance, and migration flows on trend growth, the relative price of investment goods prices, and the impact of higher defense spending on debt. The impact of reduced saving flows to the United States, shifts in inequality, and trade barriers adding to inflation, are explored in more detail in Chapters 9, 12, and 14 respectively. To get to an aggregate view of the impact of a Cold War II scenario, we borrow headline numbers from those chapters.

The main conclusions:

- From 1970 to 2022, the lower price of investment goods, higher inequality, and capital flows from China and other emerging markets to the United States resulted in a net drag on the natural rate of about 70 bps. If all the peace dividend savings from lower defense spending had been banked, that could have added a further 35-bps drag.
- In our baseline slowbalization scenario, there's virtually no further impact on the natural rate. In our Cold War II scenario, the combined impact of higher investment prices, reduced inequality, and emerging

> market savings exiting the United States add approaching 20 bps to the natural rate by 2035. Throw in higher debt-financed defense spending as the world becomes less secure, and the impact rises to 70 bps.

In past decades, globalization was a notable drag on the natural rate. Slowbalization has already neutralized the impact and, in the years to come, remains the most plausible base case. In a Cold War II scenario, a world divided into rival blocs could mean significant pressure for the natural rate to rise—adding stress at a moment a lot of other things would likely also be going wrong.

Trump's second term in the White House – just getting underway as this book goes to press – adds a new and volatile element to the mixture. Early moves to impose fresh tariffs on China and a clear message that United States allies need to raise their defense spending stop some way short of our Cold War II scenario, whilst also suggesting our slowbalization base case may be too optimistic.

Deglobalization and Growth

Globalization impacts growth—and from there the natural rate—through three broad channels: trade, capital flows, and migration. We explore two scenarios for how those channels may evolve: a baseline where current trends continue; and a Cold War II, where the world fractures into rival US and China blocs, and the flow of goods, services, capital, and workers between them is effectively turned off.

In our baseline scenario:

- US–China tariffs imposed during the trade war in Trump's first term, and the UK's post-Brexit trade relationship with the European Union, remain in place. Digitalization continues to lower trade costs, especially for services.
- The stock of foreign investment—including both direct and portfolio investment—holds steady as a share of recipient countries' GDP for most countries. The exception is United States–China, where we assume the stock of bilateral investment trends down to zero over the next 20 years.
- Migrant flows evolve as set out in the United Nations 2015 projections.

In our Cold War II scenario:

- The world splits into US-led and China-led blocs. We determine which bloc a country belongs to based on its formal treaty commitments and strongest trade relationships. We further distinguish between strong and weak alliances within each bloc. In the US bloc, for example, the UK is strongly aligned, and Brazil is weakly aligned.

- We assume tariffs on goods between the blocs rise to the level China imposed on the rest of the world in 1992. That's an increase in average tariffs from 7.7% to 39.7%. The increase for individual sectors is shown in Figure 8.1. The digitalization process that lowers costs in services trade occurs within, not between, blocs.
- Investors pull funds from the rival bloc. Strong US allies withdraw all their capital from the China bloc. Weaker allies withdraw half. Funds are repatriated to investors' own bloc. So, for example, as of 2022, the United States had $126 billion invested in China. We assume all those funds are gradually divested (through active sales or by letting the capital depreciate without reinvesting).
- Migration between strong US-bloc and strong China-bloc countries dries up, and we assume that some Chinese migrants currently living in strong US-bloc countries return home. Between 2010 and 2015, the US foreign-born population has risen by close to 4 million people. Close to 20% of those newly arrived migrants came from China. Losing some of these migrants and inflows of new ones could leave the US labor force close to 4% smaller by 2050.

To estimate the impact, we use a suite of models:

- Tariffs affect the economy through multiple channels. Exporters become less competitive, creating a drag on growth. Importers must pay more,

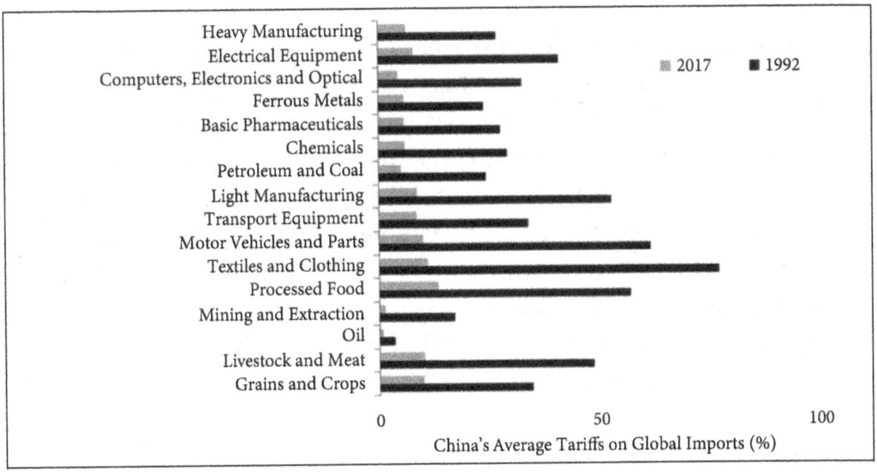

Figure 8.1 Tariff Shock—China's Average Tariffs on Imports Are Down From 1992

Source: Bloomberg Economics.

also dragging on growth and pushing prices up. A slowdown in technology transfer means advances in productivity are reduced.

- To capture all of these dynamics, we use the World Trade Organization (WTO)'s dynamic recursive Computable General Equilibrium model, known as the Global Trade Model.[2] This model integrates detailed data on trade flows, production, consumption, and tariffs—enabling simulations of how changes in trade policies affect different sectors and economies.[3]
- Foreign investment provides a boost to productivity—both by adding to the stock of capital and by transferring more advanced technology to the recipient country. We use estimates from the International Monetary Fund (IMF), which suggest a 10% drop in the ratio of foreign direct and equity investment to GDP lowers productivity by 4% after 10 years.[4]
- For recipient countries, higher migration increases the size of the labor force and so boosts output. In addition, like inflows of foreign capital, inflows of migrants typically boost productivity—bringing new skills and an entrepreneurial spirit. Following a separate IMF study, we lower total factor productivity by 0.6% for each percentage point decline in migrants as a share of the workforce.[5]

Under this Cold War II scenario, we find virtually all countries and regions are worse off. After 25 years, global GDP is 7% lower than it would have been under our baseline. In today's economy this would be equivalent to a cost of nearly $8 trillion.

- Globally, the trade shock is—by some distance—the most important channel. China is severely affected, losing over 10% of its output. For small, open economies in the China bloc—notably those in Southeast Asia—the loss of foreign investment adds a further significant drag.
- The impact on the United States bloc is more modest. As Figure 8.2 shows, United States output ends up 2.6% smaller, despite a substantial drop in net migration. Advanced economies have less to gain from globalization, partly because they're nearer the technology frontier, so they lose less when it swings into reverse. They also benefit from the reallocation of foreign capital away from China's bloc.
- Japan and Australia stand out for having more to lose, as they are more exposed to Chinese demand and migration flows.

[2] See Aguiar et al. (2019).
[3] See Goes and Bekkers (2022).
[4] See Kose, Prasad, and Terrones (2008).
[5] See IMF (2020).

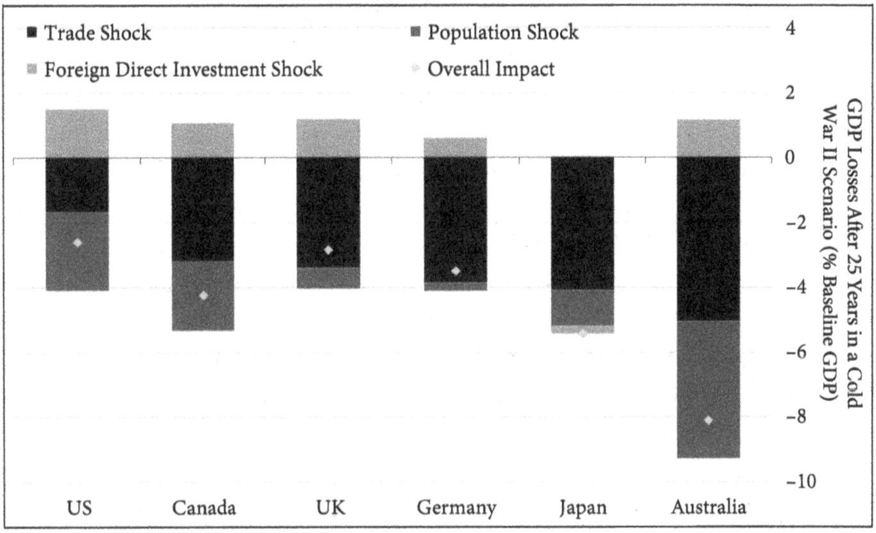

Figure 8.2 GDP Impact of Cold War II on Selected Advanced Economies
Source: Bloomberg Economics.

What does all of that mean for the natural rate?

- In the two decades before the global financial crisis, globalization contributed to stronger growth at home and abroad, creating more opportunities for profitable investment. That created modest upward pressure on the natural rate of about 0.1 ppt.
- In our baseline scenario, trend growth for the United States slows from an average of around 1.8% in the last few years, to 1.6% in the coming decades, with that slowdown creating a modest downdraft on the natural rate.
- In our Cold War II scenario, a substantial hit to the level of US GDP at the 25-year horizon translates into an additional 0.1 ppt drag on the annual growth rate. That means the drag on the natural rate is limited. Using the model set out in Chapter 3, we estimate the impact is about 7.5 bps over the next 20 years.

Summing up the discussion of growth, in the 1980s, 1990s, and early 2000s, globalization was a modest positive contributor to trend growth in the United States and other advanced economies, putting gentle upward pressure on the natural rate. In the years ahead, in our slowbalization base case, there's little impact on the natural rate. In our Cold War II scenario, a drag appears—but only a small one.

Deglobalization and the Cost of Investment

Trend growth is one channel by which globalization—and the potential for global ties to swing into reverse—impacts the natural rate. It's not the only one. Nor, it turns out, is it the most important. More significant is the relationship between globalization, productivity in electronics and information technology, and what happens to the price of investment goods.

Central banks focus their attention on the prices of goods and services faced by households. In the United States, UK, and Japan, the consumer price index covers everything from the cost of food in the supermarket to the price of buying automobile insurance. In the euro area, the harmonized index of consumer prices plays the same role.

Getting less attention: the price companies pay for things like computers, buildings, and transport equipment. Collectively known as investment goods, those products are a crucial part of the production process. Falling investment prices are one of the key reasons that borrowing costs have tumbled in advanced economies over the past few decades.

Since 1960, the price of investment goods in the United States has risen fivefold. The price of consumption goods has risen eightfold. As Figure 8.3 shows, that means capital goods have become about 30% cheaper, relative to the goods and services households spend their money on. A GDP weighted average of the 12 advanced economies we have included in our natural rates analysis points to a similar drop globally.

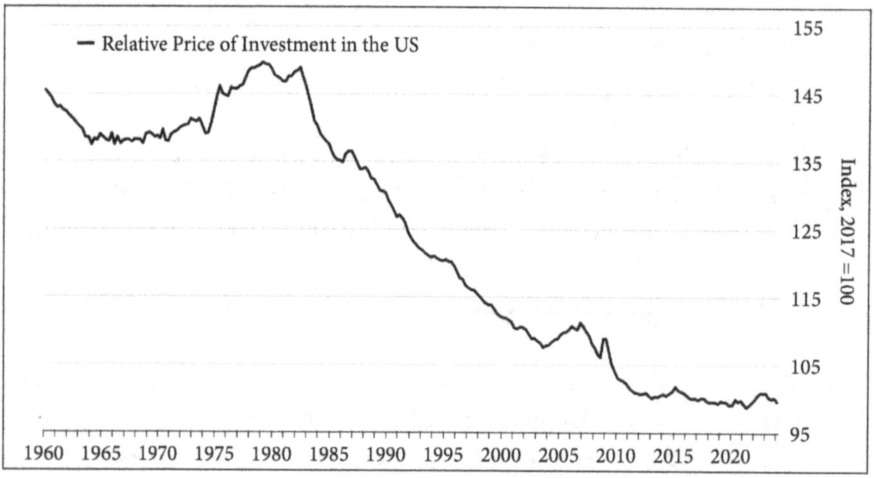

Figure 8.3 Relative Price of Capital Goods Has Tumbled

Source: BEA, Bloomberg Economics.

As Figure 8.4 shows, it has been the price of machinery and equipment that has driven the fall, with intellectual property also contributing. Within machinery and equipment, a sharp drop in the relative price of information communication technology has been the main driver. Structures—residential and nonresidential—have closely followed the path of consumer prices.

Researchers at the IMF have shown that the main driver of falling capital goods prices has been intensifying trade ties. That's partly because lower barriers to trade reduce the cost of imports—making it cheaper for US firms to import computers from China, for example. It's also because trade sharpens competition, driving efficiency gains.[6]

A more rapid pace of technological advancements and innovation in the capital goods sector—especially in information and communication technologies (ICT)—also contributed. In 1965, Intel founder Gordon Moore predicted—correctly, as it turns out—that the number of transistors in an integrated circuit would double every year, or two. There's no Moore's Law for groceries or haircuts—another reason the relative price of investment goods has been falling.

As Figure 8.5 shows, the IMF estimates about two-thirds of the fall in the relative price of capital goods between 2000 and 2011 can be explained by greater trade integration. Within that, 40% can be explained by the direct impact of lowering trade barriers with the remainder coming from the productivity-induced boost from higher trade. Outside of the impact of

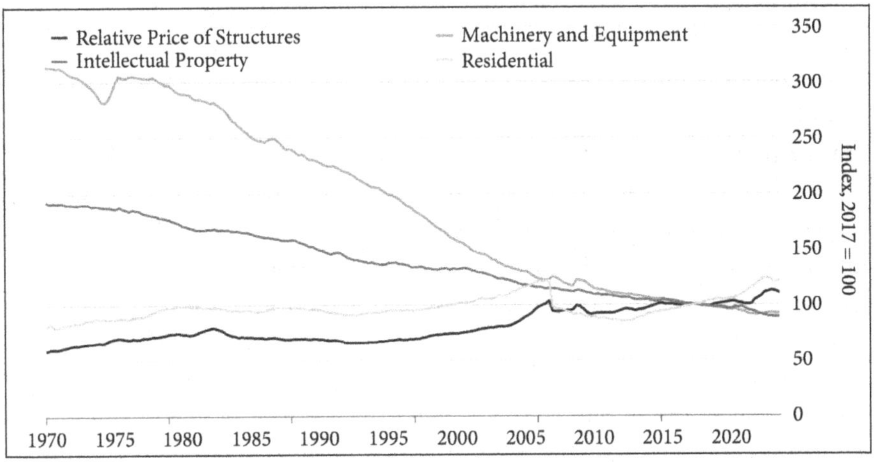

Figure 8.4 Machinery and Equipment Explain Most of the Decline
Source: BEA, Bloomberg Economics.

[6] See Lian et al. (2020).

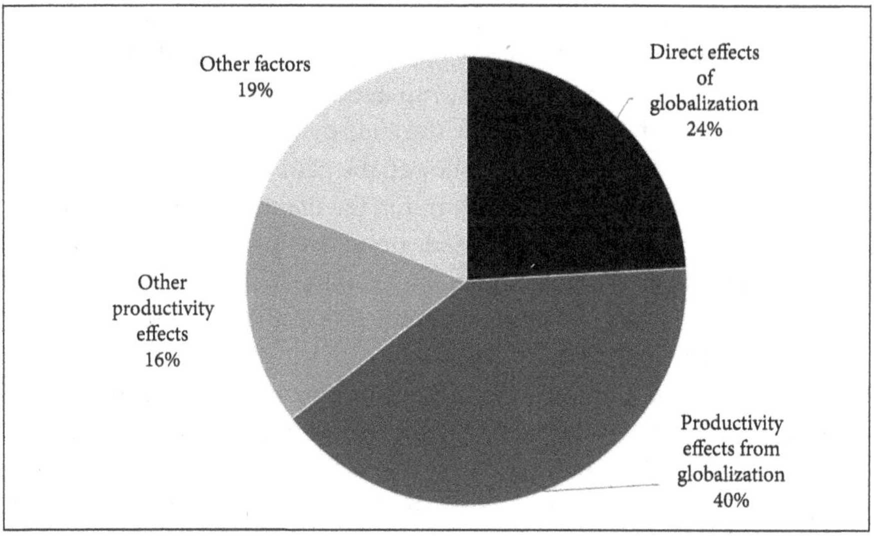

Figure 8.5 Globalization Accounts for Most of the Fall in Relative Price of Investment Goods
Source: IMF, Bloomberg Economics.

globalization, the IMF found that the biggest impact came from improvements in productivity.

For spending on investment, and so also the natural rate, to fall, lower relative prices of investment goods are a necessary—but not a sufficient—condition. After all, if relative investment prices are falling, and capital goods can replace workers in the production process, a profit-maximizing business would fire all their workers and replace them with robots. Investment prices would fall, but that could be more than offset by an increase in the quantity of investment.

As Rana Sajedi and Gregory Thwaites—then researchers at the Bank of England—demonstrated, what matters for the natural rate is whether capital goods are substitutes for workers (meaning a robot can be used to replace a worker), or complements (meaning robots make workers more productive).

That question has been the focus of extensive research by the economics profession, with a range of different answers. The key takeaway for our purposes is that all the studies conclude that capital goods are complements, not substitutes, for workers. That means the condition for a falling relative cost of investment to lower the natural rate is met.[7]

[7] See Sajedi and Thwaites (2016) and Chirinko (2008).

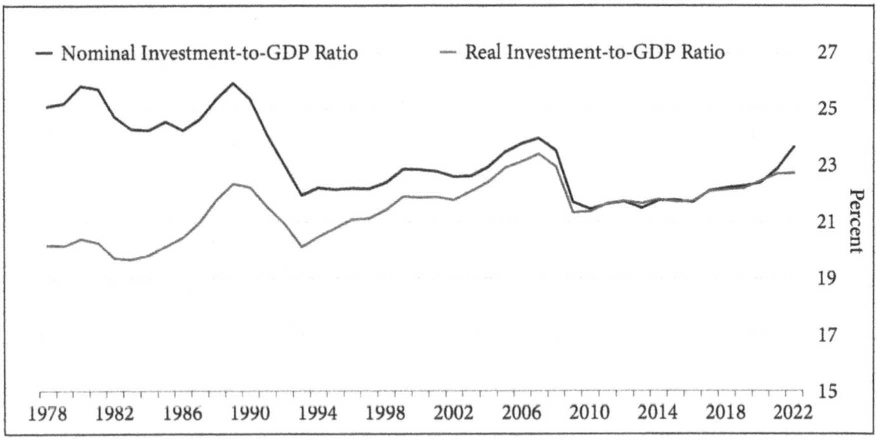

Figure 8.6 Real Investment Share of GDP Rising, Nominal Investment Share Falling
Source: OECD, Bloomberg Economics.

The evidence from surveys of the factory floor is confirmed by trends in the macroeconomic data—shown in Figure 8.6. In advanced economies, from the late 1970s to 2022, investment as a percentage of GDP rose in real terms but fell in nominal terms. Pulling the pieces together, the evidence from economic theory, micro-data, and macro-data agree: falling prices for capital goods are associated with businesses buying more of them—but not enough to prevent a drop in overall investment spending.

What Is the Impact on the Natural Rate?

Motivated by these facts, we have included the relative price of investment in our model of the natural rate.

Our model suggests that the US natural rate fell from almost 5% in 1970 to a shade above 2% in 2022, with the falling relative price of investment contributing about 40 bps to the 2.5 ppt decline. After slower trend growth and shifts in the age structure of the population, the price of investment is the third most important determinant of the drop. Within that 40 bps, two-thirds is explained by globalization.

How do our results stack up when compared with other estimates? As an often overlooked contributor to the fall in the natural rate, estimates for the contribution of the relative price of investment are in short supply. We uncovered two examples:

- Drawing on work by Sajedi and Thwaites, Bank of England economists Lukasz Rachel and Thomas Smith suggest the drop in the price of capital goods could have contributed about 50 bps to the 450-bps decline in long-run real rates, globally.[8] Their analysis focused on actual interest rates—not the natural rate.
- Ambrogio Cesa-Bianchi and others, also at the Bank of England, take a different view and argue that the relative price of capital has only a modest effect on the equilibrium real interest rate.[9] As a calibrated structural model, their approach is different from our own—which is estimated on the data.

Where Is the Relative Price of Investment Heading?

After falling sharply through the 1980s, 1990s, and early 2000s, in more recent years, the relative price of investment has leveled off. That break in the trend has coincided with a slowdown in the pace of globalization and a slackening in the pace of productivity growth in advanced economies since the global financial crisis.

It's plausible those trends will persist—with global trade ties increasing at a slower pace and technologies like artificial intelligence slow to deliver on their promise. In our baseline projection for the natural rate, we have assumed that the relative cost of capital goods remains flat. If that happens, the 40-bps drag on the natural rate stays in place, but there's no further downward pressure.

In our Cold War II scenario, we consider what would happen if tariffs between a US-led and a China-led economic bloc rose to levels seen in the early 1990s. For the United States, we estimate that would mean trade as a share of GDP drops from 27% in 2022 all the way back to 23%. Drawing on the relationship between trade and capital goods prices estimated by the IMF and feeding that into our model, we find that would result in a 5-bps increase in the natural rate.

Summing up, at a minimum, the significant drag from lower relative capital goods prices on the natural rate appears to be over. In a risk scenario where global ties unravel, rising capital goods prices could even push the natural rate a little higher.

[8] Rachel and Smith (2015).
[9] Cesa-Bianchi, Harrison, and Sajedi (2023).

Goodbye Peace Dividend, Hello Guns-or-Butter Deficit

In the late 1980s and early 1990s, with the Cold War ending, the United States looked forward to a "peace dividend"—with reduced risk of war allowing defense spending to fall. Sure enough, as Figure 8.7 shows, military spending as a share of GDP dropped from 6.8% in 1982 to 3.3% in 2022. Looking at the other 11 advanced economies in our study over the same period, defense spending fell from a simple average of 2.6% in 1982 to 1.4% in 2022.

In theory, lower defense spending should have significant benefits. Spending can be reallocated to other priorities—like raising education standards, amping up infrastructure investment, or investing in research and development. Alternatively, taxes could be cut—sharpening incentives for entrepreneurs. Or debt could be reduced—as indeed occurred, with US debt falling from 44% of GDP in 1991 to 32% in 2001.

For the natural rate of interest, lower government borrowing impacts through two channels:

- A reduction in the net supply of safe assets is a drag. Our model shows that a 1-ppt drop in the global supply of net safe assets as a share of GDP reduces the natural rate in the United States by 7 bps.
- Lower government debt means that investors demand a smaller premium as insurance against the risk of default or inflation. Our model

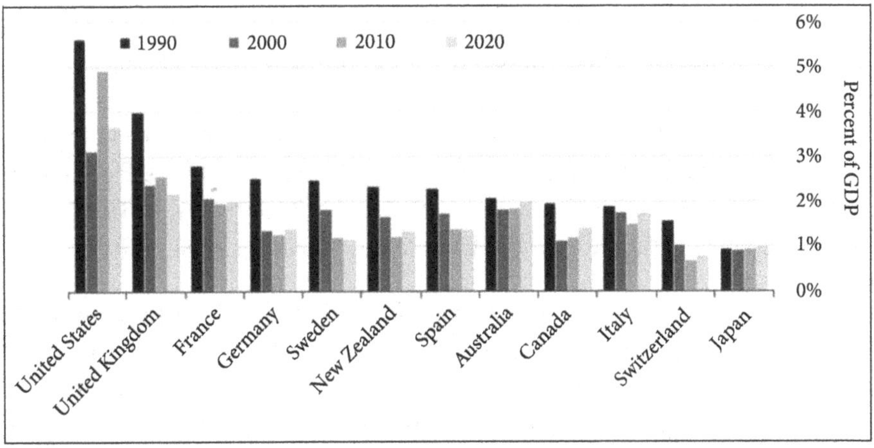

Figure 8.7 Defense Spending as a Share of GDP
Source: Stockholm International Peace Research Institute.

shows a drag of just under 2 bps on the US natural rate for each percentage point decrease in the national debt-to-GDP ratio.

Putting that all together, a 1-ppt drop in the US debt-to-GDP ratio cuts about 3 bps from the long-term cost of financing. As a thought experiment, if the US government had banked all the savings made whenever defense spending dipped below 4% of GDP between 1995 and 2022, the drag on the natural rate would have been about 35 bps.

Three decades on from the collapse of the Soviet Union, talk of a peace dividend has been replaced by fears of a renewed "guns-or-butter" trade off. Russia's invasion of Ukraine, war in the Middle East, and concerns about China's rise, are spurring the United States and its allies to invest more in their militaries. For US allies, signs that Washington DC is growing tired of paying for their security further sharpens incentives:

- In 2022, Japan announced plans to increase defense spending to 2% of GDP—after decades of keeping it below 1%—citing increased concerns about China and North Korea.
- In 2024, Britain committed to raise defense spending to 2.5% of GDP as fast as resources allow—a modest increase relative to 2023 spending of 2.3% but an indication of the global direction of travel.
- In 2024, 23 of NATO's 32 members were expected to meet its target of defense spending at 2% of GDP, up from six prior to Russia's invasion of Ukraine.

To see what happens if geopolitical tensions continue to escalate, in our Cold War II scenario we assume that defense spending as a share of GDP rises to 4% across all advanced economies in the US bloc for the decade to 2035. Overall, that would take total defense spending as a share of GDP across the 12 economies covered in our analysis back to levels observed in 1990, albeit distributed evenly rather than the United States bearing most of the burden.

- It wouldn't take much for the United States to lift defense spending to 4% of GDP, as it was already at 3.4% of GDP in 2023. Assuming the entire increase is financed by higher borrowing, by 2035, debt could reach 117% of GDP compared with 109% in our baseline forecast.
- For the other 11 economies in our study, where the GDP-weighted average spending on defense was just 1.5% of GDP in 2023, the effort needed is more substantial. By 2035, we estimate this scenario would

increase the GDP-weighted debt to GDP ratio to 152% compared with our baseline of 121%. Projections for individual countries are shown in Figure 8.8.

Plugging those numbers into our model, the combined impact of a higher global supply of safe assets and higher domestic debt means the natural rate in the United States could face a bump of 50 bps by 2035. To put a sharper point on it, debt at 117% of GDP and 10-year borrowing costs 50 bps higher would mean that, in 2035, the US government spends an extra 0.6% of GDP on debt servicing than it would have done without the upward pressure on defense spending—that's more than it spent on schools in 2022.

Adding It Up

A more fragmented global economy and increasingly fractious geopolitics has significant implications for the natural rate:

- Slower global growth means fewer opportunities for productive investment, exerting a modest drag on the natural rate between 2025 and 2050.

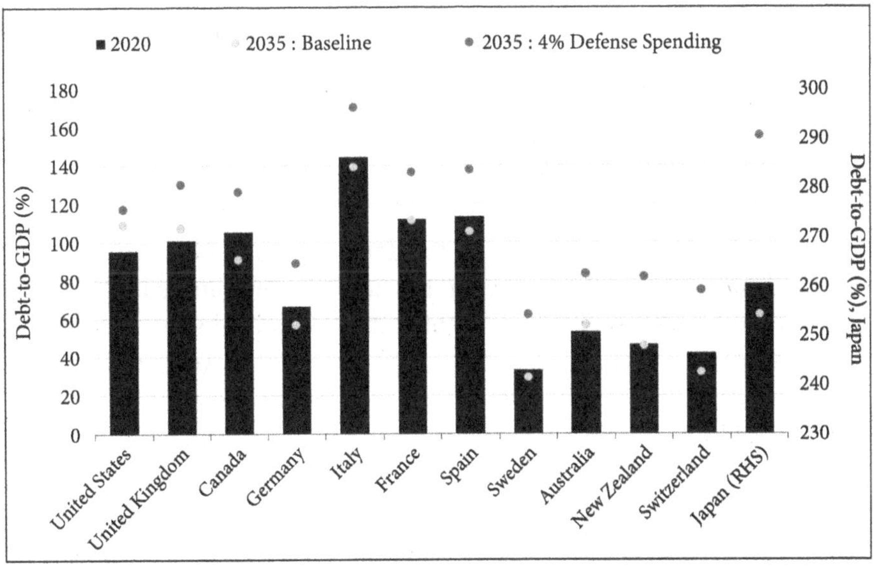

Figure 8.8 Debt Forecasts for Different Levels of Defense Spending
Source: Bloomberg Economics.

In our Cold War II scenario, we estimate that at 7.5 bps on US long-term borrowing costs.

- Reduced productivity gains from trade means the relative price of investment goods is set to stay steady and potentially edge higher. In our base case, that draws a line under a 40-bps drag on the natural rate. In our Cold War II risk scenario, it pushes it up a modest 5 bps.
- Higher defense spending means a peace dividend risks being replaced by a war penalty—with higher public debt adding to upward pressure on the natural rate. In our Cold War II scenario, that pushes the natural rate up by 50 bps.

Fracturing global ties also have implications for inequality, explored in Chapter 12. We estimate that globalization boosted the proportion of income going to top earners in the United States, increasing saving and lowering the natural rate by a bit less than 10 bps between 1970 and 2022. As jobs get reshored and workers are protected from global competition, inequality could fall—this could push the natural rate up a few basis points.

In the past, dollar asset accumulation from China also depressed the natural rate. That flow of saving has already dried up, and we expect Beijing to slowly divest its dollar holdings in the years ahead. In Chapter 9, we calculated that could add about 10 bps to the natural rate by 2035. In an extreme scenario, if China and other emerging economies divest from the United States rapidly, that could add another 20 bps.

Adding it up, as Figure 8.9 shows, between 1970 and 2022, the drag on the natural rate from deeper global ties was about 70 bps. If all the savings from the peace dividend had been banked, the drag would have increased to more than 100 bps.

In the years ahead, in our base case for global ties continuing to deepen, but at a much slower pace, the impact on the natural rate is limited. The 70-bps drag shrinks to 60 bps by 2035 as China diversifies its dollar holdings, but there's little impetus for either a further drop or shift to pressure for higher borrowing costs.

If our Cold War II scenario crystalizes, the combination of more expensive investment goods, higher defense spending, reduced inequality, and global savings fleeing a weaponized dollar could push it 70 bps above our baseline.

History, to return to Fukuyama's point, is back—maybe it never really went away. At a minimum, that means the globalization drag on borrowing costs is over. If history returns with a vengeance, substantially higher borrowing costs would be a likely consequence and an additional source of stress.

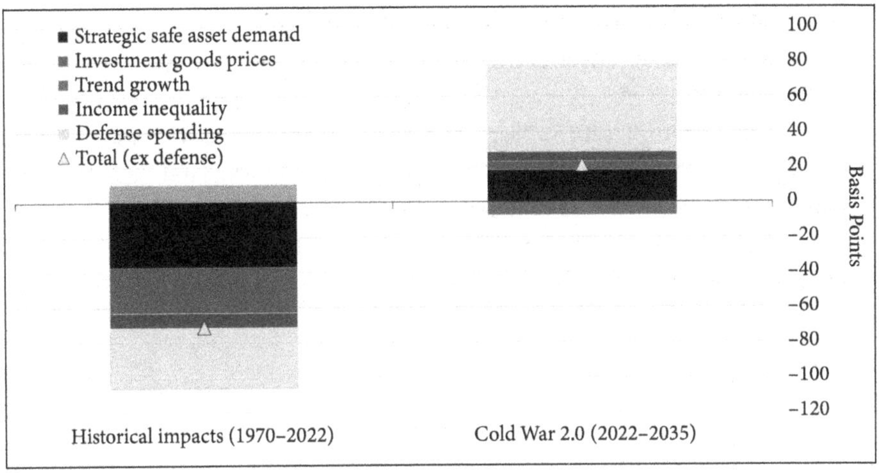

Figure 8.9 Globalization Impacts on the Real Natural Rate of Interest

Note: Historical trend growth impact refers to the two decades to 2008, it has faded since.
Source: Ademmer and Rush (2024), Bloomberg Economics.

Bibliography

Ademmer, M. and Rush, J. (2024). "Drivers of the Natural Long-Term Rate of Interest (and Why the Economy Hasn't Tanked)." *Oxford Open Economics*, 3, odae012. https://doi.org/10.1093/ooec/odae012

Aguiar, A., Chepeliev, M., Corong, E. L., McDougall, R., & van der Mensbrugghe, D. (2019). "The GTAP Data Base: Version 10." *Journal of Global Economic Analysis*, 4(1): 1–27.

Cesa-Bianchi, A., Harrison, R. and Sajedi, R. (2023). "Global R* (No. 18518)." CEPR Discussion Papers. https://cepr.org/publications/dp18518

Chirinko, R. S. (2008). "σ: The Long and Short of It." *Journal of Macroeconomics*, 30(2): 671–686.

Fukuyama, F. (1989). "The End of History?" *National Interest*, 16(16): 3–18.

Goes, C., and Bekkers, E. (2022). "The Impact of Geopolitical Conflicts on Trade, Growth, and Innovation." World Trade Organization Staff Working Paper ERSD-2022-09. https://www.wto.org/english/res_e/reser_e/ersd202209_e.htm

IMF (International Monetary Fund). (2020). "World Economic Outlook, April 2020." Chapter 4. https://www.imf.org/en/Publications/WEO/Issues/2020/04/14/weo-april-2020

Kose, M., Prasad, E., and Terrones, M. (2008). "Does Openness to International Financial Flows Raise Productivity Growth?" IMF Working Paper 08/242. https://www.imf.org/external/pubs/ft/wp/2008/wp08242.pdf

Lian, W., Novta, N., Pugacheva, E., Timmer, Y., and Topalova, P. (2020). "The Price of Capital Goods: A Driver of Investment Under Threat." *IMF Economic Review*, 68(3): 509–549.

Rachel, L., and Smith, T. (2015). "Secular drivers of the global real interest rate." Bank of England Staff Working Paper, 571. https://www.bankofengland.co.uk/working-paper/2015/secular-drivers-of-the-global-real-interest-rate

Sajedi, R., and Thwaites, G. (2016). "Why Are Real Interest Rates So Low? The Role of the Relative Price of Investment Goods." *IMF Economic Review*, 64(4): 635–659.

9 China Shock

How China's Saving Impacts US Borrowing Costs

Chang Shu, David Qu, Eric Zhu, and Tom Orlik

What was the cause of the global financial crisis (GFC) that tipped the United States and much of the rest of the world into recession at the end of the first decade of the 21st century? Candidates are many and various. Some blame the bankers—Wall Street whizz kids hiding ever-increasing leverage behind ever-more-complex trades in pursuit of ever-increasing bonuses. Some blame Washington, DC do-gooders, engineering social policies that aimed at helping low-income families buy a home and ended by saddling them with an unsustainable burden of debt. Some blame the Federal Reserve: perhaps America's central bank was too cautious in raising interest rates in the years ahead of the crisis, with bargain basement borrowing costs fueling Wall Street bets and low-income home purchases alike.

The Fed has another candidate to propose: China. In the years ahead of the crisis, then-Fed Governor Ben Bernanke introduced the idea of a global savings glut—a mountain of cash stashed away in the foreign exchange (FX) reserves of China, other Asian exporters, and oil producers like Saudi Arabia—which was channeled into purchases of US Treasuries. In 2007, then-Fed Chair Bernanke said that "played an important role in the decline in long term rates"—the same decline in long-term rates that pumped air into the housing bubble. In 2010, with the first intensity of the financial crisis over, but the long slog of recovery just beginning, he returned to the theme. In a speech to the American Economic Association, he argued that "capital flows from emerging markets can help to explain asset price appreciation and low long-term rates in the countries receiving the funds."[1]

In a bit more detail, the saving glut argument goes something like this: In 1997 and 1998, the Asian Financial Crisis demonstrated that emerging market currencies were vulnerable to speculative attacks—often with disastrous consequences. Responding to that, China and other countries with

[1] Bernanke (2010).

Chang Shu, David Qu, Eric Zhu, and Tom Orlik, *China Shock*. In: *The Price of Money*. Edited by: Jamie Rush, Tom Orlik, and Stephanie Flanders, Oxford University Press. © Oxford University Press (2025).
DOI: 10.1093/9780197800942.003.0009

a trade surplus used those funds to amass huge FX reserves—a buffer that could be used to defend their currencies against speculative attack. In China's case, reserves—which by the time of Bernanke's 2007 speech had already reached close to $1.5 trillion—were also a consequence of the People's Bank of China (PBOC) buying dollars to slow yuan appreciation. As Figure 9.1 shows, with the bulk of those reserves invested in Treasuries, US borrowing costs stayed low, despite moves by the Fed to raise the short-term interest rate. Those low, long-term interest rates were the fundamental reason for the property bubble, which burst, tipping first the United States and then the world into crisis.

There is, of course, a certain self-serving "look, over there, a bear!"—or perhaps, as it's China, "a panda!"—quality to the argument. Whether it is the Fed setting interest rates excessively low, the unscrupulous brokers saddling low-income households with unsustainable mortgage debt, the Wall Street traders slicing and dicing that debt into ever more exotic assets, or the regulators that turned a blind eye, to many, the GFC looks much more "Made in America" than "Made in China." At the same time, Bernanke's core insight—that a global savings glut was a factor keeping US borrowing costs low—has the ring of truth. At a fundamental level, it's not the Federal Reserve but the balance of savings and investment that determines interest rates. And in the first decade of the 21st century, China saved a lot and sent a lot of those savings to the United States.

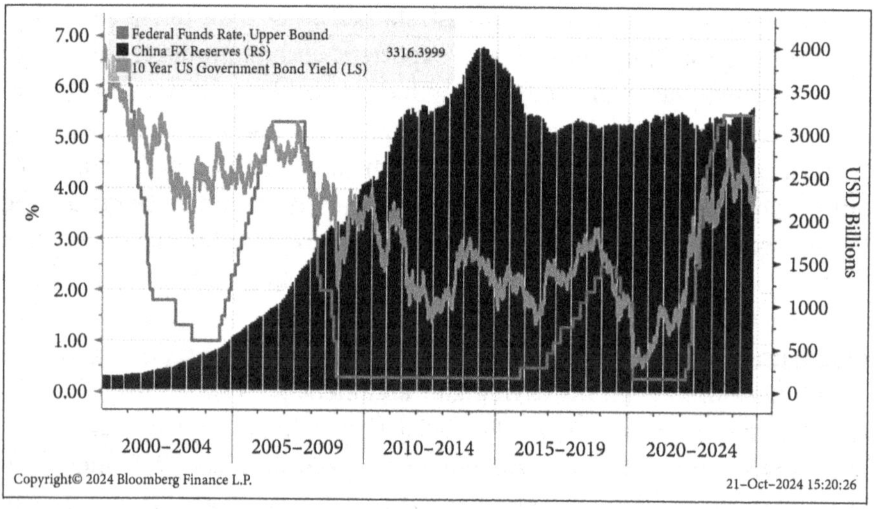

Figure 9.1 Ten Year Treasury Rate Stayed Steady Even as Fed Funds Rate Rose
Source: Bloomberg LP.

Since then, a lot has changed. China's currency has moved from a "crawling peg"—with the PBOC actively buying dollars to prevent yuan appreciation—to a "dirty float," with the central bank largely absent from the market. China's current account surplus—the underlying source of the funds that flowed into FX reserves and from there to US Treasuries—has shrunk from an outsize 10% of GDP in 2007 to less than 2% in 2023. That means China's FX reserves have already stopped growing. Indeed, in a moment of near-crisis in 2015, China's central bank sold hundreds of billions of dollars of reserves to prevent a slide in the yuan. In the years ahead, the shrinking share of the United States in global GDP and rising role for the yuan in trade settlement will reduce the incentive for China to hold reserves in dollars. In a risk scenario, where geopolitics continue to fracture and China follows Russia's path of rapid divestment, it could move out of dollars rather quickly.

In this chapter, we forecast the outlook for China's current account surplus and explore market-driven and geopolitical scenarios for how it allocates its FX reserves. We then use our model of drivers of the natural rate to estimate how much China's saving contributed to low US borrowing costs in the past and how that will evolve in the years ahead. The big conclusion is that at its peak in 2014, China's saving contributed an almost 30-bps drag on US 10-year borrowing costs. Taking account of other big savers—Japan, the East Asian tiger economies, petrostates like Saudi Arabia and Russia, as well as Brazil and Mexico—the impact doubles to about 60 bps. With the overall decline in the natural rate between 1970 and 2014 more than 300 bps, that suggests Bernanke's savings glut hypothesis wasn't wrong but is only part of the explanation for low US rates. Our model points to slowing growth and demographic factors playing a larger role. With China's current account surplus set to stay small, and the share of its FX reserves allocated to dollars expected to fall, the modest drag is set to shrink close to zero in the years ahead.

What Drives China's Current Account?

The current account balance is the sum of a country's goods and services transactions with the rest of the world. A country that sells more than it buys—like China for the entirety of its recent history—has a current account surplus. A country that buys more than it sells—like the United States over the same period—has a deficit. More than a dry set of accounting numbers, the current account balance captures the zero-sum dimension of international economics. For countries lucky enough to have one, a current account surplus means more growth and more jobs. China's supercharged economic expansion in the first decade of the 21st century was thanks in no small part to its ability to export more than it imported. A current account deficit can mean less growth and more unemployment. Donald Trump's campaign for the US presidency on a promise to "beat China" tapped into the deep resentment at US manufacturing jobs lost as a result of that dynamic.

In the US telling, China's surging current account surplus reflected grabby mercantilism: policies from Beijing that boosted the competitiveness of the country's exports while erecting a barrier to imports. There's an element of truth in that story. An undervalued yuan, high tariffs, state ownership of the commanding heights of the economy, and incentives to lure foreign firms to relocate production all helped boost exports while keeping a lid on imports. At a deeper level, though, shifts in China's current account balance are driven by structural forces that have little to do with the exchange rate and trade policies. Demographics, relative growth rates, macro-economic policy, and the social safety net all factor in. From both the grabby mercantilism and the structural forces perspectives, China's current account—already much reduced from its 2007 peak—looks set to stay low in the years ahead.

An undervalued yuan, low wages, and easy access to global markets—the drivers of China's export boom—are no longer in play. In the first decade of the 21st century, as China's current account balance roared higher, economists at the Peterson Institute for International Economics estimated that the yuan was undervalued against the dollar by as much as 40%. Back then, the PBOC was overseeing steady appreciation of the yuan, but not enough to quickly undo that undervaluation or strip China's exports of the competitive benefits. Fast forward to 2024 and the PBOC has stepped back from day-to-day intervention in the currency markets, and the pressure on the yuan is for depreciation not appreciation. The benefit that China's exports—and so also its current account balance—received from a cheap yuan are long gone.

An additional driver of China's booming exports, lagging imports, and surging current account surplus came from low wages. In 2001, when China joined the World Trade Organization, average manufacturing wages were just 3% of the level in the United States. After two decades of rapid pay gains for Chinese workers, the gap is still significant, but it's also substantially reduced. Compared to other emerging markets, China's workers are no longer cheap. Wages for factory workers are now in line with those in Mexico and many times higher than those in India and Vietnam. Adding to the stress on exports, growing friction with the United States—reflected in the trade war that erupted in the first Trump presidency —means exporters face higher tariffs and new barriers to market entry. As a share of the global total, China's exports peaked in 2016 at 14% and have been on a declining trend since then.

How about the deeper factors at work? Here we refine a framework used by the International Monetary Fund (IMF) to project current account balances across countries, zooming in on the factors that matter most for China:

- Growth rate compared to key trade partners. In general a country that is growing faster than its main trade partners would be expected to import more, dragging the current account surplus down. Based on Bloomberg Economics projections, China's growth rate is set to slow from about 5% in 2024 to just 1% in 2050. Over the same period, the GDP-weighted average of growth in the United States, Japan, and Germany is set to just slow slightly from 1.4% in 2024 to 1.2% in 2050. That narrowing growth differential should be a moderate push factor expanding the size of China's surplus.
- Life expectancy. The longer people expect to live the more they must save to prepare for retirement. Higher saving means less demand for imports and so tends to increase the size of a country's current account surplus. In China, projections from the United Nations show life expectancy is expected to rise from 80.8 years in 2024 to 84.7 years in 2050, also pointing to a sustained push for current account surplus.
- Trade openness. Higher openness to trade—especially for a net exporter—will allow more trade flows and so increase the current account surplus. The gauge for China, measured as the ratio of goods exports and imports to GDP, has declined to 34% in 2023 from above 60% in the mid-2000s. With potentially more trade tensions going forward, diminished openness is projected to continue pulling down China's surplus.
- Macro-economic policy. Expansionary monetary and fiscal policy boosts demand for imports and so drags on the current account balance. Our baseline projections assume an incrementally expanding fiscal deficit over the long term. Credit—measured by the private credit-to-GDP ratio—is assumed to continue mild expansion until 2030 before gradual declines over the following two decades. Overall, the combination of these policy trajectories would mean a modest drag on China's surplus in the next decade.

The model isn't perfect. There are factors that it doesn't include—for example, currency and capital controls. Our assumptions on the outlook for trade

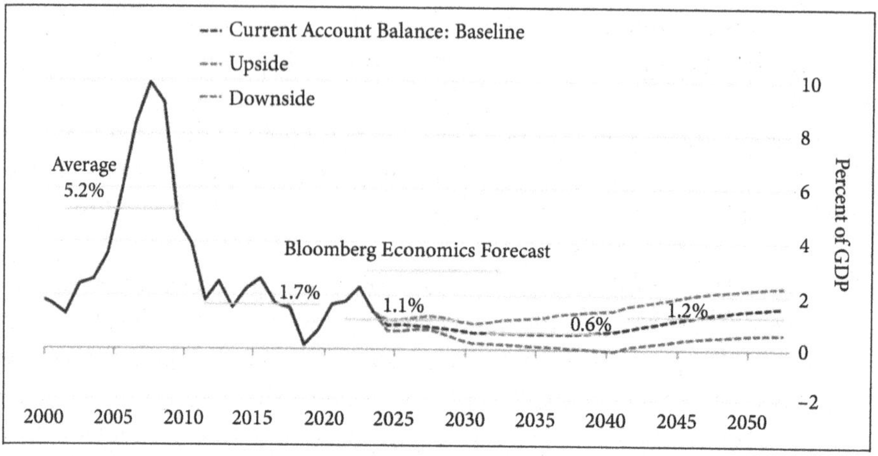

Figure 9.2 China's Current Account Surplus Set to Stay Low
Source: Bloomberg Economics.

openness and macro-economic policy might prove to be wide of the mark. Still, it brings together a number of important structural drivers, and the results align with our intuition—China's current account balance is set to stay low. As Figure 9.2 shows, we project a dip from an average of 1.1% of GDP in the 2020s to a low of 0.6% of GDP in the 2030s and a modest revival to 1.2% of GDP in the 2040s.

De-dollarization and China's FX Reserves

China's current account balance was the source of its savings glut. What mattered for US interest rates, though, is what it did with those savings. For the first decade-plus of the 21st century, the answer was simple. The PBOC maintained first a yuan peg to the dollar then, from 2005 on, a crawling peg with the yuan strengthening against the greenback at a managed pace. Doing so required the PBOC to buy up dollars coming into the country through the current account at a fixed price. Those dollars fueled the rapid increase in China's FX reserves, which climbed from a meager $150 billion at the start of the century all the way up to a peak of close $4 trillion in summer 2014.

In 2014, that changed. After years of gradual appreciation, the yuan was close to fair value against the dollar. That meant the PBOC could step back from day-to-day intervention—still wading back in from time to time to prevent volatility—but allowing the markets to play the main role in setting the exchange rate. For China's FX reserves, that shift in the yuan regime from a crawling peg to a dirty float had profound consequences. No more day-to-day intervention meant no more dollars piling up in the PBOC's coffers. China's FX reserves stopped rising. Indeed, in 2015, a moment of panicked capital outflows forced the PBOC into sales of dollars to defend the yuan. Total reserves fell to just above $3 trillion—a level at which they have stayed ever since.

What is the outlook for the allocation of China's remaining FX reserves? To answer that question, we explore two scenarios. First, assuming geopolitics won't be a major factor, we adapt a model developed by Serkan Arslanalp and Chima Simpson-Bell, of the IMF, and Barry Eichengreen of Berkeley College, University of California to explore how economic and market drivers might impact the dollar share.[2] Second, assuming growing tensions between China and the United States (and the willingness of Washington to weaponize the dollar), will be a factor, we use Russia's de-dollarization of reserves as a template for the path China might follow.

As a starting point for the analysis, we need to estimate the share of China's FX stash—some $3.2 trillion as of summer 2024—that's allocated to dollars. China's policymakers are, understandably, tight-lipped about the exact composition of their reserves. After all, if you're managing one of the world's largest pots of cash, anything you say you want to buy is going to get rather expensive, anything you want to sell rather cheap. Still, China's policymakers have in the past said that their allocation roughly aligns with the global pattern. The IMF's Composition of Foreign Reserves data suggest that as of end-2023 about 58.4% of the total—or $1.9 trillion - is invested in Treasuries or other dollar assets, down from a peak of 71.5% in 2001. Our estimate of China's dollar holdings is shown in Figure 9.3.

Based on the framework developed by Arslanalp, Eichengreen, and Simpson-Bell, a number of factors explain the diversification of reserves so far, and point to continued reduction in the dollar share in the years ahead:

- Economic size. As the share of the United States in global GDP falls, the case for holding dollar reserves weakens. The US share has already fallen from a peak of 30.1% in 2000 to around 26% in 2023. Bloomberg Economics forecasts that it will continue edging down to 17% in 2050.
- Trade settlement. Reduced use of the dollar to settle the bill in China's trade reduces the need to hold dollar reserves. Data from the PBOC show that the share of yuan invoicing reached 8.7% in current-account transactions in 2022 compared to 2.4% in 2010.

[2] See Arslanalp, Eichengreen and Simpson-Bell (2022).

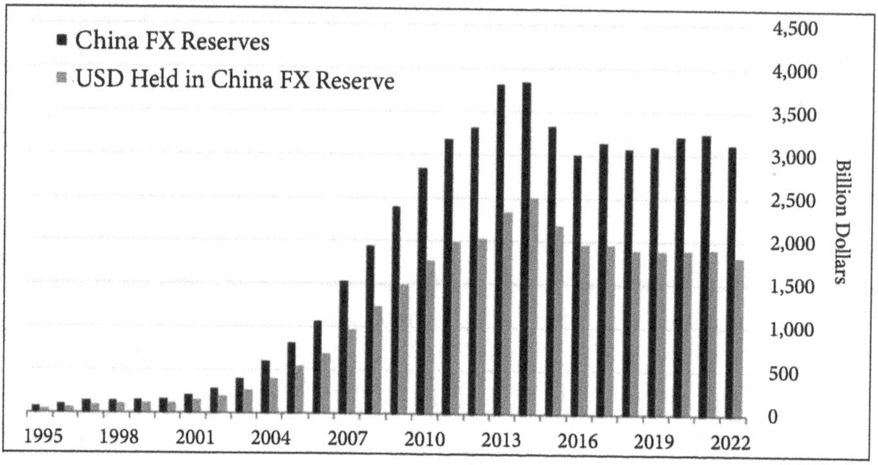

Figure 9.3 China's Holding of Dollars in FX Reserves
Source: Bloomberg Economics.

- Public debt. Higher debt levels raise the chance of default by the United States and the temptation to erode the value of debt by inflation. The GFC and Covid pandemic have already pushed US debt sharply higher. Unchecked deficits mean it has further to rise.
- Market liquidity. Reductions in the cost of yuan trading mean China's FX reserve managers can diversify at lower cost. The Bank of International Settlements tri-annual FX market survey showed yuan trading grew 14.5 fold between 2010 and 2022, and its share of the global total rose from 0.5% to 3.5%.
- Risk-adjusted returns. Low and unstable returns on US Treasuries add an incentive to diversify. From 2012 to 2021, the 10-year yield averaged just 2%. In 2022 and 2023, yields rose, but any gains from the small volume of purchases that year were more than offset by massive valuation losses on the broader portfolio.

We pull these factors together in a model. As Figure 9.4 shows, the results suggest that the share of US safe assets in China's reserves is set to continue falling, dropping from 48.5% end-2023 to 19.5% at end-2050. Assuming no change in total reserves, that points to a drop from $1.6 trillion to $600 billion—a fall of close to $1 trillion. The range of uncertainty around that forecast is wide. Factors in the model could evolve in a way that's out of line with our forecasts. And not all the factors that impact the size and allocation of China's FX reserves are in the model. A repeat of 2015's capital outflows, for example, could force the PBOC to sell dollars to defend the yuan, resulting in a drop in both total reserves and the share allocated to dollars.

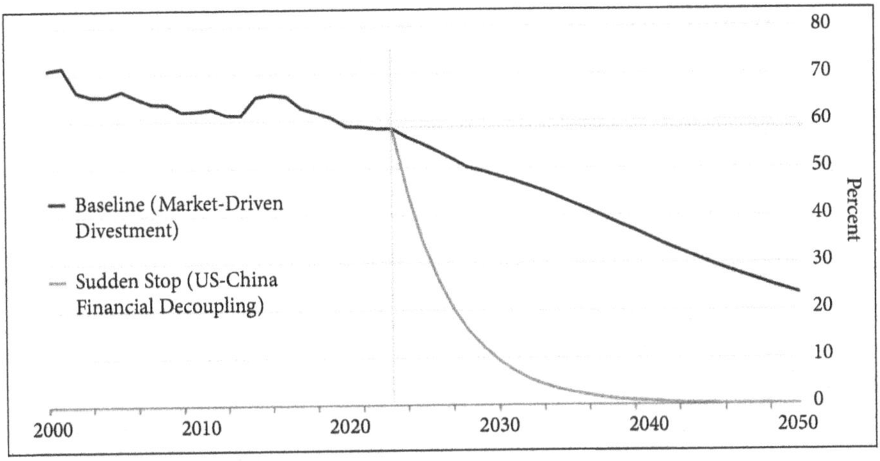

Figure 9.4 Forecasts for Dollar Share of China's FX Reserves

Source: Bloomberg Economics.

Geopolitics is another wildcard. In February 2014, Russia annexed Crimea—prompting sanctions from the United States and Europe. Anticipating a broader breakdown in relations, Russia's central bank began diversifying its reserve holdings away from dollars. From 40% in 2016, the dollar share of Russia's reserves fell to 11% at the end of 2021. Even that didn't prove fast enough to protect Russia's national treasure from the long arm of US sanctions. In February 2022, following Russia's invasion of Ukraine, the United States and its allies froze $300 billion of its central bank assets.

In China, policymakers were paying close attention. "The security of Chinese holdings has increasingly become a geopolitical issue" wrote Yu Yongding, a former policy advisor to the central bank. "The weaponization of the US dollar has completely destroyed the national credit on which the international monetary system is based," he added.[3] If China followed the same path as Russia from 2016 to 2021, its holdings of dollar assets would fall to almost zero in a short period of time. Reflecting on the lesson of what happened in 2022, it's possible Beijing would go even further than that, and attempt to diversify away from the euro and sterling as well.

There are, of course, powerful and persistent reasons why the dollar remains the world's reserve currency. The United States has the world's biggest economy, largest financial markets, and most powerful military. No other market matches the depth and liquidity of the US Treasury market. US institutions—from an independent central bank to a free press and rule of law—provide structural support. Still, the shift in global reserve allocation

[3] See South China Post (2023).

from 71.5% in dollars in 2001 to 58.4% in 2022 shows that those factors are not barriers to diversification. China's reserves are so large that they'd have more difficulty than Russia in finding a new home for them. The US weaponization of the dollar following Russia's invasion of Ukraine gives them an incentive to try.

How China's Savings Impact US Rates

How might that shift in China's reserve allocation impact borrowing costs in the United States? To estimate the impact, we turn to the model of the natural rate introduced in Chapter 3. As Figure 9.5 shows, at its peak in 2014, Chinese saving contributed about a 30-bps drag on US borrowing costs.

In the years ahead, in our baseline of market-driven diversification for China's FX reserves, that drag moderates gradually to near zero in 2050. In our sudden stop scenario, where fractious geopolitics push China to follow Russia's path of rapid divestment, it falls to zero in the early 2030s. Either way, our results suggest that the downward pressure Chinese saving exerted on US rates was never very strong and is set to fade close to nothing in the years ahead.

Why are our estimates of the impact of Chinese saving on US borrowing costs so small? Bernanke's savings glut thesis wasn't just about China. Taking

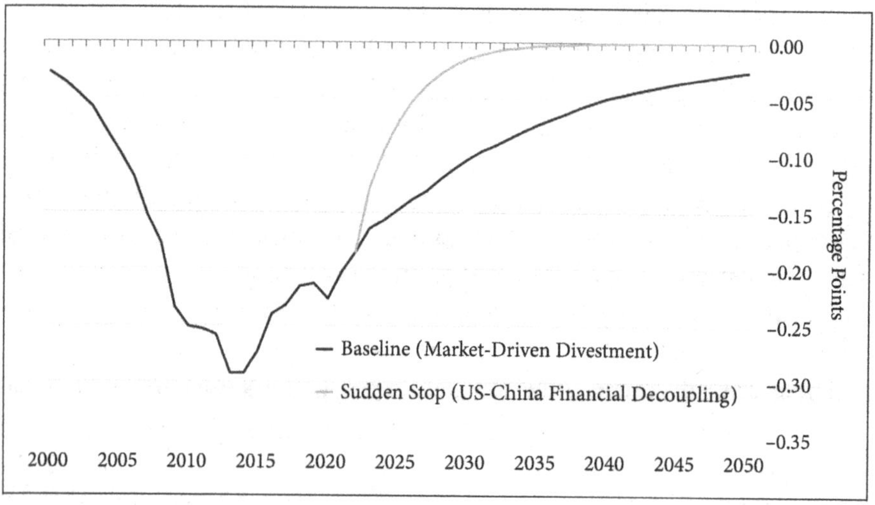

Figure 9.5 Scenarios for China Saving Impact on R*

Source: Ademmer and Rush (2024), Bloomberg Economics.

account of safe asset accumulation by Japan, the Asian tiger economies, oil exporters like Saudi Arabia, as well as Brazil and Mexico, the peak drag on US rates doubles to 60 bps. Still, our model shows that even by 2014, when the savings glut was in full force, other factors—notably slowing trend growth and demographic factors—played a larger role.

Another possibility is that our model is getting it wrong:

- It's possible that safe asset supply (Treasury debt issuance) and safe asset demand (China's purchases of Treasury debt) might have different impacts on borrowing costs. We, like others, have estimated our model on net safe asset demand and so would miss that distinction.
- It's also possible that cyclical but persistent shocks to the market, like the Fed's asset purchases, have blurred the evidence on the impact of China's purchases of Treasury debt.
- Or maybe we're just including too many explanatory variables in our model. Perhaps some of them have a spurious connection to the natural rate and are drowning out the impact of China in our results.

So we have considered three alternatives: the coefficient for the impact of safe asset demand on the natural rate is at the upper bound of our plausible interval; rising safe asset demand has the same (but inverse) impact on yields as the IMF assumes in its sensitivity analysis when debt rises above 60% of GDP; and the coefficient is as big as Fed economists Thiago Ferreira and Samer Shousha find in their 2020 study, which includes fewer drivers of the natural rate.

As Table 9.1 shows, the results for these three variations show impacts on US borrowing costs that are larger than in our model, but still not enormous. The biggest impact comes from applying the Ferreira and Shousha coefficient, which implies that, at its peak in 2014, China's saving contributed a 65-bps drag on US borrowing costs.

Pantomime Villain Revealed to be Pipsqueak

In the drama of recent US economic history, China often plays the role of villain.

China's exports, the story goes, decimated US manufacturing jobs. A bulging trade surplus should have caused the yuan to appreciate—hitting export competitiveness and solving the problem. But the dastardly PBOC intervened—buying up US Treasuries to block yuan appreciation. The same

Table 9.1 Alternate Estimates of China Saving on US Rates

	2014 Impact	Change 2022–2050	Coefficient	Definition
Ferreira and Shousha (2020)	-0.65	0.36	0.16	(1% of world GDP)
Baseline	-0.29	0.16	0.07	(1% of world GDP, ex China)
Upper plausible bound	-0.43	0.23	0.11	(1% of world GDP, ex China)
IMF debt rule of thumb	-0.47	0.26	0.04	(4bp per 1% of domestic GDP)

Source: Ferreira and Shousha (2020) Ademmer and Rush (2024) Alcidi and Gros (2018) Bloomberg Economics.

process kept US long-term borrowing costs too low for too long, pumping air into the housing bubble and triggering the GFC.

The big takeaway from our analysis is that while the signs on that model of the world are correct, the magnitudes are wrong. China did save a lot and did recycle those savings into Treasuries, and that did weigh on Treasury rates. But our best estimate is that the peak impact was about 30 bps in 2014; and in 2005, when China was supposedly sowing the seeds of the housing bubble, it was a mere 10 bps.

Broadening the definition out to include other big savers, the impact of the global savings glut was about 35 bps in 2005 and 60 bps by 2014—still small compared with the 3-ppt decline in the natural rate of interest over the same period. In the years ahead, with China's current account surplus expected to stay low, and the dollar share of China's FX reserves to fall, the drag is set to fade toward zero.

Bibliography

Ademmer, M., and Rush, J. (2024). "Drivers of the Natural Long-Term Rate of Interest (and Why the Economy Hasn't Tanked)." *Oxford Open Economics*, 3, odae012. https://doi.org/10.1093/ooec/odae012

Alcidi C., and Gros, D. (2018). *Debt Sustainability Assessments: The State of the Art.* European Parliament. https://www.europarl.europa.eu/RegData/etudes/IDAN/2018/624426/IPOL_IDA(2018)624426_EN.pdf

Arslanalp, S., Simpson-Bell, C., and Eichengreen, B. (2022). "The Stealth Erosion of Dollar Dominance: Active Diversifiers and the Rise of Nontraditional Reserve Currencies." *IMF Working Papers*, 2022(058).

Bernanke, B. (2007). "Global Imbalances: Recent Developments and Prospects." Board of Governors of the Federal Reserve System. https://www.federalreserve.gov/newsevents/speech/bernanke20070911a.htm

Bernanke, B. (2010). "Monetary Policy and the Housing Bubble." Board of Governors of the Federal Reserve System. https://www.federalreserve.gov/newsevents/speech/bernanke20100103a.htm

Ferreira, T. R. T., and Shousha, S. (2020) "Scarcity of Safe Assets and Global Neutral Interest Rates." International Finance Discussion Papers 1293. Washington DC: Board of Governors of the Federal Reserve System.

Phillips, S., Catão, L., Ricci, L., Rudolfs Bems, D. M., Julian Di Giovanni, F. U., Castillo, M., Lee, J., Rodriguez, J., and Vargas, M. (2013). "The External Balance Assessment (EBA) Methodology." *IMF Working Paper*, 2013(272): 1.

South China Morning Post. (2023). "China Exposure to US Dollar 'Weaponisation' Demands Rethink on Yuan Internationalisation as Geopolitical Woes Intensify, Yu Yongding Warns." https://www.scmp.com/economy/china-economy/article/3229877/china-exposure-us-dollar-weaponisation-demands-rethink-yuan-internationalisation-geopolitical-woes

10

The Problem with Petrodollars

How Cristiano Ronaldo, an Artificial Moon, and Flying Taxis in the Desert May Push US Interest Rates Higher

Ziad Daoud

Saudi Arabia wants to spend $500 billion to build Neom—a futuristic city in the desert. The city will be home to millions of people, an even larger number of robots, and the most Michelin-starred restaurants per inhabitant in the world. If the vision of its planners is fulfilled, it will also be the only city in the world where you can hail a flying taxi.[1]

The kingdom is also spending billions on sports. Its sovereign wealth fund acquired Newcastle United Football Club in 2021.[2] Its local clubs were the second-largest spenders in the world in 2023, pouring billions of dollars into transfer fees and wages for footballers, including Cristiano Ronaldo.[3] It'll even host the 2029 Asian Winter Games at a yet-to-be-built ski resort in the heart of the desert.[4]

Other oil producers in the Gulf Cooperation Council (GCC) are also opening their wallets. Abu Dhabi's billions have helped Manchester City to become one of England's most successful football clubs. Neighboring Qatar spent $300 billion upgrading its infrastructure to host the FIFA World Cup in 2022. Kuwait is setting up a sovereign wealth fund to invest more at home.[5]

Politically, the Gulf's "oil for security" pact with the United States is fracturing. Trade ties with China are deepening. The region's two largest economies, Saudi Arabia and the UAE, have been invited to join the BRICS, the emerging market bloc that counts China, Russia, and Iran among its members. And the Saudi-led OPEC+ group cut oil output in 2022 and 2023, despite US lobbying to raise it.

[1] For more on the outlandish plans for Neom, see Hubbard (2020), Nereim (2022), and Scheck, Jones, and Said (2019).
[2] See Hellier (2021).
[3] See Miller (2023).
[4] See Reuters (2022).
[5] See MacDonald (2023).

Ziad Daoud, *The Problem with Petrodollars*. In: *The Price of Money*. Edited by: Jamie Rush, Tom Orlik, and Stephanie Flanders, Oxford University Press. © Oxford University Press (2025). DOI: 10.1093/9780197800942.003.0010

In the past, the oil exporters of the GCC were among the biggest and most reliable purchasers of US Treasury debt. From 2005 to 2014, with rising oil prices swelling their coffers, the GCC parked more than $800 billion in international reserves, mostly in US debt securities.

Taken together with purchases from China and other Asian exporters, that helped keep borrowing costs in the United States at bargain basement lows. The petrodollar contribution to what Fed Chair Ben Bernanke called the global savings glut could have shaved as much as 0.25 ppt off US borrowing costs. Over the period from 2005 to 2023, that saved the US taxpayer some $700 billion—more than the annual GDP of the UAE.

In the future, the combination of ambitious spending plans at home and weaker political ties to the United States mean those purchases can no longer be relied on. With Middle Eastern buyers reducing their presence in the market, a significant force keeping US borrowing costs low will be removed.

How Petrodollars Reduced US Borrowing Costs

In February 2005, Alan Greenspan, then Fed Chair, identified what became known as the Greenspan conundrum.[6] In testimony to Congress, he observed that "long-term interest rates have trended lower in recent months even as the Federal Reserve has raised the level of the target federal funds rate by 150 basis points."[7]

This, Greenspan continued, was puzzling because it "contrasts with most experience, which suggests that, other things being equal, increasing short-term interest rates are normally accompanied by a rise in longer-term yields." The simple math of the yield curve suggests that when the Fed moves short-term rates, long-term rates should move in the same direction.

Just a month after that testimony, then Fed governor (and Greenspan's successor as chair) Ben Bernanke proposed a path out of the perplexity: the savings glut hypothesis. Bernanke's theory says the recycling of global savings—including the GCC's income from oil exports—into purchases of US Treasury debt was driving down long-term borrowing costs even as the Fed hiked short-term rates.

Bernanke's explanation had three building blocks:

- First, rising oil prices. The market moved from a low of about $10 per barrel in 1998 to above $50 in 2005. The uptrend continued after

[6] See Coughlin and Thornton (2022).
[7] See Greenspan (2005).

Bernanke set out his thesis, with prices above $100 for most of the period between 2011 and mid-2014.

- Second, significant GCC trade surpluses. As Bernanke wrote in 2015, "the current account surplus of the Mideast/North Africa region was large in 2006 and remained large in 2013, reflecting continued profits from oil sales."[8]
- Third, the GCC recycled its extra savings into US government debt, pushing down rates. In Bernanke's words: "Because the supply of savings exceeds the demand for investable funds, savings earn lower returns than in the past."[9] Low returns were a loss for GCC investors, but a win for the United States—which could live beyond its means at lower cost.

How large was the GCC's contribution to the decline in US yields? Our ballpark estimate: petrodollars have lowered yields by between 10 and 25 bps between the early 1990s and the 2010s.

How do we arrive at this answer? The model in Chapter 3 is one guide. It throws everything at the wall—inflation, demographics, growth, debt issuance—and overseas demand for US debt, including that from the GCC. It uses state-of-the-art tools to estimate the relative importance of each driver, concluding that GCC holdings depressed the natural rate in the United States by about 10 bps.

It's worth considering other evidence from research more tightly focused on the impact of capital flows on borrowing costs. A Chicago Fed paper estimates that flows from Asia and the Middle East combined reduced US borrowing costs by 0.5 ppt between 1992 and 2019. The two sets of flows had comparable contributions, implying a 0.25-ppt contribution from the GCC.[10]

A comparison with the impacts of quantitative easing provides a third point of reference. In these operations, the Fed buys US government debt to bring down borrowing costs. Petrodollars from the GCC going into US debt might have roughly the same effect.

- Between 2007 and 2019, the Fed bought $3.3 trillion of assets in response to the global financial crisis. Reviewing the extensive literature on the effect of quantitative easing, Bernanke concluded the operations reduced US interest rates by just over a percentage point.[11]

[8] See Bernanke (2015).
[9] See Bernanke (2022).
[10] See Barsky and Easton (2021).
[11] See Bernanke (2022).

- From 2005 to 2014, the GCC's international reserves, excluding gold, rose by about $800 billion. That's about a quarter the size of the Fed's purchases, so the impact on Treasury yields should also be about a quarter—more than our model suggests, but aligned with the 0.25-ppt estimate suggested by the Chicago Fed paper.

In 2019, US debt stood at $23 trillion. That means a 0.25-ppt reduction in debt costs would have saved the US Treasury around $60 billion a year. That's double the amount the US Federal government spent on science, space, and technology in 2019.

The savings to the US taxpayer from recycling of GCC petrodollars into Treasury debt are unlikely to persist. Instead, in the years ahead they'll probably reverse. Why? The three underpinnings of the savings glut thesis as it applies to the GCC—high oil prices, outsized trade surpluses, and investment of these surpluses into US debt are all breaking down.

Peak Oil, Spending at Home, and Risky Investments

Oil prices go through cycles. As of mid-2024 the market is riding an uptrend. Prices averaged $99 per barrel in 2022, and $82 in 2023. That's much higher than the $58 average between 2015 and 2021. The logic of past cycles, the energy transition, and national security concerns mean that high prices are unlikely to be sustained.

Oil booms carry the seeds of their own bust, as high prices attract new producers to the market. The downturns of the 1980s and 1990s followed the boom of the 1970s as new discoveries in the North Sea came online. US shale output flooded the market, bringing to an end the 2005–2014 boom. The pattern is clear: high prices lead to additional supply, which lowers prices.

The threat to oil prices today doesn't just come from supply. Weaker demand—as the world transitions toward clean energy—could be an additional factor. The International Energy Agency estimates that demand will peak before 2030 and needs to shrink to a quarter of its current level by 2050, if the world really wants to achieve net-zero carbon emissions.[12]

The Middle East will likely be the main provider of these last few barrels of oil due to low extraction costs, but they're unlikely to generate a significant windfall. The IEA estimates that the required reduction in fossil fuel

[12] See Smith (2023a), and IEA (2021).

consumption will drive prices to $25 per barrel by 2050. No GCC country can cover its public spending or imports at that price.

There could certainly be slippage in the transition to a net-zero world. The early days of the second Donald Trump presidency – for example - suggest that for the world's biggest economy tackling climate change is no longer a priority. That means demand might not fall as sharply as the IEA predicts. Saudi Aramco—Saudi Arabia's giant national oil company—described the IEA predictions as unrealistic.[13]

OPEC is more bullish. The oil cartel sees consumption rising through 2045.[14] But even in the case of partial adjustment, and demand falling less rapidly than anticipated, the effect on prices could still be significant. Covid offers a case study: the loss of 15% of global demand in the first half of 2020 halved oil prices.

The need for energy security is an additional threat to long-term oil demand. Russia's war in Ukraine lit a fire under Europe's efforts to reduce its fossil-fuel dependence. Russia's decision to turn off Europe's gas sent inflation soaring. It was only an unseasonably warm winter in 2022 that saved the economy from recession. Europe's policy makers responded by increasing efforts to diversify supply—including accelerating investments in renewable energy.

Falling crude prices will mean less money flowing into GCC coffers. Higher spending at home will mean that not only is the petrodollar savings pool smaller, but the share devoted to purchase of US Treasury debt is reduced.

There's spending on construction. Saudi Arabia wants to build the futuristic city Neom with a price-tag of $500 billion. The final cost will probably exceed that. One part of Neom, a linear city called The Line, could alone cost $1 trillion.[15] Neom isn't the only large investment—the total project pipeline for eight years from 2023 will amount to $2.1 trillion.[16] Not to be outdone by its bigger neighbor, Kuwait is starting a sovereign wealth fund dedicated to domestic investments.[17]

There's spending on sports. Saudi Arabia wants to host the 2034 FIFA World Cup.[18] Neighboring Qatar poured $300 billion to upgrade its infrastructure ahead of hosting the same tournament in 2022. It's also splashing billions more on golf [19] and winter sports.[20] Against the monumental cost

[13] See Ferman (2023).
[14] See Smith (2023b).
[15] See Nereim (2022).
[16] See Takla (2023).
[17] See MacDonald (2023).
[18] See Kadabashy (2023).
[19] See Martin (2023a).
[20] See Descalsota (2022).

of those endeavors, the $2 billion Saudi Arabian clubs spent on recruiting footballers in the 2023–24 season doesn't look that significant—but it's another indicator of how petrodollars are now flowing anywhere except into US Treasuries.

The evolution of the current account balance for GCC countries provides a window into how patterns of spending and saving are shifting. For the GCC, the current account balance would improve with high oil prices or elevated savings. To neutralize the effect of oil prices and isolate the impact of the savings piece of the equation, we compare the current account balance in 2022 versus 2013—two years in which oil prices were about $100 per barrel.

As Figure 10.1 shows, most GCC countries ran a smaller current account surplus in 2022 compared with 2013. For the GCC as a whole, the current account balance fell from 21% of GDP in 2013 to 16% in 2022. At the macro level, that shows more spending and less saving, bigger transfer fees for football stars, more rivets to fix wings onto taxis, and so less money going into US Treasuries, and higher borrowing costs for the United States.

Lower oil export income will mean reduced flows into GCC coffers. Higher spending at home means a smaller share of that income will be devoted to investment. The last piece of the puzzle: a shift in investment focus from safe, low-return Treasury debt to riskier, high-return assets. Before discussing how the GCC invests its wealth, though, it's useful to get a sense of its size.

The GCC is rich. Taken together, Saudi Arabia, UAE, Qatar, Kuwait, Oman, and Bahrain own more than $5 trillion of assets abroad.

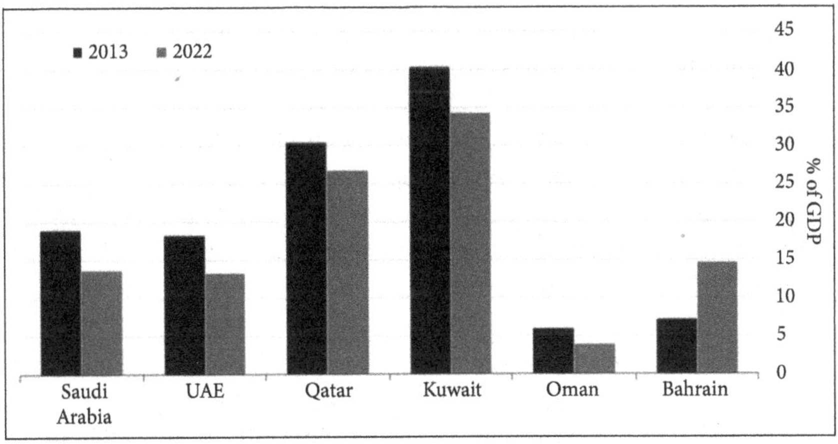

Figure 10.1 GCC Current Account Balance

Source: IMF.

Saudi Arabia, which publishes data on its international investments, had overseas assets of $1.2 trillion in 2021. The holdings range from dollar deposits to shares in companies like electric vehicle giant Lucid Group, ride-sharing app Uber, and Newcastle United FC. If the assets were divided equally, each of Saudi Arabia's 20 million citizens would have $60,000.

The figures for some of the other GCC nations are even more striking. Unlike Saudi Arabia, other oil exporters in the region don't publish data on international investments, so we rely on the External Wealth of Nations database, maintained by Gian Maria Milesi-Ferretti at the Brookings Institution. The data are based on his earlier work with Philip Lane, who became the European Central Bank's chief economist.

The data show the United Arab Emirates with about $2 trillion of assets abroad. Divided by its one million citizens, that means $2 million of overseas wealth per citizen. Qatar's $800 billion in overseas assets—including luxury London store Harrods—means its 400,000 population have a claim on about $2 million each.[21]

Of course, GCC countries have debts as well as assets. Based on the External Wealth of Nations dataset, obligations in the form of overseas debt and foreign stakes in GCC companies add up to about $2 trillion. Netting that out, net foreign assets for the GCC is still a hefty $3.5 trillion.

If fully invested in US debt, that $3.5 trillion would be roughly equal to all the Fed's quantitative easing programs from 2008 and 2020. And we know, from Bernanke's estimates on the impact of quantitative easing, that this could lower the interest rate on US debt by a bit over 1 ppt, saving Washington $300 billion in debt-servicing payments each year.

Unfortunately for the United States, the GCC doesn't invest all its wealth in US Treasury debt. If anything, it has been shifting away from it. Multiple data sources show a tilt toward riskier investments.

- Data from the International Monetary Fund show the GCC is parking a smaller share of its trade surplus in foreign exchange reserves. Between 2005 and 2014, the GCC accumulated $2.3 trillion in trade surpluses, and parked 37% of these in reserves. Since 2017, the GCC added nearly $800 billion in cumulative trade surplus, but reserves didn't increase at all.
- The External Wealth of Nations database combined with Saudi central bank's data show a higher share of GCC wealth is heading to risky assets, like stocks, at the expense of safe investments like debt. As Figure 10.2 shows, at end-2021, the GCC had 44% of its wealth invested in risky assets. That's up from just 17% in 2007.

[21] See Daoud (2024).

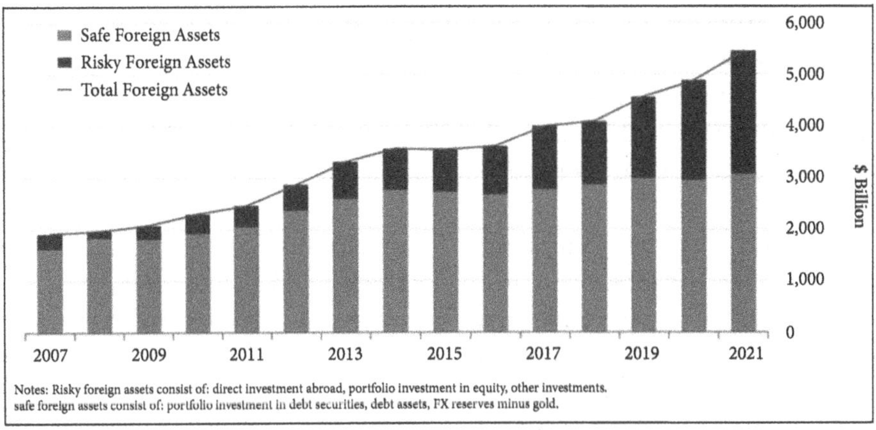

Figure 10.2 GCC External Investments

Source: Milesi-Ferretti (2022), External Wealth of Nations database, Brookings Institution, Saudi Central Bank, Bloomberg Economics.

- The US Treasury Department data show a decline in GCC's holdings of US Treasuries. For Saudi Arabia, the stockpile fell to a six-year low in June 2023.[22]

The change in investment strategy has implications at home. Investing in riskier assets may generate higher returns over the long term, but it can also lead to losses in some years. In 2022, Saudi Arabia's Public Investment Fund lost $11 billion on its investments—likely linked to the poor performance of global stocks.[23]

For the United States, the combination of lower oil prices crimping GCC export income, more spending of that income by GCC countries at home, and a pivot toward investing in riskier assets points in one direction: fewer petrodollars flowing into the US Treasury market and higher borrowing costs for the government.

Steadying the Social Contract, Breaking the Security Pact

Two general principles govern policy in the GCC. At home, there's an implicit social contract between monarchs and citizens, a pact where political consent is traded for economic benefits. Abroad, the Gulf has a pact with the United States which exchanges oil for security. Both principles face challenges, and that means a change in policy.

[22] See Abu Omar (2023).
[23] See Martin (2023b).

A story from the Iraqi-Israeli-British historian Avi Shlaim sheds light on the social contract in the GCC and its limits. In his memoirs, Shlaim recounts the story of his great-grandfather, who was left an inheritance "in the shape of forty keys to forty houses . . . that their family should be able to live from the rent of these houses alone for seven generations without having to do any other work."[24]

The good news for Shlaim's family: inherited wealth meant an easy life. The bad news: with no incentive to work, the result could be a lot of lazy children. Poor stewardship of the inheritance, or shifts in the real estate market, could reduce its value. And after seven generations, a bigger family might find that even income from 40 houses is spread a little thin.

For the GCC, oil wealth plays a similar role. A steady stream of oil income allows rulers to provide citizens with benefits in the form of cushy jobs, subsidized utilities and housing, and free education and healthcare. At the same time, oil wealth means a disincentive to work. And a drop in the price of oil, expansion in the population, or both, might mean not enough funds to go around—breaking the social contract.

It's against this backdrop that GCC states have pivoted from safe but low-yielding investments in US Treasuries to riskier but higher-yielding bets—typically channeled through their sovereign wealth funds. The aim is to hedge against the risk of falling oil prices by making investments that can generate an alternative source of income, funding the maintenance of the social contract without political changes.

In 2016, Saudi Arabia's then-Deputy Crown Prince Mohammed bin Salman set out the strategy.[25] Bin Salman said he planned to beef up the Kingdom's sovereign wealth fund, "making investments the source of Saudi government revenue, not oil." In the years since, the kingdom has expanded its sovereign wealth fund, while shrinking the size of its international reserves.

Shlaim's family wealth didn't last for seven generations. The eldest son squandered it after he acquired a taste for gambling. An unkind assessment would be that the GCC's risky bets on electric vehicles and ride-sharing apps could take them in the same direction. Fundamentally, though, the plan makes sense—diversify sources of income to ensure the social contract can be funded no matter what happens to oil prices.

If the oil-funded social contract is the basis of the domestic political system in the GCC, then the "oil for security" pact is the pillar of its international relations. Symbolized by the 1945 meeting between US President Franklin D. Roosevelt and Saudi King Abdul Aziz Ibn Saud aboard a US cruiser in the

[24] See Shlaim (2023).
[25] See Fattah, Bartenstein, and Avis (2022).

Suez Canal, the pact is simple: the GCC provides the United States with oil; the United States guarantees the GCC security.

Iraq's invasion of Kuwait in 1990 shows how the pact is meant to work. The United States was quick to dispatch its troops to Saudi Arabia to protect its territory from further Iraqi incursion, form an international coalition, and begin a military campaign to kick Iraqi troops back across the border.

The pact is no longer what it used to be. In 2017, when Qatar faced a Saudi-led blockade, and Trump accused it of funding extremism, Doha had to turn to Turkey for protection.[26] Resentment toward the United States has festered in the UAE after the 2015 Iran nuclear deal under President Barack Obama.[27] Saudi Arabia, sidelined by President Joe Biden over the murder of journalist Jamal Khashoggi, slashed oil production despite US pleas, and restored ties with Iran through Chinese mediation.[28]

Dissimilar though presidents Obama, Trump, and Biden are, one thing they have in common is a determination to spend less time on the Middle East, pivoting toward China as the main focus of US foreign policy.

The GCC feels the US shift has left a gap, and it's searching for new partners to fill it. With the "oil for security" pact breaking, the incentive for GCC states to recycle their petrodollars into US Treasuries is further reduced.

Pegged to the Dollar

Could the gap between the United States and the GCC widen further? Two questions will prove critical. First, whether the Gulf will sell its oil in non-dollar currencies—a shift from the dollar to China's yuan would be a major rupture. Second, whether GCC countries will weaken their currency peg to the dollar. On both questions, there is a stronger case for stability than change.

Could the GCC pivot from the United States toward China also mean a shift from selling oil in dollars to accepting payments in yuan? For China, such a move would support efforts to dethrone the dollar as the world's dominant trade and investment currency. For the GCC, though, the move doesn't make sense:

- The GCC runs a trade surplus with China, meaning accepting payments in yuan would lead to rapid accumulation of yuan savings. In international trade or investment, yuan are not as useful as dollars.[29] The greenback dominates cross-border commerce in the same way English

[26] See Kozok and Ant (2017)
[27] See Fattah et al. (2022).
[28] See Daoud and McBride (2023).
[29] See Bertaut, von Beschwitz, and Curcuru (2023).

dominates other languages in cross-border communications.[30] Unless a country is under sanctions—like Russia or Iran—it's unlikely to trade oil in non-dollar currencies.
- An important reason why accumulating savings in yuan isn't particularly appealing is that China's controlled capital account makes the currency hard to invest. Concerns about persistent currency depreciation as China's growth prospects slow, further reduce the appeal.
- Finally, GCC countries have currency pegs to the US dollar. That means they need to hold dollars to back up their local currencies. As long as the pegs are in place, GCC countries are unlikely to shift away from the dollar in oil trade settlement.

If the dollar-peg restricts the GCC's ability to trade oil in other currencies, could this currency arrangement change in the next few years? Probably not.

De-pegging would mean that the GCC currencies become volatile, moving up and down with swings in oil prices. That's the case even with diversified economies, like Canada and Norway. The volatility will be more pronounced for the Gulf—where oil is a larger part of the economy. And it would inject instability into import costs and consumer prices.

Volatile currencies and inflation would make it harder for the region to attract foreign workers and investments. The majority of the region's labor force—in some cases as many as 90% of workers—are noncitizens.[31] There's appetite—indeed competition—to attract more. A currency that's fixed against the dollar provides attractive predictability. A currency that's as volatile as the oil price would not.

The downside of moving from pegged to floating currencies is significant. The upside is limited. The main exports for GCC countries are oil and gas—both are denominated in dollars. A weakness in the Saudi riyal isn't going to make a Saudi barrel of oil more attractive versus, for example, a Venezuelan barrel of oil.

De-pegging the currency would bring all the negatives of a flexible exchange rate, without the main benefit of boosting exports. The GCC is unlikely to make that switch willingly.

A New Conundrum for US Rates

The oil boom of the early 2000s funded massive GCC investments in US Treasury debt. The move was part of a global trend after the Asian Financial Crisis,

[30] See Kindleberger (1967).
[31] See GCC-Stat (2021).

when many emerging markets built up foreign-exchange reserves as a buffer against the risk of capital flight.

That helped drive down the cost of borrowing for the American government. The GCC alone contributed a reduction of interest rates of as much as 0.25 ppt. That might not seem a lot. But as the United States is the world's largest economy, and its public debt is even bigger than its annual output, the savings on debt servicing costs were meaningful.

The drivers of high GCC savings and investment in US debt are now swinging into reverse. Peak oil demand means exports may not give the GCC the same windfall they provided in the past. The region is consuming more domestically, which shrinks the pool of funds it can deploy abroad. And the need to diversify sources of income mean a pivot toward riskier investments with higher returns and away from US Treasuries.

The shift is likely to endure. The social contract is becoming costlier as the GCC population grows—meaning a pressing need to park oil revenue in higher-return investments. A changing global landscape—with the GCC diversifying security and economic links away from the United States and toward China and India—is another factor behind the investment shift.

Add vanity projects, flashy footballers, and flying taxis to the mix, and it seems the oil savings glut that helped keep debt costs low for the United States has come to an end. The conundrum facing the next generation of US central bankers might be why long-term borrowing costs stay high, even when short-term interest rates are cut.

Bibliography

Abu Omar, A. (2023). "Saudi Arabia's Hoard of US Treasuries at Six-Year Low in Embrace of Risk." https://www.bloomberg.com/news/articles/2023-08-16/saudi-hoard-of-us-treasuries-at-six-year-low-in-embrace-of-risk

Barsky, R., and Easton, M. (2021). "The Global Saving Glut and the Fall in U.S. Real Interest Rates: A 15-Year Retrospective." *Economic Perspectives*. Federal Reserve Bank of Chicago, No. 1. https://doi.org/10.21033/ep-2021-1

Bernanke, B. (2015). "Why Are Interest Rates So Low, Part 3: The Global Savings Glut." Brookings. https://www.brookings.edu/articles/why-are-interest-rates-so-low-part-3-the-global-savings-glut/#:~:text=My%20conclusion%20was%20that%20a,for%20low%20global%20interest%20rates

Bernanke, B. (2022). *21st Century Monetary Policy: The Federal Reserve from the Great Inflation to COVID-19*. New York: W. W. Norton.

Bertaut, C., von Beschwitz, B., and Curcuru, S. (2023). "The International Role of the U.S. Dollar." Post-COVID Edition. https://www.federalreserve.gov/econres/notes/feds-notes/the-international-role-of-the-u-s-dollar-20211006.html

Coughlin, C. C., and Thornton, D. L. (2022). "Further Evidence on Greenspan's Conundrum." *Federal Reserve Bank of St. Louis Fed Review*, First Quarter 2022, 104(1), pp. 70–77.

Daoud, Z. (2024). "Gulf States Learn the Power and Limits of Petrodollar Persuasion." *Bloomberg Markets, Vol 33, No. 2.* https://www.bloomberg.com/news/articles/2024-04-24/gulf-states-learn-the-power-and-limits-of-petrodollar-persuasion?srnd=undefined

Daoud, Z., and McBride, C. (2023). "US-Saudi Oil Pact Breaking Down as Russia Grabs Upper Hand." https://www.bloomberg.com/news/features/2023-04-12/recession-odds-inflation-fears-jump-as-us-saudi-oil-pact-breaks-down

Descalsota, M. (2022). "Saudi Arabia Just Won A Bid For The 2029 Asian Winter Games. The $500 Billion City They're Set To Be Hosted In Doesn't Exist Yet." Business Insider. https://www.businessinsider.com/saudi-arabia-500-billion-city-asian-winter-games-2022-10

Fattah, Z., Bartenstein, B., and Avis, D. (2022). "Iran Nuclear Talks: UAE, Israel Pressure U.S. for Security Guarantees." https://www.bloomberg.com/news/articles/2022-03-14/uae-israel-pressure-u-s-for-iran-security-guarantees

Ferman, M. (2023). "Peak Oil Demand 'Wilting Under Scrutiny,' Aramco CEO Says." https://www.bloomberg.com/news/articles/2023-09-18/peak-oil-demand-view-wilting-under-scrutiny-aramco-ceo-says

GCC-Stat (2021). "Quarterly Report on Labour Statistics in the Gulf Cooperation Council for the Second Quarter 2020." Muscat, Oman. https://gccstat.org/images/gccstat/docman/publications/labour_statistics2020_1.pdf

Greenspan, A. (2005). Testimony, Monetary Policy Report to the Congress, U.S. Senate—February 16, 2005. Federal Reserve Board. https://www.federalreserve.gov/boarddocs/hh/2005/february/testimony.htm

Hellier, D. (2021). "Saudi Wealth Fund Buys Newcastle United After League Backing." https://www.bloomberg.com/news/articles/2021-10-07/saudi-fund-chief-staveley-in-talks-for-newcastle-board-seats

Hubbard, B. (2020). *MBS: The Rise to Power of Mohammed Bin Salman.* New York: Tim Duggan Books.

IEA (International Energy Agency). (2021). "Net Zero by 2050 A Roadmap for the Global Energy Sector." International Energy Agency. https://iea.blob.core.windows.net/assets/deebef5d-0c34-4539-9d0c-10b13d840027/NetZeroby2050-ARoadmapfortheGlobalEnergySector_CORR.pdf

Kadabashy, K. (2023). "Saudi Arabia Confirms Bid to Host 2034 FIFA Football World Cup." https://www.bloomberg.com/news/articles/2023-10-05/saudi-arabia-confirms-bid-to-host-2034-football-world-cup

Kindleberger, C. (1967). "The Politics of International Money and World Language."
Essays in International Finance no. 61, International Finance Section, Department of Economics, Princeton University.

Kozok, F., and Ant, A. (2017). "Turkey Fast-Tracks Qatar Troops Bill Update in Symbolic Move." https://www.bloomberg.com/politics/articles/2017-06-07/turkey-fast-tracks-qatar-troops-bill-amendment-in-symbolic-move

MacDonald, F. (2023). "Kuwait Plans New Sovereign Investment Fund to Boost Growth." https://www.bloomberg.com/news/articles/2023-07-16/kuwait-plans-new-sovereign-investment-fund-to-boost-growth

Martin, M. (2023a). "PGA Golf Merger Is Saudi Arabia's Biggest Soft Power Win Yet." https://www.bloomberg.com/news/articles/2023-06-07/pga-golf-merger-is-saudi-arabia-s-biggest-soft-power-win-yet

Martin, M. (2023b). "Saudi Arabia Public Investment Fund Reports $11 Billion Investment Loss for 2022." https://www.bloomberg.com/news/articles/2023-07-11/saudi-wealth-fund-reports-11-billion-investment-loss-for-2022

Milesi-Ferretti, G. M. (2022). "The External Wealth of Nations Database," The Brookings Institution (based on Lane, P. R. and Milesi-Ferretti, G. M. (2018). "The External Wealth of Nations Revisited: International Financial Integration in the Aftermath of the Global Financial Crisis." *IMF Economic Review* 66, 189-222.)

Miller, H. (2023). "Saudi Arabia Leapfrogs Football Powerhouses With $875 Million Splurge." https://www.bloomberg.com/news/articles/2023-09-08/saudi-arabia-s-spending-spree-on-football-players-nears-1-billion

Nereim, V. (2022). "MBS's $500 Billion Desert Dream Just Keeps Getting Weirder." https://www.bloomberg.com/features/2022-mbs-neom-saudi-arabia/

Reuters. (2022). "Saudi Arabia Win Bid to Host 2029 Asian Winter Games at Desert Megacity." The Guardian. 4 Oct. https://www.theguardian.com/sport/2022/oct/04/saudi-arabia-to-host-2029-asian-winter-games-at-desert-megacity-neom-trojena

Scheck, J., Jones, R., and Said, S. (2019). "A Prince's $500 Billion Desert Dream: Flying Cars, Robot Dinosaurs and a Giant Artificial Moon." Wall Street Journal. https://www.wsj.com/articles/a-princes-500-billion-desert-dream-flying-cars-robot-dinosaurs-and-a-giant-artificial-moon-11564097568

Shlaim, A. (2023). *Three Worlds*. London: Oneworld Publications.

Smith, G. (2023a). "Oil Demand Growth to Slow Sharply as Peak Nears, IEA Says." https://www.bloomberg.com/news/articles/2023-06-14/oil-demand-growth-to-slow-dramatically-as-peak-nears-iea-says

Smith, G. (2023b). "OPEC Boosts Oil Demand Forecast to 2045 Despite Climate Crisis." https://www.bloomberg.com/news/articles/2023-10-09/opec-boosts-oil-demand-forecast-to-2045-despite-climate-crisis

Takla, R. (2023). "Saudi Arabia's Construction Pipeline for Next 8 Years Is Worth $2.1 tn: Top Executive." Arab News. https://www.arabnews.com/node/2397856/business-economy

11
Russia's Revenge
How Sanctioned States Dodge the Weaponized Dollar

Alex Isakov

As the World War II alliance between the USSR and United States started to crumble in the late 1940s, Moscow worried it could lose access to its dollar reserves. To reduce this risk, the Kremlin capped dollar holdings at $5 million and moved liquid assets to the UK and European countries it viewed as politically neutral.[1] The geopolitics of the move turned out to be correct: Soviet reserves remained free from restrictions. Confidence in the British pound proved to be less well-founded: the currency lost 30% of its value.[2]

The Soviet experience highlights two forces shaping demand for safe assets. First, countries' international reserve allocation is driven by geopolitics. Countries allocate their international reserves based in part on their place in the global system of alliances and enemies, taking account of the threat of sanctions. Second, geopolitical drivers of reserve allocation often clash with economic drivers—the imperative to retain value over time, the need to diversify exposure to country-specific risks, and the preference for deep and liquid markets.

In this chapter, we explore whether the weaponization of the dollar presents a threat to its status as the world's dominant reserve currency. We conclude that increased geopolitical fracture is likely to reduce global demand for safe assets, as external surplus nations ramp up domestic investment and consumption and accumulate less savings. Still, if the United States manages to maintain a broad coalition of countries supporting its financial sanctions, the dollar's dominant position in the composition of international reserves will remain secure.

[1] In Belgium, Luxemburg, and the Netherlands.
[2] See Polak (1951).

Alex Isakov, *Russia's Revenge*. In: *The Price of Money*. Edited by: Jamie Rush, Tom Orlik, and Stephanie Flanders, Oxford University Press. © Oxford University Press (2025). DOI: 10.1093/9780197800942.003.0011

There are two reasons why studying Russia provides clues about prospects for the dollar's continued dominance:

- Over the last 20 years, Russia has faced radically different external environments, from being generally free from sanctions to being among the most heavily sanctioned economies in the world—the consequence of its invasion of Ukraine.
- Russia publishes detailed data—including on the currency composition of its reserves, trade settlement, and the central bank's foreign exchange (FX) market interventions. Data availability exceeds that from other heavily sanctioned states—Iran, North Korea, and Venezuela.

Even as we focus on Russia, our conclusions also apply—at least in broad strokes—to other countries making reserve allocation decisions in the face of sanctions risk. Russia has already been at the sharp end of a weaponized dollar. China very likely fears it will suffer the same fate.

Sanctions Shift Incentives for Safe Asset Accumulation

When the Soviet Union collapsed in 1991, Russia's government was left with around $50 million dollars' of reserves.[3] This soon dwindled to $30 million—an amount so low that when prime minister Yegor Gaidar was sharing the numbers, newspapers would mark up the units to billions out of disbelief. Over the following decade, the country went through an International Monetary Fund (IMF)-supervised fiscal adjustment, saw the value of its currency collapse, and suffered the ravages of high inflation.

In the 1990s, many emerging markets suffered the trauma of abrupt fiscal adjustment and capital flight. Learning the lesson from a rolling series of crises, in the years that followed, countries with a current account surplus began using it to build up their reserves—aiming to have a buffer against future shocks. Over the decade from 2002 to 2012, emerging markets increased their reserves from around $2.2 trillion to $11.1 trillion, according to our estimates.

Research by Olivier Jeanne and Romain Rancière of the International Monetary Fund and Mengxue Wang of Columbia University identifies four drivers of reserve accumulation: maintaining financial stability; managing the exchange rate; smoothing the commodity cycle; and, attracting foreign direct investment. Their conclusions are summarized in Table 11.1.[4]

[3] See Matyukhina (2017).
[4] See Jeanne and Rancière (2006), and Wang (2019).

Table 11.1 Safe Asset Demand Drivers

Driver	Impact of financial sanctions
Hedge against capital sudden stops	Sanctions reduce global capital market integration, so less reserves are required to offset capital flight
Exchange rate management	Sanctioned countries are usually forced to adopt a flexible exchange rate, so less reserves are required to manage the currency
Commodity cycle buffer	Sanctioned countries struggle to accumulate hard currency liquid assets that are safe from sanctions freezes and so hold fewer reserves
FDI collateral	Sanctioned states struggle to attract foreign direct investment. Reserve accumulation does not provide a strong enough assurance of safety for foreign investors. [a]

[a]See Harold and Nader (2012).
Source: IMF, Bloomberg Economics

The first driver is maintaining sufficient liquid foreign assets to offset the risk to financial stability from capital flight. In the 1980s, emerging markets tended to hold reserves close to 4% of GDP. In the 1990s, they started to accumulate more. Starting from around zero in the early 1990s, by 2009 Russia had accumulated enough reserves to service about 2.5 years of debt. By 2020, the Kremlin had enough in its coffers to cover five years.[5]

Maurice Obstfeld, then a professor at University of California, Berkeley, argued that the motivation was partly softer capital controls—which meant funds could enter and exit emerging markets more easily, and partly deeper financial markets—which meant bigger fund flows and so more potential for system-shaking shocks.[6] Financial sanctions reduce access to global capital and so, also, the need for safe assets as a buffer against capital flight.

Russia's external sovereign debt declined by around 50% between late 2013, just before President Vladimir Putin ordered the annexation of Crimea, and late 2015, when it reached around $30 billion. Reduced access to foreign capital markets meant less need for reserves as a buffer against capital flight. It also accelerated Russia's transition away from a second driver of safe asset demand: a managed exchange rate.

The second driver of safe asset demand is exchange rate management. Countries running rigid exchange rate regimes, for example, pegging their currency to the dollar, need to keep their stock of reserves high to maintain

[5] See Edwards (1984).
[6] See Obstfeld, Shambaugh, and Taylor (2009).

market confidence. Atish R. Ghosh and coauthors at the IMF calculate that, in general, central banks with an exchange rate peg keep reserves 5% of GDP higher than those with flexible regimes.[7]

Financial sanctions make it hard to maintain a managed exchange rate. It would not be possible for Hong Kong, for example, to maintain a peg with the US dollar if the United States sanctioned the Hong Kong Monetary Authority. Holding the outsize reserves necessary to defend managed exchange rates also exposes countries to greater losses if their overseas assets are frozen. With those incentives in operation, sanctioned countries tend to move to a flexible exchange rate.

After the collapse of the Soviet Union, Russia ran a rigid exchange rate regime, pegging the ruble first to the dollar and later to a basket of dollars and euros. As Figure 11.1 shows, every major shock pushed the central bank further toward flexibility:

- The 1998 currency crisis triggered a move from peg to managed float.
- The 2008 global financial crisis was a catalyst to widen the trading bands for the ruble.
- In 2014, sanctions following the invasion of Crimea gave the central bank no choice but to overcome its fear of floating.

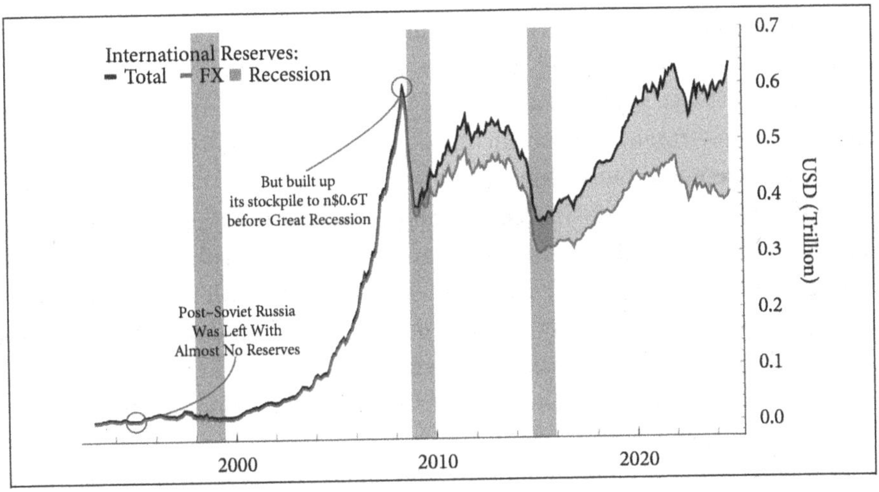

Figure 11.1 The Rise and Fall of Russia's FX Reserves

Source: Bank of Russia, Bloomberg Economics

[7] See Ghosh, Ostry, and Tsangarides (2011).

The third driver of safe asset demand—especially for commodity exporters—is fiscal policy. From 1990 to 2024, the price of oil touched a high of close to $140 a barrel, and a low of $10. Prices for other commodities were similarly volatile. Without some kind of cushion, the result for commodity exporters would be sharp swings between bumper earnings and bare cupboards.

The solution: set up a sovereign wealth fund, paying a portion of commodity earnings into it in the good times, and drawing them down to cover the cost of social spending in the bad. Financial sanctions reduce the strength of this driver of safe asset demand for three reasons:

- Minimizing the impact of sanctions typically requires countries to be flexible in their policy decisions, making it hard to be disciplined in managing commodity income.
- Accumulation of a large amount of foreign assets exposes the government to sanctions risk.
- Sanctions—like the oil export price caps faced by Russia following its invasion of Ukraine—can reduce export earnings.

In the last 20 years, Russia has employed a variety of fiscal rules, starting with the creation of its first sovereign wealth fund—the Stabilization Fund—in 2004. When oil prices were above $20 a barrel—and back in 2004 the average price was $38 a barrel—export earnings above that benchmark were channeled into the Stabilization Fund and invested in foreign safe assets.

In the years that followed, the rules governing operations changed, and the fund itself was split into a National Wealth Fund and Reserve Fund. The core purpose—smoothing out the impact of the commodity cycle on Russia's economy—remained unchanged.

In the run-up to the 2014 occupation of Crimea, Russia had accumulated around $180 billion of reserves between the two funds, with over 90% in dollars and euros. As Figure 11.2 shows, after Russia was hit with sanctions in 2014, the government swiftly exhausted the Reserve Fund, using the stash of safe assets to fund fiscal measures. In subsequent years, Russia also reduced the share of dollar assets in the National Wealth Fund—taking it from 45% to 0% by mid-2021.[8]

The final reason emerging markets stockpile safe assets is to signal to foreign investors that their funds will be safe. Seen from that perspective, FX reserves are a kind of collateral which countries post to persuade foreign investors that their funds won't be expropriated.

[8] See Arutyunov (2021).

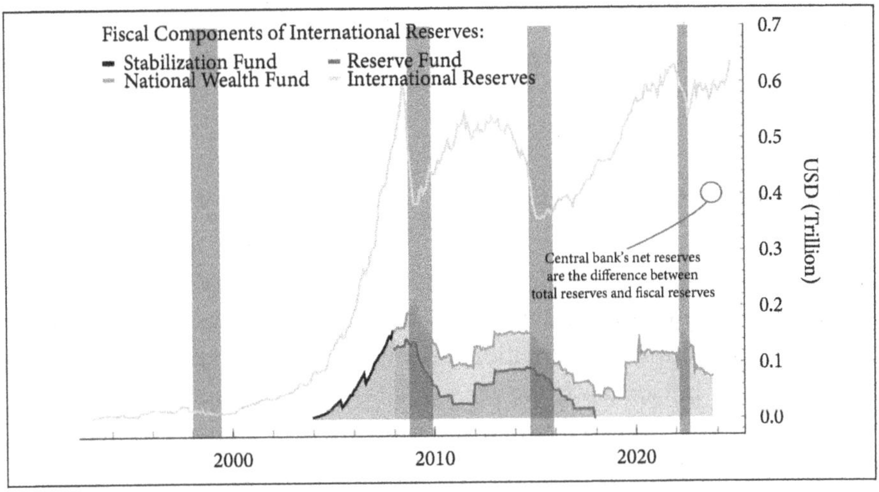

Figure 11.2 Rise and Rise of Russia's Sovereign Wealth Fund
Source: Bank of Russia, MinFin, Bloomberg Economics

The Foreign Direct Investment (FDI) collateral theory of safe asset demand has substantial empirical support. Michael Dooley at Deutsche Bank, for example, showed that around 2008, China's holdings of US Treasuries relative to the stock of US FDI in China were consistent with collateral requirements in US markets. It also helps explain one of the biggest puzzles in international finance: why capital flows uphill from developing nations—where capital is scarce and returns high—to developed economies, where capital is abundant and returns lower.[9]

It also helps explain what's going on with Russia's safe asset demand. On the brink of Russia's 2022 invasion of Ukraine, G7 countries including the UK, Germany, and France were the biggest owners of FDI in Russia, excluding tax havens and Ireland. Russia's total FX reserves were roughly equal to its total stock of inward FDI.

By imposing barriers to capital, trade, and technology flows, sanctions make it harder for countries to attract FDI. That, in turn, reduces the incentive to accumulate reserves. In Russia, annual net inflows of FDI have fallen from $69 billion before the invasion of Crimea in 2014 to negative $11 billion in 2023. In parallel, holdings of hard currency reserves have fallen.

Summing up, in normal times the need to hedge against capital flight, manage the exchange rate, smooth the commodity cycle, and attract FDI provide a powerful motive for emerging markets to accumulate safe assets. As the

[9] See Dooley, Folkerts-Landau, and Garber (2008).

experience of Russia demonstrates, sanctions that block access to global capital markets, and close avenues for trade and technology transfer, significantly reduce that motivation.

Adapting to Sanctions

Addressing an audience of Russian foreign policy experts in October 2022, President Vladimir Putin lamented that "the US and the West have discredited the whole institution of international reserves." In Putin's telling, the United States had first inflated away the value of Russia's foreign assets and then simply stolen them.[10] Missing from the story—Putin's invasion of Ukraine, which was the trigger for the asset freeze.

On February 24, 2022, Russia's tanks rolled across the border into Ukraine. Days later, the United States and members of its sanctions coalition—including the EU, Japan, and UK—restricted the Russian government's access to their reserves. Around $300 billion—built up by the Bank of Russia over decades—had been frozen.

The sanctions—which also blocked Russia's access to international trade and capital markets—sent shockwaves across the financial system. Russian households rushed to the bank to withdraw their savings. By early March, the ruble had lost 62% of its value against the dollar relative to the end of 2021. The consensus among economists was that Russia faced dire consequences, with a financial crisis imminent and deep recession to follow.

Predictions of doom proved wide of the mark. By late June, the ruble had rebounded to its strongest level in five years. For 2023 as a whole, GDP declined 2.1%, and—looking longer-term—barriers to trade and investment threatened to erode Russia's growth potential. Economic prospects were less rosy than they had been before the invasion. Still, relative to the financial crisis and economic collapse many had predicted, the damage wasn't that bad.

Why didn't sanctions land with the expected force? An important part of the explanation: the complexity of the international trade and financial system. For Russia, a major economy with trade and financial ties stretching east and south as well as west, and competent economic policy leadership, that complexity opened up numerous paths to dodge the full force of sanctions.

Among Russia's early efforts to stabilize the financial system and economy were the sale of reserves held in Chinese yuan and a steep increase in the central bank's policy rate to defend the ruble, a raid on hard currency received

[10] See Putin (2022).

by exporters, and tough controls to stem capital flight. The longer-term adaptation strategy, however, reflects the nature of the sanctions.

What does it mean to weaponize the dollar? By preventing sanctioned countries from using its currency, the United States is blocking access to the dollar's functions as a store of value, unit of account, and medium of exchange. The limited effectiveness of sanctions suggests that countries like Russia are good at finding alternatives, as summarized in Table 11.2.

Reserve currencies retain value over time. Over the last 50 years, the dollar index—a weighted average of the greenback's value against a basket of other currencies—has risen strongly. Over the same period, Argentina's peso—to pick a striking counter example—has lost almost all of its value. The dollar is a reserve currency. The peso is not.

What do sanctioned states—which lose access to dollar's function as a stable store of value—look for in a substitute? In general, they prefer to hold assets in a currency that meets the following criteria:

- Issued by a neutral country—there's no sense in shifting out of dollars into sterling if the UK is going to join a US sanctions coalition.
- With free movement of capital—so reserves can be tapped when they are needed and are not subject to controls which limit access.
- Negatively correlated with the shocks they are likely to face—for example, as an oil exporter, Russia might aim to invest in a currency that typically appreciates when oil prices fall.

Table 11.2 Sanctioned States' Dollar Substitution Strategy

Dollar Function	Substitution Strategy
Store of value	- Reduce demand for financial assets - Raise demand for physical assets like gold - Increase investment in productive assets - Reduce saving
Unit of account	- De-dollarization of home financial system - Higher reserve and capital requirements for FX liabilities and assets
Medium of exchange	- Bilateral trade settlement - National payments systems - Barter

Source: Bloomberg Economics

Those criteria are easier to identify than to meet. That means countries facing a broad sanctions coalition tend to have limited options for where to park their funds.

For Russia, the only real options are Turkey and China. Turkey is politically neutral, has an open capital account, and the lira typically appreciates when oil prices fall. China is Russia's strategic ally. Its currency—the yuan—is remarkably stable. The one drawback from Moscow's perspective is that its capital account remains controlled—adding friction to cross-border fund flows.

In the wake of the invasion of Ukraine and the retaliatory sanctions imposed by the United States and its allies, Russia has tapped both options. Billions of dollars have been wired to Turkey to fund the Akkuyu nuclear power plant construction.[11] Other reserve assets have been shifted out of G7 currencies into Chinese yuan and gold.

Even in neutral countries, financial assets remain at risk of asset freezes, as the holding companies may be subject to US sanctions. Companies in the United Arab Emirates, Kazakhstan, and Kyrgyzstan have fallen foul of the United States, accused of facilitating restricted activities for Russia. That's why sanctioned states often have a preference for physical assets as a store of value. Russia has channeled funds into a shadow tanker fleet—around 600 ships that carry Russia's crude oil and refined products—and added at least 20 tons to its gold hoard.[12]

A second adaptation strategy is minimizing external imbalances. Current account surpluses generate foreign assets which are vulnerable to sanctions. With that in mind, sanctioned states prefer keeping their trade with the world roughly in balance—exporting and importing in roughly equal amounts. In Russia, the March 2022 sanctions shock prompted the government to introduce cut price loans to boost imports, and – after the initial ruble panic was over - lower the policy rate to stoke domestic demand.

Sanctioned countries often find that their ability to settle trade in a sanctioning country's currency is reduced. In particular, banks in the sanctioned country can be blocked from using the SWIFT system that is the backbone of international payments.[13] The United States restricted financial transactions with North Korea in the 1950s, Chile under the Pinochet dictatorship in the early 1970s, South Africa during apartheid in the 1990s, and Afghanistan following the September 11th 2001 attack on the World Trade Center.

[11] See Kozok (2022).
[12] See Zulfiqar and Longley (2023).
[13] See Cipriani, Goldberg, and La Spada (2023).

Following the invasion of Ukraine, Russia has received the same treatment. The United States and EU have restricted access to SWIFT for Sberbank and VTB Bank—Russia's biggest banks—hindering their ability to process cross-border payments. Reflecting Washington's desire to punish Russia without imposing excessive costs on the rest of the world, other banks—including Gazprombank, which facilitates natural gas trade—retained their access to the system.[14]

Even as some of their banks retain access, the recent Russian experience illustrates some of the dodges that sanctioned countries can employ to get around the dollar system. Four tactics stand out: switching from the dollar to the yuan; using local currencies and barter; channeling trade through offshore hubs; and, exotic schemes using crypto currencies.

It's the first of those options—switching to trade settlement in yuan—where Moscow has had the most immediate success. As Figure 11.3 illustrates, the share of Russia's exports that are settled in yuan has surged from 0.5% in January 2022 to 16% in March 2023. Over the same period, the yuan's share in Russia's FX turnover increased from around 0.4% to 48%, and the share of FX corporate loans in China's currency soared from near zero to 28%.

Yuan settlement works for Russia's trade with China, and with some other countries like Pakistan—which are already connected to China's global network. It doesn't work for all of Russia's trade partners. The prominent

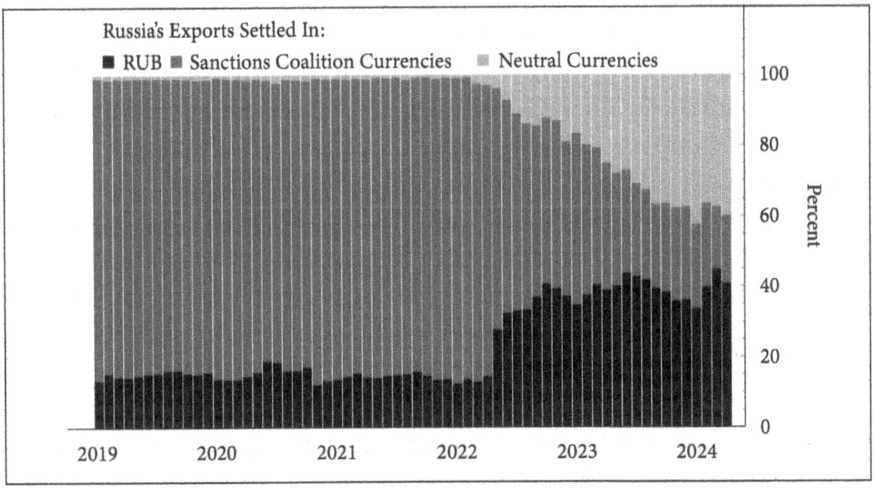

Figure 11.3 Russia Shifts to Yuan for Trade Settlement

Source: Bank of Russia, Bloomberg Economics

[14] Gazprombank was ultimately sanctioned as part of the "farewell" sanctions package by the outgoing Biden administration in late 2024: https://home.treasury.gov/news/press-releases/jy2725.

example is India, which has become Russia's second largest market for oil and views China as a strategic rival.

For India, paying for imports from Russia in rupee would be a significant positive—giving the country a taste of the "exorbitant privilege" enjoyed by issuers of reserve currencies. There's precedent for India to pay for its Russian oil in its own currency. This is how the Indian economist Dr Narottam Shah described rupee trade settlement with the Soviet Union back in 1983:

> The rupee-trade arrangement with Russia is the most marvelous thing on our export front. We can buy whatever we want from them, and for the most part it is essential items like crude oil and fertilizers, and after that we need do no export promotion to generate revenues to buy them back, since it becomes their headache to purchase Indian goods and services and utilize the rupees generated from our imports.[15]

For Russia, settlement in rupee is less positive—for several reasons. India maintains capital account restrictions which means that rupee revenues cannot be readily converted to hard currency and moved elsewhere. Russia doesn't have the appetite to accumulate a large stock of Indian financial assets. And trade between the two countries is unbalanced, with India's bilateral deficit around $55 billion in 2023—meaning there's not a lot of Indian exports Russia can use its rupee to pay for.

That's why, despite India's strong interest in paying for Russian oil in its currency, bilateral trade is mainly settled in dollars, United Arab Emirates dirhams, and euros, with only a sliver settled in rupee. According to estimates from the Institute for Energy and Finance (a Russian think tank) India paid for most of its imports of Russia's oil in US dollars before February 2023 but paid in dirham for around 60% in the remainder of the year.

Trading with other sanctioned countries involves even more exotic solutions. In its trade with Iran and North Korea, Russia has resorted to barter and experimented with the use of crypto currencies.[16] Russia has purchased military supplies from both countries, making payments directly with grain, oil, and its own military technology.

In early 2023, Russia indicated that its trade with Iran could be settled in a gold-based stablecoin, backed with collateral contributed by both countries. As of mid-2024, the project appears to have fizzled. Instead, Russia's government switched to allowing corporations to mine cryptocurrencies like Bitcoin to fund a portion of cross-border trade settlement.

[15] See Singh (2013).
[16] See Frank Media (2023).

Financial Sanctions and the Future of the Dollar

Increased use of sanctions and efforts of some economies to sanction-proof their financial systems do not mean the imminent decline of the dollar as the main international currency. That position is propped up by three structural factors: the ability of the United States to build broad sanctions coalitions, dollar pegs in the Middle East and elsewhere, and the relative lack of appeal of China with its closed capital account.

First, if the United States is able to maintain broad sanctions coalitions, including major developed and emerging markets, then the motivation to diversify reserve holdings away from the dollar will remain weak. That's because safe asset holdings in currencies issued by other countries in the coalition will remain as vulnerable to freezes and seizures as if they are held in dollars. Russia's decision to reduce the dollar share of its reserves in favor of euro assets did not insulate it from sanctions.

Second, major holders of dollar reserves—notably Saudi Arabia and the UAE—have currencies that are pegged to the dollar. That means they have a strong incentive to hold dollar assets and little motivation to switch into other currencies.

Third, China is the only non-US bloc country with a big enough trade and financial system to merit safe asset status for its currency. Even two years after the US freeze of Russia's assets, other central banks have been slow to shift funds into yuan. China's controlled capital account makes it hard to move funds in and out of yuan and limits its appeal as a reserve currency.

At the same time, fear of a weaponized dollar, and Russia's partial success at dodging US sanctions, have strengthened the motive—and highlighted the opportunity—to search for alternatives. These conditions also reduced overall demand for safe assets. The decline in safe asset demand from China, Russia, and oil exporters in the Middle East will force the United States to start living more closely within its means or face higher borrowing costs. Exorbitant privilege may have to come back to earth.

Bibliography

Arutyunov, A. (2021). "The Finance Ministry Has Got Rid of Dollars: Is It Time to Follow Its Example?" https://www.forbes.ru/finansy-i-investicii/434243-minfin-izbavilsya-ot-dollarov-pora-li-posledovat-ego-primeru

Cipriani, M., Goldberg, L. S., and La Spada, G. (2023). "Financial Sanctions, SWIFT, and the Architecture of the International Payment System." *Journal of Economic Perspectives*, 37(1): 31–52.

Dooley, M., Folkerts-Landau, D., and Garber, P. (2008). "Asia, Interest Rates, and the Dollar." Deutsche Bank. https://www.researchgate.net/publication/242366353_Asia_Interest_Rates_and_the_Dollar

Edwards, S. (1984). "The Role of International Reserves and Foreign Debt in the External Adjustment Process." https://www.elibrary.imf.org/downloadpdf/display/book/9780939934287/ch07.pdf

Frank Media. (2023). "Russia and Iran May Create a Stablecoin for Gold." https://frankmedia.ru/108598

Ghosh, A. R., Ostry, J. D., and Tsangarides, C. G. (2011). "Exchange Rate Regimes and the Stability of the International Monetary System." https://www.elibrary.imf.org/display/book/9781589069312/9781589069312.xml

Harold, S. W., and Nader, A. (2012). "China and Iran: Economic, Political, and Military Relations." https://www.rand.org/pubs/occasional_papers/OP351.html

Kozok, F. (2022). "Russia Is Wiring Dollars to Turkey for $20 Billion Nuclear Plant." https://www.bloomberg.com/news/articles/2022-07-29/russia-is-wiring-dollars-to-turkey-for-20-billion-nuclear-plant

Jeanne, O., and Rancière, R. G. (2006). "The Optimal Level of International Reserves for Emerging Market Countries: Formulas and Applications." IMF Working Paper WP/06/229. https://www.imf.org/external/pubs/ft/wp/2006/wp06229.pdf

Matyukhina, A. (2017). "Mau, Prikhodko, Reznik: On the 90s as a Springboard for the 2000s." https://yeltsin.ru/news/mau-prihodko-reznik-o-90h-trampline-dlya-nulevyh/

Obstfeld, M., Shambaugh, J. C., and Taylor, A. M. (2009). "Financial Instability, Reserves, and Central Bank Swap Lines in the Panic of 2008." *American Economic Review*, 99(2): 480–486.

Polak, J. (1951). "Contribution of the September 1949 Devaluations to the Solution of Europe's Dollar Problem." *IMF Staff Papers*, 1951(002): 1–32.

Putin, V. (2022). "Remarks at Meeting of the International Discussion Club Valdai." https://www.kremlin.ru/events/president/news/69695

Singh, C. U. (2013). "Indo-Soviet Trade Drops Drastically as USSR Stops Imports From India." India Today. https://www.indiatoday.in/magazine/economy/story/19830531-indo-soviet-trade-drops-drastically-as-ussr-stops-imports-from-india-770709-2013-07-19

Wang, M. (2019). "Foreign Direct Investment and Foreign Reserve Accumulation." *Economic Fluctuations Colloquium and Monetary Colloquium*, 8: 1–61.

Zulfiqar, A., and Longley, A. (2023). "Russia's Shadow Oil Tanker Fleet Becomes Everyone Else's Problem ." https://www.bloomberg.com/news/articles/2023-02-18/russia-s-shadow-oil-tanker-fleet-becomes-everyone-else-s-problem

12

The Rich Get Richer, the Rates Get Lower

How Rising Inequality Pushed the Natural Rate Lower and Artificial Intelligence Could Extend the Trend

Selva Bahar Baziki and Adriana Dupita

The march of globalization has boosted profits for multinationals at least partly at the expense of lower wage growth for the victims of offshoring job losses. Advances in technology, from the Information and Communications Technology (ICT) revolution to industrial robots, benefited high-skill workers while pushing many low-skill workers into unemployment. Both have widened the gap between the haves and the have-nots. Progressive tax systems have cushioned the impact but not eliminated it.

Around a decade ago, French economist Thomas Piketty brought income inequality to the forefront of academic and policy discussion.[1] Piketty posited that income and wealth inequality rise whenever the real return on capital—proxied by the interest rate—exceeds the return on labor, assumed to be roughly consistent with the pace of economic growth. That's not a rare combination, and Piketty's analysis pointed to a certain inevitability in the ever-widening gap between rich and poor.

But what if a rise in inequality has a feedback effect on the rate of interest? The main channel connecting the two variables is saving. High-earning households tend to save a large share of their income—after all, there are only so many luxury cars that one person can usefully own. Low-earners, whose income is mostly swallowed up by spending on food, shelter, and other necessities, don't tend to save very much.

When the income distribution tilts in favor of high-earners, therefore, that leads to more saving and downward pressure on the natural rate of interest. Piketty's case for an ever-rising income gap as a result of the return on capital outstripping rewards to workers overlooks that potential feedback. The

[1] See Piketty (2014).

Selva Bahar Baziki and Adriana Dupita, *The Rich Get Richer, the Rates Get Lower*. In: *The Price of Money*. Edited by: Jamie Rush, Tom Orlik, and Stephanie Flanders, Oxford University Press.
DOI: 10.1093/9780197800942.003.0012

evidence from the literature and our own model suggests it's a real force, if not the dominant one.[2]

The share of US post-tax income commanded by the richest 10% of households rose from 25.6% in the early 1980s to above 30% in the early 2020s. Over the same period, we estimate that the natural rate of interest on 10-year Treasury bonds fell by a little more than 250 bps. Our model of the drivers suggests rising inequality in the United States contributed some 25 bps of the drop. Spillovers from rising inequality in other advanced economies explain a further 10 bps.

In other words, while there might well—as Piketty suggests—be a dynamic from higher interest rates to higher inequality, our work reveals that there is also an impulse in the other direction, with higher inequality resulting in lower interest rates.

In this chapter, we review the evolution of income inequality in advanced economies over the last four decades, summarize the literature on the relation between inequality and the natural rate, and use our model to estimate the contribution of inequality to the drop in borrowing costs. Finally, we explore scenarios for how globalization, technology, and government policy could impact inequality—and from there the natural rate—in the decades ahead.

The Rich Get Richer

There are lots of different ways of measuring inequality. For the natural rate, what matters is the share of post-tax income commanded by high-income households. After all, it's post-tax income that households are making their spending and saving decisions with; and it's the aggregate of all those decisions which are driving the supply of saving and, so, influencing the natural rate.

With that as the destination, our analysis starts by looking at pre-tax income shares going to the top 10% of earners in 12 advanced economies from the United States to New Zealand. That's where we should see the impacts of globalization and technological change most clearly. It is also the measure for which comparable data are most widely available with the longest timespan.

- In the United States in 2022, 48% of pre-tax national income was in the hands of the 10% of highest earning households—the highest share of any of the 12 advanced economies in our study.
- The United States also saw the biggest jump in inequality since 1980, with the pre-tax income share of the top 10% climbing from 33.8%.

[2] See Ademmer and Rush (2024).

- The United States might be an extreme example of rising inequality, but it's not the only one. As Figure 12.1 shows, between 1980 and 2022, 10 of the 12 economies saw an increase in pre-tax income inequality.

Shifting the focus to post-tax income—where we have data for 10 advanced economies, with Japan and New Zealand dropping out of the sample—we see inequality still increasing, but by a considerably smaller amount. In the past four decades, the share of post-tax income for the top 10% of households rose on average 1.2 ppt, a bit more than one-fifth of the average 5.8 ppt-jump in pre-tax inequality over the same period.

As Figure 12.2 shows, post-tax income inequality in the United States is still the highest among its advanced peers and rose the most in the past four decades, with the share of the top 10% rising from 25.2% in 1980 to 30.1% in 2021.

Why has the gap between the haves and have-nots in advanced economies widened? Three factors stand out: automation, globalization, and social policy.

- The number of US manufacturing jobs has fallen from a historical peak of 19.6 million in 1979 to 12.8 million 40 years later. David Autor, an economics professor at MIT, estimates that about a quarter of the drop comes from competition from cheaper imported goods—mainly from China. With manufacturing jobs among the highest-paying for high-school educated workers, that is a significant contributor to rising inequality.[3]

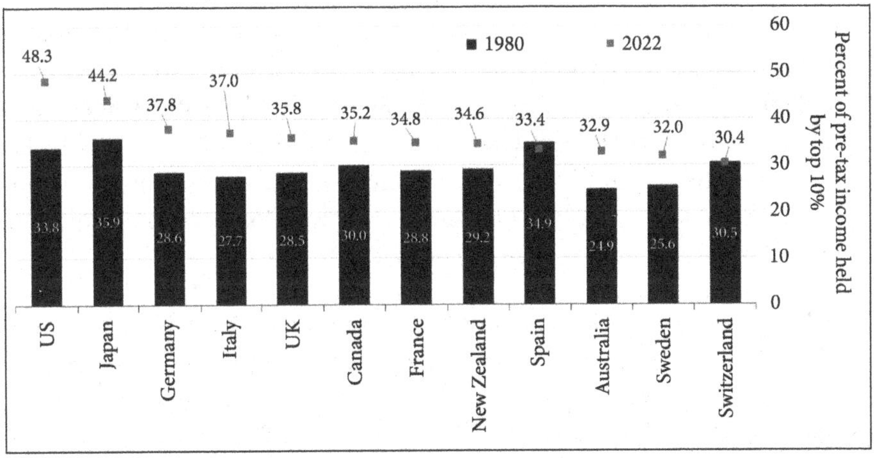

Figure 12.1 Pre-Tax Income Inequality Rose in Most Advanced Economies

Source: World Inequality Database

[3] See Autor, Dorn, and Hanson (2016).

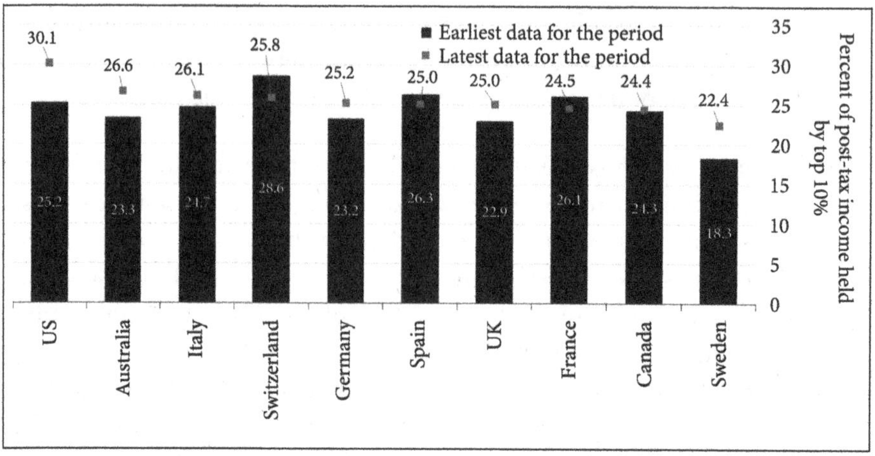

Figure 12.2 Over the Past Four Decades, Post-Tax Income Inequality Also Rose in Most Countries but by Less

Earliest available datapoint for the past four decades: 1980 for the United States, the UK, and Spain; 1981 for Australia, Canada, and Sweden; 1982 for Switzerland; 1984 for France; 1986 for Italy; and 1991 for Germany. Latest available datapoint: 2018 for Australia and Switzerland; 2019 for Germany and Canada; 2021 for the United States; and 2020 for all others. Source: World Bank (World Development Indicators).

- In 1980, computers were still at an early stage of development and factory automation remained rudimentary. By 2022, powerful computers were cheap, ubiquitous, and connected. Industrial robots can now do everything from assembling to packaging and harvesting. MIT's Daron Acemoglu and Boston University's Pascual Restrepo estimate that labor-replacing technology explains between 50% and 70% of the increase in wage inequality in the United States from 1980 to 2016[4].
- In the 1980s, a revolution in social policy, dreamed up by free-market champions like University of Chicago economist Milton Friedman and implemented by President Ronald Reagan in the United States and Prime Minister Margaret Thatcher in the UK, reduced the role of the tax and benefit system in redistributing income. In 1980 the top US income tax rate was 70% and the minimum wage was 46.6% of the median. In 2022, the same figures were 37% and 27.4%.

A literature survey by University of Oxford professor Brian Nolan expands the list. He and his coauthors flag how reduced union power and increased concentration in product markets hit workers' income and consumers' purchasing power.[5] They also identify the rise of the financial sector as a factor contributing to the emergence of a winner-take-all version of capitalism.

[4] See Acemoglu and Restrepo (2020).
[5] See Nolan, Richiardi, and Valenzuela (2019).

Branko Milanovic—a professor at City University of New York—flags a shift in social norms that has made inequality more acceptable.[6]

How Big Is the Impact of Inequality on the Natural Rate?

A number of studies have attempted to uncover the key factors driving the decline in the natural rate in recent decades, with productivity growth and demographic change the main focus of attention. More recently, a body of research has investigated the possible role of rising income inequality.

- Using a calibrated model of the global neutral rate, Lukasz Rachel and Thomas Smith, economists at the Bank of England, estimate that rising inequality can explain about one-tenth of the 450 bps-decline in long-term real interest rates around the world between 1980 and 2015.[7]
- Adrien Auclert from Stanford and Matthew Rognlie from Northwestern explore how inequality impacts growth. Their calibrated model attributes about one-fifth of the decline in the US natural rate since the 1980s to the rise in income inequality.[8]
- IMF economist Josef Platzer and University of Sydney professor Marcel Peruffo stage an analytic horse race between the variables most commonly cited as drivers of the natural rate. Their results suggest that 70 bps of the decline in the neutral rate from 1975 to 2015 can be explained by rising inequality.[9]
- Using data from a survey on consumer finance, Princeton's Atif Mian, Harvard's Ludwig Straub, and Chicago's Amir Sufi disentangle the impact of rising inequality and demographic change on savings and the neutral rate, finding the former more influential than the latter.[10]

Our Model

Our model—set out in detail in Chapter 3—suggests that every 1 ppt-increase in the post-tax income held by the top 10% is consistent with a decline of about 5 bps in the natural rate in the United States. Estimates for the UK and other advanced economies are of a similar magnitude.

[6] See Milanovic (2011).
[7] See Rachel and Smith (2015).
[8] See Auclert and Rognlie (2020). The authors highlight that inequality caused by higher income risk (which tends to raise precautionary savings) weighs significantly more on aggregate demand and the natural rate than a temporary change in inequality or a permanent shift caused by fixed factors (such as differences in households' education).
[9] See Platzer and Peruffo (2022).
[10] See Mian, Straub, and Sufi (2021).

In the period from 1970 to 2022, the US natural rate fell by more than 250 bps. We think rising inequality in the United States explains about 25 bps of the decline—about a tenth of the total. Spillovers from rising inequality in other advanced economies explain another 10 bps of the drop.

Our estimated impacts are a little lower than those reported by Rachel and Smith and substantially lower than some other estimates in the literature. One possible explanation is that we consider an expanded set of drivers. In addition to the productivity and demographic variables that most models include, ours also considers the relative price of investment, demand and supply for safe assets, and how the natural rate in each economy responds to global influences.

Another possible cause for the difference could be the choice of the inequality measure. We estimate our model using a post-tax measure of income inequality. Some other studies use measures based on pre-tax income. We think post-tax measures offer a better representation of the forces at play, and they have risen by much less than pre-tax measures.

To Them That Hath Shall Be Given: Forecasting Inequality

What does the future hold? We build a simple dynamic model to forecast inequality out to 2050. It builds on the 2013 work by Florence Jaumotte, Subir Lall, and Chris Papageorgiou of the IMF, who explore the impact of globalization and technological progress on inequality for a large panel of countries.[11]

We expand the model to incorporate labor market and human capital variables, leaning on work by Marina Gindelsky at the Bureau of Economic Analysis and her 2018 approach to modeling inequality in the United States.[12]

The main variables in our inequality forecast model are:

- Inequality: In line with the historical evidence, we assume inequality is persistent, and so future levels will depend in part on current levels. We focus on the share of pre-tax income claimed by the top-10% of earners and use data from the World Inequality Database.[13]

[11] See Jaumotte, Lall, and Papageorgiou (2013).

[12] See Gindelsky (2018).

[13] The data on income inequality in this study come from the World Inequality Database. We have continuous (pre-tax) inequality data for the United States, Canada, Australia, New Zealand, and France from 1950 to 2022. For the UK, Japan, Germany, Italy, Spain, and Sweden, we have data for the turn of each decade from 1950 through 1980 and continuous data from there on. We fill missing data for these countries

- Productivity growth: Rising levels of productivity are good for growth, but the bulk of the gains are typically captured by high-skill, high-income households. This means that faster productivity gains typically increase inequality. We use Bloomberg Economics forecasts for trend productivity growth and flex them with an assumption of more rapid gains in our high-inequality scenario.
- Globalization: In advanced economies, a higher trade share of gross domestic product (GDP) is typically good news for high-skill workers and bad news for low-skill workers, who find themselves competing with low-wage rivals in China, Mexico, and other emerging markets. In our base case, we assume exports and imports as a share of GDP increase only modestly. In a risk scenario, we assume geopolitical tensions drive an extended period of deglobalization.
- Women's labor force participation: The historical evidence shows that by adding to the supply of low-skilled labor, the entry of women into the labor force adds to inequality. We use data from the International Labor Organization (ILO) on historical female labor force participation and project forward using detailed data on participation by age cohort and United Nations demographic forecasts.
- Average years of schooling: For most of the population—and especially for those in the lower end of the distribution—wages are the main source of income. Building on earlier work on the education premium on wages, we use data from Barro and Lee's Education Attainment Dataset on average years of schooling.[14]
- Unemployment and inflation: We attempt to capture movements in the business cycle and labor market slack by including inflation and unemployment rates in our calculations.
- Despite its relative parsimony, our model captures about 98% of the variation in levels of inequality over past decades for the countries in our sample.

With that as a starting point, we consider three scenarios for inequality and their implications for the natural rate, assuming post-tax inequality changes in tandem with our forecasts for the pre-tax metrics:

going back linearly and only use the full set from 1950 for descriptive charts. We restrict our data analysis for these countries to data from 1970 onward. Due to lack of earlier data, the analysis for Switzerland starts in 1980.

[14] See Florida and Mellander (2013), and Barro and Lee (2013).

- A baseline scenario, where productivity and trade exposure are in line with the Bloomberg Economics long-term forecasts. The result is a small increase in inequality and only a modest further drag on the natural rate.
- A low-inequality scenario where deglobalization drives reshoring of low-skill jobs, reducing income inequality and raising the natural rate.
- A high-inequality scenario where artificial intelligence and other new technologies deliver significant productivity gains, and the bulk of those gains are captured by high earners, resulting in higher inequality—and a decline in the natural rate.

In the base case, as Figure 12.3 shows, pre-tax inequality continues rising in the next three decades but at a much slower pace than it did in earlier decades. The reason for the slower ascent is that we assume only modest further deepening of global trade ties. Rising education levels also moderate the upward pressure from other sources.

For the United States, the top 10% end up with just over half of pre-tax income by 2050—up from about a third in the 1980s and 48.3% in 2022. A GDP-weighted average of the other countries in our sample of advanced economies shows the share of the top 10% rising to 38.2% in the next three decades from 36.3% in 2022.

If government redistribution continues to narrow the gap between pre- and post-tax inequality by the same degree as in recent years, the impact would be small—with a drag on the natural rate of about 5 bps. As Figure 12.4 shows, our base case is that inequality is set to shift from a

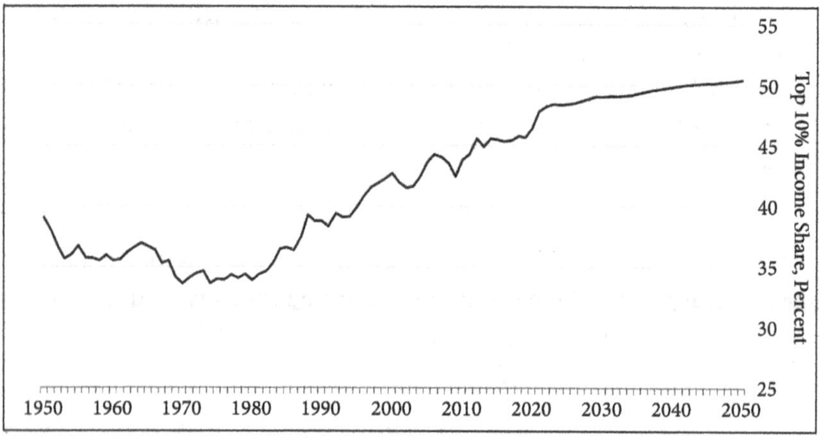

Figure 12.3 Outlook for Pre-Tax Inequality in the US
Sources: WDI, World Bank, Bloomberg Economics

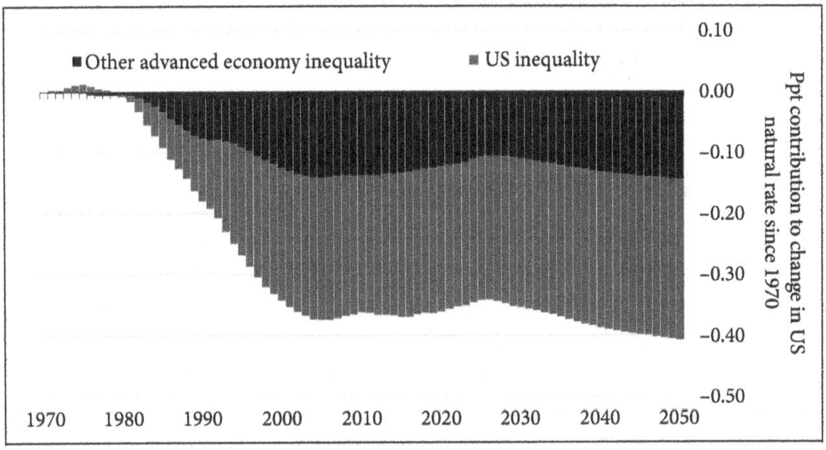

Figure 12.4 Inequality Impact on US Natural Rate, 1970–2050
Source: Ademmer and Rush (2024), Bloomberg Economics

significant drag on the natural rate in the last 40 years, to a non-zero but negligible drag in the decades ahead.

Reduced Global Ties, Lower Inequality

In our deglobalization scenario—in line with the assumptions in Chapter 8—we assume a drop in trade to levels last seen in the 1990s, before China joined the World Trade Organization. As jobs move home from abroad the result is a relative increase in demand for low-skilled workers, raising wages for that group and so reducing inequality.

- Our model shows that a 1-ppt fall in the trade share of GDP lowers the share of income for the top 10% in the United States in 2050 by 0.6 ppt.
- A drop in trade back to 1990s levels would mean a reduction in imports and exports as a share of US GDP from 30% in 2023 to below 26%. That would shave just under 3 ppt off the share of income going to the top 10% of earners.
- Taking into account global spillovers, the reduced share of income for the top 10% would add about 17 bps to the 2050 natural rate, assuming the government does not stand in the way as inequality falls.
- As a thought experiment, we explore what happens if a future US government not only reduces global trade ties but also flexes the tax and welfare system to reduce the level of post-tax inequality in line with that of Sweden. That would mean a drop of about 8 ppt in the share of income

going to the top 10% of earners. We estimate that would add more than 40 bps to the natural rate.

AI Revolution, Higher Inequality

In our rising-inequality scenario, we assume new technologies like AI trigger a leap forward in productivity—in line with the possible future set out in Chapter 4.

- In line with the experience of the IT revolution in the 1990s, we assume AI and other technologies will deliver a 10% boost to productivity, with gains spread out over a decade starting in the 2030s.
- Plugging those assumptions into our forecast model, the results show the share of income for the top 10% of US earners rising around an additional 1 ppt. Taken together with the 2-ppt gain in our baseline—mainly the result of ongoing trade deepening—that takes the share of pre-tax income for the top 10% of earners up to 51% in 2050.
- Together with global spillovers, a 3-ppt increase in inequality might be expected to push down on the natural rate of interest by as much as 20 bps in years to come, unless the government steps in.
- How about if advances in technology turn out to have a dystopian impact on inequality, with all the gains captured by high earners and all the losses suffered by everyone else? If that happens, the pre-tax share of income for the top 10% of US earners could rise to 60%. If that happened, drag on the natural rate would rise to 50 bps.

Our model does not include all the factors that impact inequality. Union membership and access to financial services—for example—are factors that are widely discussed in the literature but which don't feature in our model. Our scenarios for deglobalization and advances in technology are highly stylized; alternative paths are possible. Uncertainties abound. Still, the main takeaways seem clear and robust enough.

Conclusion

Piketty's research shone a powerful light on the problem of inequality and the way in which high interest rates and low growth widen the gap between the haves and have-nots. Missing from his worldview is the dynamic from widening inequality to lower interest rates, a function of the high savings rate among high earners.

Our model suggests that in the period from 1980 to 2022, widening inequality in the United States and other advanced economies shaved 35 bps off the natural rate. Throwing the analysis forward, our base case is that a slower deepening of trade ties will mean a more modest increase in inequality in the years ahead, adding a modest drag of about 5 bps by 2050.

We also consider low- and high-inequality risk scenarios. In the low-inequality scenario, deglobalization could add approaching 20 bps to the natural rate. Amped up tax and welfare transfers to significantly lower the share of total income for the top 10% of US earners could raise the natural rate by 40 bps.

In the most extreme of our high inequality scenarios, rapid advances in technology—with those gains captured entirely by high earners—result in a markedly higher share of incomes for the top 10% and the natural rate falling by as much as 50 bps.

Bibliography

Acemoglu, D., and Restrepo, P. (2020). "Robots and Jobs: Evidence from US Labor Markets." *Journal of Political Economy*, 128(6): 2188–2244.

Ademmer, M., and Rush, J. (2024). "Drivers of the Natural Long-Term Rate of Interest (and Why the Economy Hasn't Tanked)." *Oxford Open Economics*, 3, odae012. https://doi.org/10.1093/ooec/odae012

Auclert, A., and Rognhlie, M. (2018). "Inequality and Aggregate Demand." NBER Working Papers 24280. https://www.nber.org/system/files/working_papers/w24280/w24280.pdf

Autor, D. H., Dorn, D., and Hanson, G. H. (2016). "The China Shock: Learning from Labor-Market Adjustment to Large Changes in Trade." *Annual Review of Economics*, 8(1): 205–240.

Barro, R. J., and Lee, J. W. (2013). "A New Data Set of Educational Attainment in the World, 1950–2010." *Journal of Development Economics*, 104: 184–198.

Florida, R., and Mellander, C. (2013). "The Geography of Inequality: Difference and Determinants of Wage and Income Inequality across US Metros." *CESIS Electronic Working Paper Series*, 304, 2–28.

Gindelsky, M. (2018). "Modeling and Forecasting Income Inequality in the United States." Bureau of Economic Analysis Working Paper, August. https://www.bea.gov/system/files/papers/WP2018-7_0.pdf

Jaumotte, F., Lall, S., and Papageorgiou, C. (2013). "Rising Income Inequality: Technology or Trade and Financial Globalization?" *IMF Economic Review*, 61(2): 271–309.

Mian, A., Straub, L., and Sufi, A. (2021). "What Explains the Decline in r*? Rising Income Inequality Versus Demographic Shifts." NBER Working Paper 2021-104, University of Chicago. https://scholar.harvard.edu/straub/publications/what-explains-decline-r-rising-income-inequality-versus-demographic-shifts

Milanovic, B. (2011). "More or Less." IMF Finance & Development, September 2011. https://www.imf.org/external/pubs/ft/fandd/2011/09/milanovic.htm

Nolan, B., Richiardi, M. G., and Valenzuela, L. (2019). "The Drivers of Income Inequality in Rich Countries." *Journal of Economic Surveys*, 33(4). https://onlinelibrary.wiley.com/doi/abs/10.1111/joes.12328

Piketty, T. (2014). *Capital in the Twenty-First Century*. London: Harvard University Press.

Platzer, J., and Peruffo, M. (2022). Secular Drivers of the Natural Rate of Interest in the United States: A Quantitative Evaluation. *IMF Working Papers*, 2022(030): 1.

Rachel, L., and Smith, T. (2015). "Secular Drivers of the Global Real Interest Rate." Bank of England Staff Working Paper, 571.

13
The Era of Falling Rates Is Over

Jamie Rush

Between 1970 and 2022, the natural rate of interest in the United States fell by more than 2.5 ppts—dropping from almost 5% at the beginning of the period to a little over 2% at the end. That propelled asset values higher, made it easier for governments and households to borrow and redistributed spending power from savers to borrowers.

Combining our model of the fundamental drivers of interest rates with projections on how those drivers will evolve, we think the decades-long decline has come to an end. In the years ahead, interest rates are more likely to shift onto a permanently higher trajectory than to drift further down. If upside risks crystallize, they could end up much higher.

Some of the biggest contributors to the decline in the natural rate over past decades are unlikely to exert much more downward pressure:

- Trend growth took a leg down in the wake of the global financial crisis. Now it appears to be stabilizing, steadying the underlying return on capital. We forecast that having fallen from 3.5% in 1970 to 1.8% in 2022, in the decades ahead trend growth in the United States will be only a little slower, averaging 1.6%.
- The baby boomers are entering retirement, meaning they're starting to draw down their pension savings. Based on United Nations demographic forecasts, there will be one dependent per adult of prime working age in the United States in 2050, up from 0.93 in 2022. That means less saving and more spending.
- Austerity is out, higher spending on pensions, healthcare, industrial policy and defense is in. Wider government deficits are increasing the competition for savings. The Congressional Budget Office projects that the United States debt-to-GDP ratio will climb to 122% by the mid-2030s, up from 97% in 2022.
- Weaponization of the dollar in sanctions against Russia, China's switch toward a floating exchange rate, and oil exporters like Saudi Arabia

Jamie Rush, *The Era of Falling Rates Is Over*. In: *The Price of Money*. Edited by: Jamie Rush, Tom Orlik, and Stephanie Flanders, Oxford University Press. © Oxford University Press (2025). DOI: 10.1093/9780197800942.003.0013

spending more on ambitious projects at home means shrinking demand from some of the main global buyers of safe assets.
- Inequality remains a reality. But the hyper-globalization that drove a widening gap between the high-saving haves and the low-saving have-nots is now fading. A slower pace of increase in inequality means a slower pace of increase in savings.

For the United States, we think the real natural rate on 10-year US bonds has already climbed from a post-global financial crisis trough of 1.7% in 2012, to 2.3% in 2022. By the early 2030s, it could move up to 2.8%. That translates into an inflation-stabilizing 10-year nominal Treasury yield of 4.5–5%.

There are upside risks to the outlook:

- Our baseline assumes governments get their finances under control and debt ratios stabilize. If instead governments keep borrowing, as they have in the past, the competition for savings will become more intense.
- If the world gets serious about tackling climate change, the investments needed to green the economy will drive borrowing costs higher. BloombergNEF estimates getting to a zero-emissions economy will cost more than $30 trillion, about 30% of 2023 world gross domestic product (GDP).
- If the promise of frontier technologies, like artificial intelligence and quantum computing, lives up to the hype, there could be a period of faster trend growth, raising the return on capital.
- If the world economy splits along geopolitical fault lines, China's savings could flee from a weaponized dollar, broken supply chains might raise the cost of capital goods, inequality may fall as jobs are reshored, and higher defense spending could push up debt.

In a risk scenario where all those drivers come into play, the balance tilts further from savings glut toward savings shortage, and the natural rate on 10-year US bonds could rise to north of 6%.

The Future of Natural

"Making predictions is difficult, especially about the future"—so said baseball hall-of-famer Yogi Berra (or possibly Nobel Prize-winning Danish physicist Niels Bohr). In the world of economics, the sentiment rings true. Disentangling what has happened in the past is hard enough. Forecasting how those forces will evolve in the future is harder still.

Still, thinking through how big structural forces driving investment and saving may evolve in years to come is a useful exercise. And while uncertainties can't be denied, they also shouldn't be exaggerated. Many of the underlying trends are slow-moving. Some—like demographic shifts—are baked in. For others—like changes in China's demand for US assets—the arguments are compelling.

Drag on Rates from Lower Growth Is Leveling Off

Trend growth—the rate of expansion that can be sustained without pushing inflation up—has slowed. In the United States, trend growth in the 1970s averaged about 3%. From there, with the exception of about a decade from the mid-1990s to the early 2000s (as the ICT revolution drove productivity gains), it has decelerated. In the 2010s, it was below 2%.

Looking ahead, our baseline forecast for the United States assumes that productivity gains remain modest and global heating adds a modest drag. The growth of labor supply is also expected to slow, reflecting population aging. Overall, we see US trend growth settling at around 1.6% in coming decades, a little slower than between the global financial crisis and the Covid pandemic.

Outside the United States, demographic trends are more challenging, meaning a bigger drag on growth from a shrinking workforce. For the other advanced economies in our model, even if productivity growth stabilizes at recent levels, we see potential growth declining from a GDP-weighted average of about 1.1% in the years before the pandemic to 0.7% in the years ahead.

Slower trend growth means fewer opportunities for productive investment. For the United States, combining our growth forecasts with our model of natural rate drivers points to a drag of about 20 bps by 2050. The direction of travel—with lower trend growth dragging the natural rate lower—remains the same. But compared with the 60-bps downdraft between 1970 and 2022, the force is much reduced.

Demographic Drag Waning

After slower trend growth, it is shifts in the age structure of the US population that has had the biggest impact on the natural rate. Between 1970 and 2022, the baby boomer generation was working and stashing away savings in preparation for retirement. The dependency ratio—the number of free-spending retirees and children per hard-saving worker—fell from 1.24 at the start of the period to 0.93 at the end. That boosted savings and, so, lowered the natural rate.

The baby boomers are now reaching retirement age and starting to spend down their savings. With too few new workers to replace them, the UN expects the US dependency ratio to climb to about 1.0 in 2050. The demographic trends that boosted saving are reversing, and that means pressure on the natural rate is shifting from down to up.

Putting some numbers on it, between 1970 and 2022, baby-boom savers and a falling dependency ratio dragged the natural rate in the United States down by about 65 bps. In the years ahead, with baby boomers retiring and the dependency ratio rising again, that down arrow turns into an up arrow, with demographic factors likely pushing the natural rate higher by about 30 bps.

Inequality Set to Continue Rising, But at Slower Pace

High earners are high savers. That means rising inequality increases saving and lowers the natural rate. In past decades, two factors drove a significant increase in inequality. Globalization meant manufacturing workers in the United States faced greater competition from low-wage workers in China and other emerging markets. Advances in technology meant they were also staving off competition from no-wage robots.

The era of hyperglobalization is now over. Before the global financial crisis, trade was growing about twice as fast as global GDP. In the years since, it has grown at roughly the same pace. Add in the trade war between the United States and China, measures announced in President Donald Trump's second term, and rifts like Brexit and it's hard to see the pace reaccelerating. Advances in technology continue - artificial intelligence could potentially be an accelerator of inequality, but it's too early to make a definitive judgment.

Our forecast for inequality in the United States in the years ahead shows a modest ongoing upward drift, but with the pace of increase markedly slower than in past decades. The share of US income going to the top 10% rose from about a third in the 1980s to 48% in 2022. We expect it to edge higher in years to come but only by a percentage point or so.

For the natural rate, the impact is similar to that seen with trend growth—not a reversal from drag to boost but rather a bottoming out of the drag. In the period from 1970 to 2022, widening inequality pulled the natural rate in the United States down by about 35 bps. From 2023 to 2050, we forecast a modest 5-bps drag.

Investment Prices Have Stabilized

Advances in technology, together with efficiency gains from deepening global trade, have made it cheaper to equip workers with the hardware and software they need. In the United States, between 1970 and 2022, the price of investment goods relative to consumer goods fell by about a third. That meant businesses could get more investment bang for less investment bucks, pushing the natural rate down.

In more recent years, as with slowing growth and widening inequality, the trend hasn't reversed but it has stabilized. Since the global financial crisis, with productivity gains slowing and trade expanding at a more tepid pace, the relative price of investment goods has steadied. In our baseline forecast, we expect that stability to persist.

For the natural rate, that turns the relative price of investment from a significant drag into a neutral factor. From 1970 to 2022, the falling cost of computers and other capital goods pulled the natural rate down by about 35 bps—making it one of the biggest contributors to the fall. From 2023 to 2050, our baseline forecast is for the impact to be close to zero.

Rising Debt Is Pushing Rates Up

The balance between the supply of safe assets—government debt issued by the United States and other major advanced economies—and demand for them is an important determinant of the natural rate. More supply means borrowing costs go up; more demand means they go down. Rising government debt also encourages investors to demand higher rates as a hedge against default or inflation.

From 1970 till 2007, debt was relatively low and stable. In the United States, the debt-to-GDP ratio started the period at 27% and ended at 35%. From the 1990s on, demand for that debt from China, other Asian emerging markets, and petrostates like Saudi Arabia was also strong. With supply of safe assets steady, and demand rising, the pressure on the natural rate was down.

Those trends have started to reverse. The global financial crisis and Covid pandemic were triggers for borrowing to rise sharply higher. In the United States, the debt-to-GDP ratio ended 2022 at around 95%. The Congressional Budget Office expects it to rise to 105% by the late 2020s. Weaponization of the dollar as a tool of economic sanctions, a shift in China's FX regime, and petrostates investing funds closer to home mean some of the biggest buyers have reduced their appetite.

Put the pieces together, and we estimate that from 1970 to 2007, net demand for safe assets and government debt levels in advanced economies took 10 bps off the natural rate in the United States. From 2007 to 2022, we estimate these factors added well over a percentage point. In the period from 2022 to 2035, we think there'll be further upward pressure of nearly half a point.

Adding It Up

We estimate the real natural rate in the United States fell from 4.9% in 1970 to a trough of 1.7% in 2012 before regaining some of its lost altitude with a move up to 2.3% by 2022—consistent with a nominal 10-year Treasury rate in the region of 4.5%.

Given our baseline projection for the structural drivers of borrowing costs, we see it rising to 2.8% by 2030, consistent with a Treasury yield of around 4.8%. If debt ratios stabilize, borrowing costs could fall back somewhat in the decades that follow. Figure 13.1 shows our estimate of the fall and rise of the natural rate, and the contributions of the main drivers.

With other advanced economies set to follow a similar trend, the big picture—captured in Table 13.1—is that the era of falling long-term real interest rates appears to be over. Our baseline projection sees global borrowing costs climbing until 2030. And while the natural rate falls back somewhat in the subsequent two decades, the post global financial crisis nadir is not reached again.

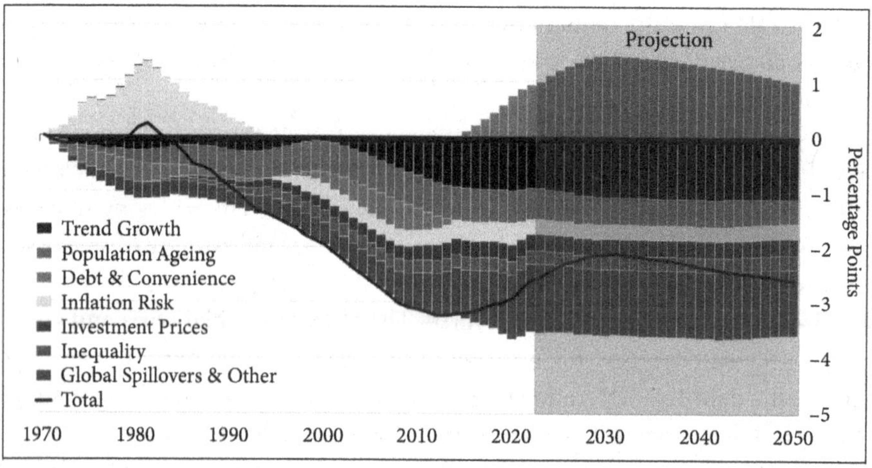

Figure 13.1 The Fall and Rise of the Natural Rate

Source: Ademmer and Rush (2024), Bloomberg Economics

Table 13.1 The Past and Future of the Natural Rate

United States	**1970 (%)**	**Change 1970–2022 ppts**	**2022 (%)**	**Change 2022–2035 ppts**	**2035 (%)**
R*	**4.91**	**−2.59**	**2.32**	**0.38**	**2.71**
Trend Growth		−1.74		−0.25	
of which, global spillovers		*−0.82*		*−0.06*	
Demographics		−0.69		0.18	
of which, global spillovers		*−0.12*		*0.09*	
Capital Goods Prices		−0.40		0.00	
of which, global spillovers		*−0.10*		*0.00*	
Inequality		−0.35		−0.02	
of which, global spillovers		*−0.12*		*0.00*	
Inflation Risk & Convenience Yield		−0.57		0.00	
Net Safe Asset Demand		0.76		0.22	
Domestic Debt Issuance		0.48		0.25	
Other		−0.07		0.00	
Advanced Economies	**1970 (%)**	**Change 1970–2022 ppts**	**2022 (%)**	**Change 2022–2035 ppts**	**2035 (%)**
R*	**5.30**	**−3.51**	**1.80**	**0.27**	**2.06**
Trend Growth		−1.96		−0.23	
of which, global spillovers		*−1.00*		*−0.12*	
Demographics		−0.65		0.20	
of which, global spillovers		*−0.23*		*0.08*	
Capital Goods Prices		−0.38		0.00	
of which, global spillovers		*−0.16*		*−0.01*	
Inequality		−0.31		−0.03	
of which, global spillovers		*−0.17*		*0.01*	
Inflation Risk & Convenience Yield		−0.82		0.00	
Net Safe Asset Demand		0.59		0.20	
Domestic Debt Issuance		0.38		0.12	
Other		−0.36		0.01	

Source: Ademmer and Rush (2024) Bloomberg Economics

Debt, Heat, Robots, War: Four Horsemen of Higher Rates

We see four main risks to our baseline forecast: rising debt, rising temperatures (actual and geopolitical), and the rise of the robots. All four tilt the balance of probabilities toward even higher rates.

In our baseline scenario, advanced economy governments stabilize their debt ratios by the early 2030s. Looming increases in spending on pensions, healthcare, and other age-related outlays, higher debt-servicing costs, and political intransigence when it comes to confronting fiscal reality raise the possibility that government borrowing could overshoot that projection.

If, instead of narrowing, deficits stay as wide as they were from 2015 to 2019, debt ratios would continue to climb. Higher safe asset supply, and investors demanding protection against the increased risk of default and inflation, could add as much as 80 bps to the natural rate by the early 2030s, as shown in Figure 13.2.

The fight against climate change will require massive investment. BloombergNEF estimates the energy infrastructure needed to support a zero-emission economy will cost more than $30 trillion globally, equal to about 30% of world GDP in 2023. Financing the capital spending needed to achieve the transition could ultimately drive US borrowing costs higher by an additional 40 bps.

Leaps forward in artificial intelligence and other technologies might yet boost productivity, resulting in faster trend growth. Drawing on early evidence from the literature on frontier technologies and assuming a similar

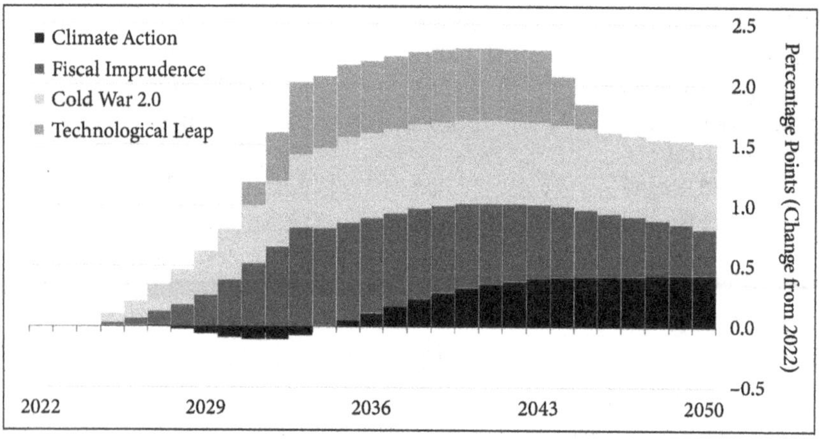

Figure 13.2 Natural Rates Risk Scenario

Source: Ademmer and Rush (2024), Bloomberg Economics

pattern to the ICT revolution of the 1990s, a 1-ppt boost to trend growth is plausible. For the United States, we estimate that could add 60 bps to the natural rate.

In our Cold War 2.0 scenario, China's savings flee from a weaponized dollar, broken supply chains raise the cost of capital goods, inequality falls as jobs are reshored, and higher defense spending pushes up debt. We estimate these factors could add as much as 70 bps to the natural rate.

Higher government borrowing, investment to fight climate change, AI creating demand for capital, and more fractious geopolitics would decrease saving and increase investment, driving the natural rate higher. If some combination of them hit together, it's not hard to imagine these factors pushing the natural rate all the way up to 4%, translating to a nominal 10-year bond yield around 6%.

The future—to return to the Berra-Bohr aphorism—is uncertain. There are downside as well as upside risks to our natural rate forecast. A world where AI widens inequality without accelerating productivity, the United States gets its fiscal house in order, and the safe haven appeal of the US dollar draws in ever greater supplies of savings is within the realm of possibility and could see the natural rate hold around bargain basement lows.

Our base case, though, is that the decades of decline in the natural rate have already ended and partially reversed. In the years ahead, the natural rate is set to edge higher still. If risks from debt, climate, geopolitics, and technology crystallize, it could rise quite a lot.

Bibliography

Ademmer, M., and Rush, J. (2024). Drivers of the Natural Long-Term Rate of Interest (and Why the Economy Hasn't Tanked). *Oxford Open Economics*, 3 odae012. https://doi.org/10.1093/ooec/odae012

14
Monetary Policy in an Age of Scarcity

Jamie Rush, Dan Hanson, and Maeva Cousin

Covid-19 and Russia's invasion of Ukraine posed the biggest challenges to central bankers since the global financial crisis in 2008.

As the virus spread, economies were shuttered and output plunged. Supply chains snarled up and governments unleashed massive fiscal stimulus. Together with the energy shock caused by Russia's invasion of Ukraine, these factors pushed price gains in advanced economies to rates last seen in the 1980s. In the United States, in June 2022, consumer price index inflation touched a high of 9.1% year on year.

At first, policymakers believed the inflation overshoot would be transitory. Fed Chair Jerome Powell said it was driven by one-off factors and set to pass without aggressive increases in interest rates. Then realization dawned: the interaction of negative supply shocks with positive demand shocks meant a robust response was required.

With prices soaring, workers demanded higher wages. Bulging pay packets created a second-round effect, prolonging and extending the run of high inflation, and—for central bankers with long memories of the wage-price spirals of the 1970s—causing conniptions. What followed was the most forceful hiking cycle in a generation.

The pandemic might be an extreme example, but it also provides a glimpse into the dynamics that are set to shape inflation in the years ahead.

As the world becomes more fragmented, the globalization tailwind that helped keep inflation low and stable in the decades before Covid lockdowns is blowing less fiercely. In the years ahead, it may even switch into a headwind—pushing prices higher. Climate change, and the cost of mitigating it, will make resources scarce, adding upward pressure on prices and making inflation more volatile.

The job of a central banker is likely to get harder—and that should color thinking on the outlook for the natural rate. Persistent negative supply shocks—the sort created by deglobalization, global heating, and efforts to

Jamie Rush, Dan Hanson, and Maeva Cousin, *Monetary Policy in an Age of Scarcity*. In: *The Price of Money*. Edited by: Jamie Rush, Tom Orlik, and Stephanie Flanders, Oxford University Press. © Oxford University Press (2025). DOI: 10.1093/9780197800942.003.0014

mitigate it—could mean the Fed, ECB, and Bank of England have to keep borrowing costs higher and run the economy cooler than they otherwise would.

We estimate fracturing global ties could add 0.1–0.3 ppt to annual inflation in the United States in the coming decade. Higher carbon prices could add a further 0.2 ppt, according to the central bank-led Network for Greening the Financial System. Taken together, the two megatrends could add a chunky 0.5 ppt upward impulse to US prices every year into the 2030s.

How much will that impact interest rates? The Taylor rule—Stanford professor John Taylor's formula for estimating where rates should be based on unemployment and inflation—suggests combating an inflationary headwind of 0.5 ppt would require rates to be higher by about 0.75 ppt. Bloomberg Economics' model of the US economy suggests offsetting the entire shock could mean policy rates have to be higher by 1.25 ppt.

Did Central Bankers Just Get Lucky?

In the decade before the global financial crisis, inflation was low and stable. Globalization pushed goods prices down, creating space for wages and services prices to rise without threatening inflation targets. Inflation expectations appeared anchored at low levels. The ramp-up of US shale output insulated the global economy from spikes in oil costs. Inflation in the United States averaged 1.8%, a shade below the Fed's 2% target.

The collapse of Lehman Brothers in 2008 and the financial havoc that followed ushered in the deepest recession in decades. Even that had only a modest impact on long-term inflation expectations, and the volatility of headline inflation receded soon after the crisis ended. As Figure 14.1 shows, relative to the high and fluctuating price changes of the 1970s and early 1980s, the Lehman shock did little to disturb a golden era for inflation management.

Economists called it the Great Moderation.[1] What was behind it? Two possibilities suggest themselves:

- The good policy hypothesis holds that central bank independence, taking inflation targeting seriously, and a stronger understanding of how the economy works meant policymakers reduced a significant source of inflation volatility—themselves. As businesses and workers came to understand that central banks were serious about hitting their targets,

[1] See Bernanke (2004).

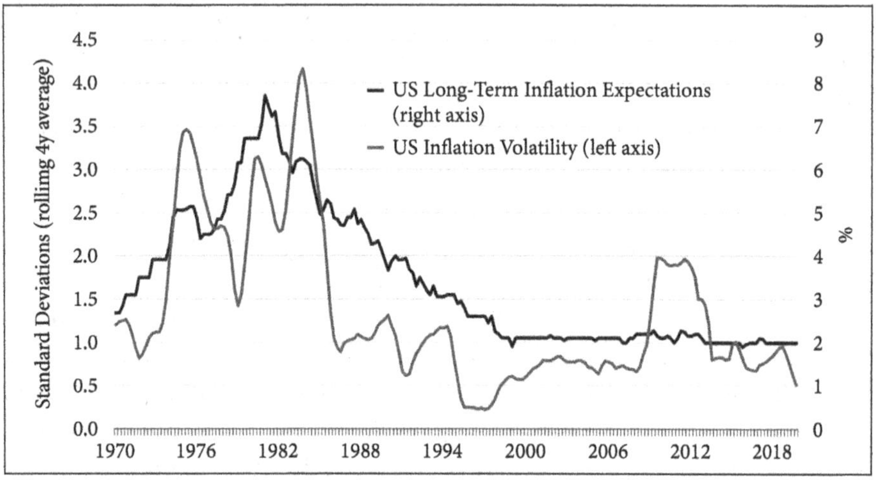

Figure 14.1 From Great Inflation to Great Moderation
Source: FRB/US, Bloomberg Economics

they moderated price hikes and wage demands—and a virtuous circle ensued.[2]

- The good luck theory is that central bankers were simply operating in a more benign environment. The integration of China's workforce into the world trading system made it easier and cheaper to source manufactured goods—making it harder for businesses to raise prices and workers to demand wage gains. In a more stable geopolitical environment, major shocks like the 1970s surge in oil prices were notable by their absence.[3]

Unsurprisingly, central bankers favor the first explanation. Former Fed chair Ben Bernanke—who coined the term Great Moderation—flags the importance of improved monetary policy in limiting volatility. The post-pandemic surge in prices challenged that view. After all, if policymakers were really so good at controlling inflation, why were they so slow to recognize that the surge which started in 2021 was not driven by transitory factors?

Even as the post-pandemic price surge suggests that good policy is less responsible for low and stable inflation than central bankers would have us believe, it also indicates the run of good luck for the global economy is running out. Covid strains on global supply chains, Russia cutting energy supplies to Europe, and a shift to protectionist policies in the United States

[2] See Cecchetti, Flores-Lagunes, and Krause (2006).
[3] See Stock and Watson (2003).

all suggest that the process of globalization which tamped down inflation in past decades faces new challenges.

When Goods Become Costly

Throughout the 1990s, emerging markets were becoming more integrated in the global trading system. China's accession to the World Trade Organization in 2001 sent that process into overdrive. A huge pool of low-cost workers were rapidly assimilated into global labor markets. China's urbanization—with hundreds of millions of farmhands flooding to factory jobs—was an additional accelerator.

Two factors meant the impact on advanced economy inflation was seen most clearly in prices for manufactured goods. First, it's harder to sell services across borders—you can buy sneakers stitched together by a Chinese worker, but it's harder to import a haircut. Second, Chinese workers were relatively low-skilled—so exports were mainly of goods assembled on factory production lines.

The impact is clear in the data. As Figure 14.2 shows, from 2000 to 2020 the average annual rate of goods price inflation in the United States was just 0.4%, with the prices of consumer electronics (like televisions) actually falling. Services price inflation, in contrast, averaged 2.6%. With goods inflation low, and services inflation high, headline personal consumption expenditure inflation was 1.8%, close to the Fed's 2% target.

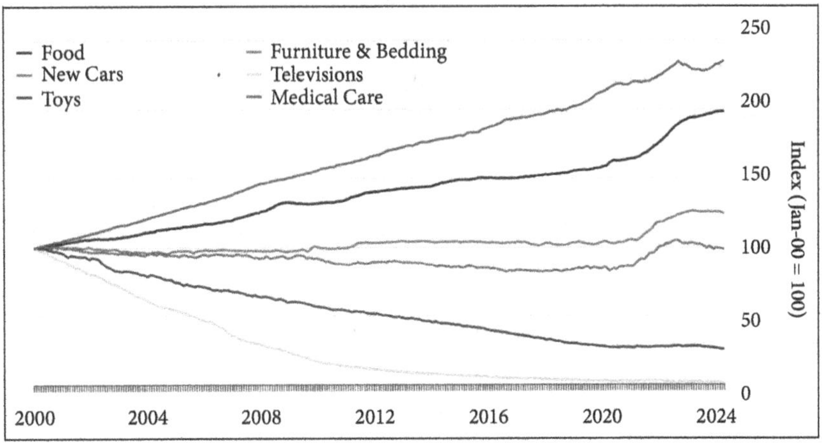

Figure 14.2 China Shock Dragged Manufacturing Prices Lower

Source: Bureau of Labor Statistics

How much of that is the China effect?

In the 20 years to 2008, the end of the Cold War and entry of China into the global economy led to a surge in trade intensity. Imports of goods and services as a share of global gross domestic product (GDP) rose from less than 17% in 1989 to more than 28% in 2008. Lower prices for imports and accelerating productivity gains both weighed on prices. Rising commodity prices as China and other emerging markets amped up demand pushed in the opposite direction.

To understand how this era of rapid globalization affected inflation and assess the risks as trade ties fracture, we use a computable general equilibrium model of the global economy, the same as the one used by the World Trade Organization. The model takes account of a range of factors that impact prices, including trade, productivity, and commodities demand.

Our results show the rapid rise in trade intensity over the two decades to 2008 lowered average annual US inflation by around 0.2 ppt. The rise in imports of consumer goods from economies with lower wages and faster productivity growth offset any upward pressure on commodity costs from higher global demand.

In our baseline forecast, globalization continues at a much slower pace. In the years ahead, we envisage a very gradual increase in trade intensity to 31%. If that happens, disinflationary tailwinds will still blow, but much less fiercely, with the impact on average annual US inflation downshifting to about −0.05 ppt.

How about if globalization swings into reverse? In a second Cold War, with the world splitting into rival geopolitical blocs and trade between the two effectively turned off, imports as a share of global GDP could drop to about 25% by 2035. Reduced global competition and lower productivity growth would lift annual inflation in the United States by around 0.2 ppt relative to our baseline scenario in the next decade.

Compared with the 2021-22 shock which saw US CPI inflation climb all the way to 9.1%, that doesn't look like much. The persistence over time means it's not something central banks would be able to ignore.

When Resources Are Scarce

Globalization wasn't the only tailwind for low and stable inflation; energy prices dynamics also contributed. True, oil at around $80 a barrel in the early 2020s is more expensive than $3 a barrel in the 1970s. But adjusting for higher prices for everything else and lower oil-intensity of output, the price has become less consequential for the world economy than it was when the 1970s shocks kicked off years of torrid price gains.

Russia's war on Ukraine and severing of energy supplies to Europe showed how the dynamic can shift. The sudden shortage of gas added 4–5 ppt to euro area inflation and created huge uncertainty about the economy's ability to adapt. In the end, inflation costs were high, but activity was less disrupted than feared—an unseasonably warm winter reduced energy demand and helped avert a recession.

Scarcity is back as an inflation driver. It's not hard to imagine more shocks from geopolitics. The United States is blocking China's access to advanced semiconductors. In recent years, China has turned trade with Japan, South Korea, and Australia off and on to exert diplomatic pressure. It's possible to envisage a scenario where emboldened oil producers jack up prices—as they did in the 1970s.

Climate change could have a slow burn impact. The world is running late on implementing the changes needed to move to a net-zero economy. Imagine governments wake up to the danger and take radical action to limit temperature increase to two degrees. According to the NGFS' delayed transition scenario, achieving that objective would require the price of carbon to go up from an average of around \$10 per ton in the early 2020s to nearly \$400 globally by 2050, and more than \$700 in the United States.

The NGFS projects that carbon prices at that level could add 0.4 ppt to average annual US inflation in the first 10 years of the transition, slightly more than an estimated 0.25 ppt impact on the euro area.

A more gradual move would, of course, have a smaller impact. In its orderly transition scenario, the NGFS estimates the impact on inflation of a more modest increase in carbon prices would be around 0.2 ppt a year for the United States, and around 0.1 ppt for the euro area. Estimates from the European Central Bank point to a similar impact.

Beyond the price impact of the transition, the greater frequency and intensity of extreme events like floods, droughts, and wildfires will increase the volatility of inflation. Leaps in prices, as harvests fail or supply chains snarl up, will likely be more common in the future than they have been in the past. In a literature review published in 2024, the European Commission takes stock of what such shocks could mean for inflation:[4]

- Ghent University professor, Gert Peersman estimates that harvest shocks and swings in prices for international agricultural commodities

[4] See Buelens (2024).

explain 25–30% of euro-area inflation volatility from 1961 to 2016. As droughts and heatwaves intensify, shocks are likely to become more frequent.[5]

- A report for Germany's Institute for the Study of Labor suggests that droughts and warmer water temperature in rivers affect electricity production and prices, through the impact on reservoir levels for hydroelectric power plants and cooling for nuclear reactors.[6]
- Research shows that manufacturing may also be affected, with water stress in Taiwan adding to disruption risks in the fabrication of semiconductors.[7]

What Is to Be Done?

Taken together, it is possible to imagine trade schisms and climate change creating upward pressure on inflation of something like half a percentage point a year over the next decade. Central banks should always be able to achieve their inflation targets on average, so long as they set the right policy. The question is: what should that policy be?

When oil or food prices spike because of one-off shocks, it's common for central banks to look through the impact on inflation. If breaking global ties and rising global temperatures exert a persistent impact, turning a blind eye won't be an option. Central banks will need to set policy tight enough to move demand in line with lower supply.

To keep inflation on target as deglobalization and climate change pushes prices up, it is likely that a meaningful part of the adjustment will have to come from services inflation running cooler than it has in the past. To make that happen, central banks will have to set interest rates high enough to keep the job market cooler and wages rising slowly.

One way to game out the implications is to use Taylor's famous model. The Taylor rule links interest rates to deviations of inflation from target and output from potential.

- Running a persistent half-point inflation shock through a version of the rule with very well-anchored inflation expectations suggests the

[5] See Peersman (2022).
[6] See McDermott and Nilsen (2013).
[7] See Lepawsky (2024).

minimum we should expect in reply from central banks is policy rates that are 25 bps higher.

- What if persistent upward pressure on inflation from geopolitical and climate shocks causes inflation expectations to rise? The original Taylor rule suggests a more vigorous response would be required, with rates 75 bps higher.[8]
- Another way to answer the question is to use a small model of the US economy to work out what size interest rate increase is required to fully offset the inflationary impact. Bloomberg Economics' SHOK model suggests it would take a sustained increase in the policy rate of about 125 bps.

Three approaches, three answers—and a wide range between the 25 bps bottom estimate and 125 bps top. Limited understanding of the scale of the likely shocks, how inflation expectations are formed, and the slope of the Phillips curve, means it's hard to zero in on a precise answer. What does seem clear is that inflationary headwinds from sustained geopolitical and climate shocks are likely to add an additional upward impulse to the natural rate.

Inflation volatility will further increase the upward pressure on interest rates. Since more volatile inflation and interest rates are not well-liked by bond holders, they may require more compensation to stay invested. A higher risk premium on bonds would add to upward pressure on long-term borrowing costs.

The Bottom Line

A shifting balance between savings and investment, moving the world from savings glut to savings shortage, has already lifted the natural rate from its post-global financial crisis nadir. In the years ahead, a further tilt in the balance away from saving is set to edge it higher still.

In addition to impacting the savings–investment balance, fracturing global ties and a higher cost of carbon may introduce fresh inflationary headwinds into the global economy. We estimate the combined impact could be in the vicinity of a 0.5-ppt impulse to US inflation every year for the next decade. Leaning against that could require central banks to run the economy cooler and keep policy rates higher by as much as 0.75–1.25 ppt.

[8] See Taylor (1993).

Bibliography

Bernanke, B. (2004). "The Great Moderation." Remarks at the meetings of the Eastern Economic Association, Washington, DC, February 20, 2004.

Buelens, C. (2024). "Climate change and its impact on prices and inflation." *Quarterly Report on the Euro Area*, 23(1): 23–39.

Cecchetti, S. G., Flores-Lagunes, A., and Krause, S. (2006). "Has Monetary Policy Become More Efficient? A Cross-Country Analysis." *Economic Journal*, 116(511): 408–433.

Lepawsky, J. (2024). "Climate Change Induced Water Stress and Future Semiconductor Supply Chain Risk." *iScience*, 27(2): 108791. doi: 10.1016/j.isci.2024.108791

McDermott, G. R., and Nilsen, O. A. (2013). "Electricity Prices, River Temperatures, and Cooling Water Scarcity." *Land Economics*, 90(1): 131–148.

Peersman, G. (2022). "International Food Commodity Prices and Missing (Dis)Inflation in the Euro Area." *The Review of Economics and Statistics*, 104(1): 85–100.

Stock, J., and Watson, M. (2003). "Has the Business Cycle Changed? Evidence and Explanations." Federal Reserve Board of Kansas City symposium, Monetary Policy and Uncertainty. https://www.kansascityfed.org/documents/3425/pdf-Stockwatson2003.pdf

Taylor, J. B. (1993). "Discretion versus Policy Rules in Practice." *Carnegie-Rochester Conference Series on Public Policy*, 39(1), 195–214.

15

A More Expensive World

What Does It All Mean?

Stephanie Flanders

The story of this book so far is that the cost of money is going up—not a lot, but a reversal after decades of decline and enough to make a difference. In our central scenario, the real long-term cost of borrowing in the United States ends up around 1 ppt higher in the 2030s than in the 2010s. Globally, the rise is a bit smaller, maybe 0.6 ppt. Compared with the 1970s and 1980s, money would still be cheap. But it won't feel that way, after decades in which the cost of borrowing seemed always to be going down.

Life will get harder for most borrowers and perhaps especially for the biggest borrowers of all—governments. For asset markets and private investors, the implications are more nuanced and would require another book to disentangle. But across the economy, it is safe to say that the stakes for economic decision-makers will be high. Put simply: the higher the opportunity cost of money, the more important it will be to invest it well.

You might think a higher real natural rate would make life easier for at least one set of policymakers: central banks. That is because, other things equal, higher average interest rates would mean more room to cut borrowing costs when recessions hit and perhaps less need to resort to alternative—less trusted—tools, such as quantitative easing, to get inflation back to target.

But other things are not going to stay the same. In the years to come, supply shocks are likely to be more frequent and the price level less predictable. That will very likely make the job of central banking more difficult. The cost of mistakes for policymakers of all kinds, whether at the central bank or the Treasury, will also be higher.

We could well be wrong on the size of the move in rates. With so much uncertainty surrounding the natural rate, the scenarios we paint here are a guideline not a blueprint. But if we are wrong, that's more likely to be because we're setting the future rate too low than too high. There are numerous

Stephanie Flanders, *A More Expensive World*. In: *The Price of Money*. Edited by: Jamie Rush, Tom Orlik, and Stephanie Flanders, Oxford University Press. © Oxford University Press (2025). DOI: 10.1093/9780197800942.003.0015

entirely plausible scenarios under which the natural rate increases by a lot more than 1 ppt.

After several decades in which money was almost always getting cheaper, an increase of that magnitude sounds like a scary scenario. The pace of change is also important. The faster it happens, the more likely it is that a more than 1 ppt rise in the cost of borrowing will cause accidents—especially in the context of climate-driven supply shocks and a more fractious and fragmented geopolitical environment.

The first reaction of borrowers and investors is that a higher natural rate is bad news because it pushes debt servicing costs higher and asset prices lower. If, however, we're right about what drives movements of the natural rate, a world in which the cost of money rises could well be one in which a number of important things are going right. It might mean, for example, that the world is working more aggressively to confront climate change—further increasing the demand for investment resources—and that productivity growth is finally picking up.

Put it another way: a world in which real rates are markedly higher might well be a world we would all prefer to live in. Eventually. But that will only be true if policymakers do their part to ease the transition and make the most of the opportunities that a more productive, zero-carbon future affords. It would definitely not be the case if the biggest factor pushing real rates up was not increased private sector dynamism and investment, but excessive borrowing by governments.

That higher premium on good policymaking and strong, adaptive core institutions is one of many reasons we would expect, if anything, more variation in cross-country economic performance in this new era compared with the first years of this century when the cost of money was falling, globalization was proceeding apace, and income inequality between countries was falling at a historic rate.

The End of the Free Lunch for Governments

To recap the key numbers: our baseline sees the 10-year real natural rate in the United States rising to 2.75% by 2030—up from a low point of 1.7% in the first half of the 2010s and around 2.3% in 2022. Over the same period, the global real rate rises from a low of 1.5% to around 2.1%. We expect borrowing costs to start falling again after that. But in the meantime, the world will have some adjusting to do, and the first to seriously feel the effects will be the biggest borrowers: governments.

As we have seen, for most of the first 20 years of this century, the cost of money was falling. But, with the exception of Japan, it was not until the global financial crisis of 2007–08 and Eurozone crises of 2010 onward that government borrowing started to climb.

Between 2007 and 2020 the average level of public debt among the advanced economies rose from around 75% of gross domestic product (GDP) to more than 130%. Remarkably, over the same period, the effective interest rate paid on that debt more than halved, from 3% to 1.4%. As a result, the average annual cost of servicing that debt actually went down, from 1.8% to 1.5% of GDP.

One of the most extraordinary moments came in the middle of the pandemic in 2020–21, when the US Treasury was able to raise funds at negative real interest rates, even at very long durations. Adjusting for inflation, investors were willing to pay the US government to borrow vast sums of money. For Washington, DC, the exceptional pandemic stimulus looked like the ultimate free lunch.

And yet, as inflation returned and central banks belatedly responded, long-term rates have jumped. Governments are finding that maturing debt has to be refinanced at sharply higher rates, and there is a bill to be paid after all. The UK—which issues a relatively high proportion of inflation-indexed debt—felt the hit sooner than most. From 2019 to 2022, net interest spending doubled from 2.1% to 4% of GDP. That's a cash increase of more than £60 billion—more than the UK's annual spending on defense, which in 2023 came to £54 billion.

Short of being paid to borrow, the next best thing for government borrowers is for the real interest rate on debt (or "*r*" as economists refer to it) to settle below the real growth rate of the economy ("*g*"). In that world, newly issued debt shrivels away relative to incomes—it is simply outgrown. And for many years, even before the pandemic, r was indeed lower than g.

Looking ahead, the Bloomberg Economics long-term forecast for real US GDP growth is about 2%. Adjusting for inflation, mid-2024 market pricing shows real 10-year yields in 10 years' time between 2.5% and 3%. That pricing is also consistent with our own projections for the natural rate which settle at around 2.75% in the 2030s.

If that's right, then r will settle above g and the free lunch will be over. The implication is that governments—in the United States and everywhere else—will need to be more selective about what they invest in and how they spend their resources.

Not everyone agrees with this assessment; governments may yet get lucky. MIT Professor Olivier Blanchard argues that we have not entered a new regime, and that r is likely to settle below g once more.[1] But given recent experience, it would be wise to calibrate fiscal policy with interest rate risks firmly in mind. The relentless upward march in debt during the low interest rate era has left many governments highly vulnerable to shifts in the rates outlook.

As Figure 15.1 shows, we estimate that interest payments as a share of US GDP will rise from about 2.4% in 2023 to about 4.5% in 2030. Over the same period, we see debt rising from 97% of GDP to around 117%. Without a shift in policy, there is little prospect of debt stabilizing. Even on the current trajectory there will be less room to spend on core government services as interest payments gobble up a rising share of revenues.

With the United States in the habit of running 5–7% of GDP budget deficits, even at close to full employment, the danger is that borrowing will run out of control. That is when the feedback loop between indebtedness and interest rates could come into play. Few seriously expect the United States to default. But there could be a tendency to tolerate higher for longer inflation, leading investors to demand a higher risk premium, meaning r moves higher, and the fiscal arithmetic gets even worse.

It's not just the United States. In the years to come, many advanced economies will need to face fiscal reality.

Italy stands out. Between 2002 and 2023, Italian public debt rose from 106% of GDP to 134%. Over the same period, debt servicing costs fell from 5.4%

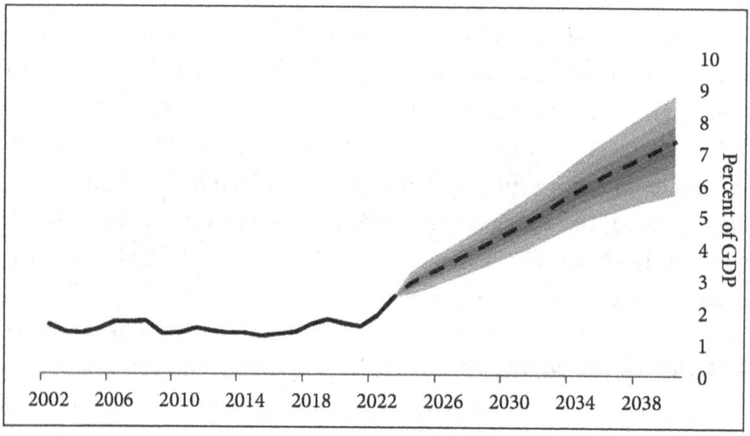

Figure 15.1 US Debt Servicing Costs
Source: Bloomberg Economics

[1] See Blanchard (2023).

of GDP to 3.6%. As Figure 15.2 shows, even if debt is stabilized at the current elevated level, on mid-2024 market pricing, servicing costs will converge on 6.5% of GDP in years to come.

Merely stabilizing Italy's debt—at a time when demographic change is shrinking the number of workers and increasing demand for health and pension spending—will be a difficult task. Getting debt falling back to safer levels, and creating space for it to rise again when fresh crises hit, would be even harder.

To achieve that objective, Italy would either need extensive reform to raise the sustainable rate of growth, fiscal consolidation on a scale that has brought down many past administrations, or debt restructuring. Put it another way: a world of higher real rates is one in which Italy will continue to pose a threat to the stability of the Eurozone.

France also has reason to worry, as was highlighted by the sharp increase in the risk premia on French sovereign debt around the surprise parliamentary election in mid-2024. France is now the euro area's biggest borrower in terms of nominal debt outstanding. Only Italy and Greece have higher debt stocks relative to GDP.

To put some numbers on the scale of the problem, as of the second quarter of 2024 Bloomberg Economics' debt sustainability model estimated only a 20% probability of French debt stabilizing or falling relative to GDP over the next 10 years. Under current market expectations, France's debt-to-GDP ratio could rise from 115% to more than 135% by 2040 and 150% by 2050.

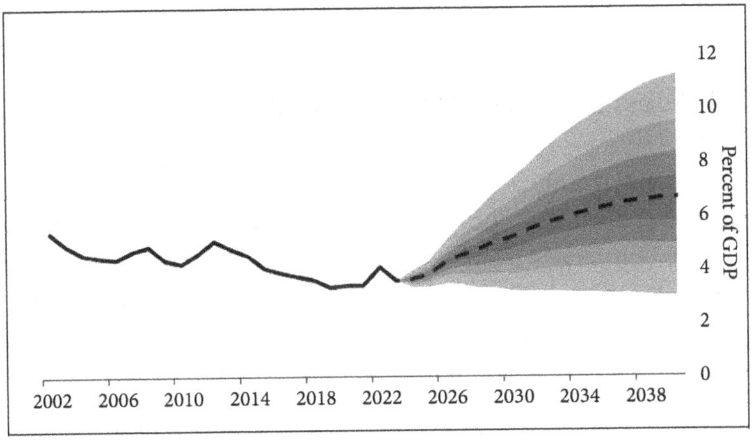

Figure 15.2 Italy Debt Servicing Costs

Source: ISTAT, Bloomberg Economics

Having emphasized the uncertainty surrounding natural rate projections, it is worth noting how much these debt forecasts depend on assumptions about the long-term, risk-free rate.

As of mid-2024, market expectations pointed to a long-term neutral policy rate around 2.3%, close to our baseline. A real long-term rate closer to 3% would push France's debt to around 145% of GDP by 2040—10 ppt higher than our baseline. Conversely, if rates were to be 1 ppt lower, roughly halfway between the current rate and the 0% implied by market pricing in 2021, the debt ratio might be contained to around 125%.

A basic lesson for all the developed country governments sitting on high—and rising—liabilities is that debt, and its management, matters again. For the better part of two decades, most developed country governments have had a free pass when it came to running up their stock of IOUs. The more they borrowed, the cheaper that borrowing often became.

The one significant exception to this unusual state of affairs was the Eurozone crisis of 2010–12, when the high level of borrowing in the European periphery briefly raised questions about the long-term sustainability of the single currency. In a world of rising global borrowing costs and heightened demand for investment resources, all higher debt countries can once again expect greater scrutiny of their fiscal sums.

There are a range of implications. Probably the most important is that fiscal frameworks should be more focused on the cost of debt servicing and more conservative in projecting these costs over time. For years, forecasts for long-term bond yields have been biased upward and the cost of borrowing has generally turned out to be lower than expected. In the future, a prudent finance minister should expect that pattern to be reversed.

Asset Prices: Discounting the Future

The falling price of money has enabled higher borrowing by governments, not all of which has been put to productive use. By definition, "risk-free" sovereign borrowers get the largest benefit from a decline in the risk-free rate. The same force that reduced the cost of debt for governments also had a sizeable impact on household and business borrowing. The impact was especially evident in real estate, as low rates meant the same salary was able to sustain higher and higher mortgages, pushing prices up.

The impact was far from trivial. In the UK, the cost of housing is as popular a topic of conversation as the weather, and the rise in the value of residential housing has accounted for the lion's share of the increase in household wealth in recent decades. Economist and former Bank of England rate setter David Miles and his colleague Victoria Monro estimate that lower long-term real interest rates lifted real home values by 108% between 1985 and 2018.[2] For context, real house prices went up by 156% in that time.

Substituting in our own estimates of the natural rate of interest for the market rates used by Miles and Monro yields a measure of the boost to real house prices from lower interest rates. We put that at about 75% over the same time period, with rising incomes similarly doing much of the heavy lifting.

Our baseline forecasts for the natural rate show a relatively flat profile for the UK in years to come. The upward impacts of higher debt issuance and a savings draw down as the population ages are checked by historically weak trend growth, which looks likely to persist, absent a shake-up in government policy.

So our baseline projection for the natural rate in the UK is consistent with a departure from historical experience. Rather than propelling real home values higher, long-term rates are more likely to act as a modest drag on UK house prices in years to come, perhaps subtracting about 4% from average prices by the mid-2030s.

That's not to say prices won't go up. Whether it's the UK or any other advanced economy, what happens to prices will also depend on the supply of housing relative to demand and on whether the general price level is going up and incomes are rising. But, absent a major change in those other factors, the pace of increase in many developed economies is likely to be slower in coming decades than homeowners have historically enjoyed.

Other things equal, a rise in the long-term cost of money should also constrain the future rise in other asset prices—not least, the price of equities. To own a share in a company is to own a claim on a stream of future profits, and you'd expect the value of a given future stream of income to fall as those future profits are discounted at a higher rate.

It seems pretty clear that the falling cost of money helped underpin the long bull market in equities that stretched over recent decades. Using the standard Gordon Growth Model—calculating the fundamental value of a stock based on estimated future dividends—and survey-based, long-term expectations for long-term rates and US economic growth, we estimate that the decline in the cost of money was responsible for about half of the increase in the S&P 500 index of US companies since 1990.

Except, life is more complicated than that.

[2] See Miles and Monro (2021).

For example, the basic dividend discount model used here fails to capture the way that share buybacks and other cash payments have overtaken the distribution of dividends for US companies in the past 20 years. In the four quarters to September 2023, dividends paid by the companies in the index totaled $580 billion and buybacks were close to $790 billion.

Using US economic growth rates to calculate "fair" value is also misleading. Major companies earn a significant chunk of their revenues overseas—meaning their earnings can be just as affected by conditions in Europe and Asia as those in the United States. Over-representation of communications, financial and technology companies in the index relative to the economy overall is another reason why the pace of GDP growth is an imperfect way of estimating the likely return on equities.

These limitations point to a broader challenge for anyone seeking to pin down exactly what an increase in the natural rate will mean for asset prices. Much will depend on what else is going on, and, specifically, whether the structural factors driving the cost of money upward happen to be making life more or less lucrative for companies and their shareholders.

Fortunes will be made and lost on corporate analysts' ability to model the interplay of these many variables. What we can say is that the opportunity cost of money over the next 10 years will be higher than it has been in recent years. That suggests break-even points for the marginal company and the marginal investment will be higher. Among other things, this suggests that over time the number of "zombie companies"—whose current profits are not sufficient to cover their debt interest costs for an extended period—should be lower.

Even that change in the operating environment for firms could have a profound effect on the composition and dynamism of the private sector in the countries where "zombies" have become a fact of life. A 2018 study by economists at the Bank for International Settlements found the proportion of undead firms across a group of 14 advanced economies grew significantly between the late 1980s and 2016, from around 2% to around 12% of all listed non-financial firms.[3] (Using a narrower criterion for a zombie firm produces lower numbers but still a significant rise: from 1% in the late 1980s to 6% in 2016.)

Tellingly, for our purposes, the most significant step change in the number of zombies seems to have occurred in the early 2000s, well before the global financial crisis. The biggest causal factor behind this increase, according to the Bank for International Settlements' analysis, was the decline in nominal interest rates. You might think that a fall in rates would have the opposite

[3] See Banerjee and Hofmann (2018).

effect—making it easier for companies to cover their interest costs and, so, cease being "zombies." But it appears to have more often had the effect of easing the pressure on companies to restructure and run down their debts.

This rise in the share of "zombies," in turn, is likely to have weakened economic performance by lowering the average productivity of the corporate sector and crowding out the growth of more productive, dynamic companies.

So here too, a world in which money is more expensive—and the pressure to restructure is more acute—could have long-run advantages for the broader economy. But there would be some painful adjustments to make along the way, particularly if the labor market and the financial sector are not in a position to find new homes for the resources that have been "liberated" from the zombies' embrace.

Greater Freedom for Central Banks—to Make Mistakes

We have tended to think a world where interest rates were further from their 0% floor would be easier for central banks because they have more room to maneuver. But that is less obvious in the environment described in Chapter 14, where supply shocks from deglobalization and climate change become more commonplace. Supply shocks will tend to make the price level more unpredictable and variable. The lesson of recent years is that taming supply-driven inflation can be more difficult—and more unpopular—than taming inflation that is caused by runaway demand.

When an economy is overheating, a central bank does not win friends when it raises interest rates to curb inflation—or "takes the punchbowl away just as the party is getting started" as Fed Chairman William McChesney Martin put it. But at least most of the households negatively affected have had the fun of going to the party, and the tightening of policy happens after a period of rising incomes.

By contrast, a central bank that raises interest rates to bring down inflation caused by a supply shock, such as Russia's invasion of Ukraine, is kicking people when they're down. Households mortgages become more expensive, just as energy and food bills are also going through the roof. No wonder central banks in 2021–22 were slow to start on that path.

Coordinating macroeconomic policies will also be more complicated. Tamping down an demand-led inflationary boom, fiscal and monetary policies act countercyclically, with the government either tightening fiscal policy or at least avoiding an expansionary stance that makes the central bank's job harder. In recent supply-side episodes, however, the two sides have worked against each other. Central banks have tightened policy even as governments are propping up demand as they cushion the cost-of-living squeeze on households.

One could argue that the recent period has been exceptional. It's not often you see a global pandemic and a European war in the space of barely two years. But energy and food are precisely the sectors that would be in the frame in the coming years in the context of both climate change itself and the global effort to transition away from carbon. A more geopolitically fragmented world is also likely to mean more frequent—and unpredictable—disruptions in global supply chains. These would not need to be as dramatic as occurred during the pandemic to cause a headache for central banks.

Simply tightening monetary policy in response to such shocks is not just unpopular for central banks: it is also suboptimal. Rate hikes respond to the side effect of the shock, when inflation has become generalized, rather than addressing the root cause of the disruption. Longer term, there's also the risk that higher rates could make it harder to finance necessary investments, for example to address climate change and so make future price shocks less likely.

Instead of relying on central banks to do the heavy lifting, a more joined-up response by other parts of government might be called for. A 2024 report for the European Parliament takes this as a starting point for proposing "a new inflation governance framework that targets shocks to systematically significant prices directly, before they are propagated throughout the economy."[4]

The report suggests an extensive microeconomic "toolbox" to do this, including the use of the Common Agricultural Policy and specific sectoral policies to address bottlenecks, for example, in computer chips and energy. These will not be a good fit in other countries and may not be up to the job even in the European Union. But the authors are almost certainly right when they say that this is a question that is not going away.

The Road Ahead

The natural rate of interest is as mysterious and difficult to pin down as it is central to the operation of the economy and financial system. Reasonable people can—and do—disagree about where it was in the past, where it is today, and where it is headed in the future.

[4] See Van T' Klooster and Weber (2024).

What we hope we have brought to the debate is a model that integrates a top-down view on the level of natural rate, a bottom-up view of the drivers, forecasts of those drivers that enable us to project its future path, and clarity on how the pieces fit together.

Our work suggests that the decades-long decline in the natural rate from the late 1970s to the 2010s is over. The last decade has already seen a modest increase. Our base case is that demographics and debt will extend that run into the 2030s. In a plausible risk scenario where geopolitical tensions rise, government borrowing stays high, the fight against climate change gets serious, and technological advances accelerate, it could rise rather a lot.

For central bankers, ministers of finance, Wall Street money managers, Main Street corporate chiefs, 401K savers and mortgage borrowers, the shift from falling to rising interest rates matters. Debt will be more expensive, asset prices less buoyant, and the environment less forgiving—especially for policymakers.

The price of money—the most important price in the global economy—is going up. So is the cost of managing it poorly.

Bibliography

Banerjee, R., and Hofmann, B. (2018). "The Rise of Zombie Firms: Causes and Consequences." *BIS Quarterly Review*, September 2018. https://www.bis.org/publ/qtrpdf/r_qt1809g.htm

Blanchard, O. (2023). *Fiscal Policy under Low Interest Rates.* Cambridge: MIT Press.

Miles, D., and Monro, V. (2021). "UK House Prices and Three Decades of Decline in the Risk-Free Real Interest Rate." *Economic Policy*, 36(108): 627–684.

Van T' Klooster, J., and Weber, I. (2024). "Closing the EU's Inflation Governance Gap." Report to the European parliament ECON Committee. https://www.europarl.europa.eu/RegData/etudes/STUD/2024/755727/IPOL_STU(2024)755727_EN.pdf

Index

For the benefit of digital users, indexed terms that span two pages (e.g., 52–53) may, on occasion, appear on only one of those pages.

Tables, figures, and boxes are indicated by an italic *t*, *f*, or *b*.